Praise for
The Magdalene Revolution

"Andrew Harvey has gorgeously written us into a new and liberatory vision of Mary Magdalene. In doing so he has opened the portals to a nurturing equality, a soul healing, radical transformation, and a luminous arrival of the Divine Feminine when we need it most."

— **V (formerly Eve Ensler)**, author of *Reckoning* and *The Vagina Monologues*

"A thoughtful, daring, exciting, well-researched study and personal story that helps move Christianity beyond the patriarchal and dualistic mindset so characteristic of the past 2,000 years. Alfred North Whitehead called for the return of a 'high hope of adventure' to religion—and Andrew delivers. His view of Mary Magdalene balances the sacred feminine and sacred masculine, sensuality and spirituality, and empowers for sacred activism. He holds Mary Magdalene up as Christ's first disciple to truly incorporate the divinization—including resurrection and ascension—that is our right and responsibility as 'other Christs.' A truly breakthrough book for a third millennium grasp of the Christ path."

— **Matthew Fox**, author of *The Beloved Will Guide You: John of the Cross and the Triple Dark Night of Our Times, The Coming of the Cosmic Christ*, and *Original Blessing*

"The true story of Mary Magdalene is at last being told. Andrew Harvey introduces us to a true female mystic, a wisdom teacher, and a healer of all divisions between body and soul, heart and mind, masculine and feminine. The real story of Mary Magdalene teaches us that Christ Consciousness is accessible to everyone, everywhere, and without exception."

— **Robert Holden**, author of *Shift Happens!* and *Higher Purpose*

"In this stunning new book, mystical revolutionary Andrew Harvey extends a ringing invitation. Not only does he dare to claim that Jesus of Nazareth and Mary of Magdala were co-equal teachers in the way of transformative love, but that their union created a seismic shift in the cosmos that calls upon all of us, people of all genders, to embody the divine balance of masculine and feminine inside ourselves and actively participate in birthing a divinized humanity that will heal, transform, and bless this world. As someone who stands outside the Christian tradition, yet deeply drawn to its mystical essence, I welcome this prophetic call with all my heart."

— **Mirabai Starr**, author of *Wild Mercy* and *Ordinary Mysticism*

"Andrew Harvey has written a blazing testament for our time. The Magdalene Revolution *unites luminous scholarship and visionary depth with a transmission of love that restores the full radiance of the Divine Feminine to the heart of the Christ path. With poetic fire and the authority of lived revelation, Harvey unveils Mary Magdalene as the co-Christ, calling us to embody the sacred marriage of the feminine and masculine as the seed of a new humanity."*

— **Banafsheh Sayyad**, founder of Dance of Oneness® and author of *Dance of Oneness: Awaken, Heal, and Transform Through Embodied Love and Light*

"Mary Magdalene is an eternal reminder of a woman's place in the consciousness of Christ. She was in a very real way who every woman is, pushed aside by those who cannot see her but loved so deeply by He who does. Andrew Harvey spells it out, literally and figuratively. This is a beautiful book."

— **Marianne Williamson**, *New York Times* best-selling author of *A Return to Love*

"The Magdalene Revolution *is a critical call for us to embody the other half of the divine story, the one that leads us back to the voice within our own hearts—the voice of a love that reminds us of our inherent worth, a love that seeks to guide us, a love that never ends."*

— **Meggan Watterson**, *Wall Street Journal* best-selling author of *Mary Magdalene Revealed*

The Magdalene Revolution

ALSO BY ANDREW HARVEY

Dialogues with a Modern Mystic, with Mark Matouske

The Direct Path: Creating a Personal Journey to the Divine Using the World's Spiritual Traditions

The Essential Mystics: Selections from the World's Great Wisdom Traditions

Heart Yoga: The Sacred Marriage of Yoga and Mysticism, with Karuna Erickson

Hidden Journey: A Spiritual Awakening

*The Hope: A Guide to Sacred Activism**

A Journey in Ladakh: Encounters with Buddhism

*Light the Flame: 365 Days of Prayer from Around the World**

Mary's Vineyard: Daily Meditations, Readings, and Revelations

Perfume of the Desert: Inspirations from Sufi Wisdom

Play Life More Beautifully: Conversations with Seymour, with Seymour Bernstein*

Radical Passion: Sacred Love and Wisdom in Action

Radical Regeneration: Sacred Activism and the Renewal of the World, with Carolyn Bake

The Return of the Mother

Son of Man: The Mystical Path to Christ

The Sun at Midnight: A Memoir of the Dark Night

Teachings of Rumi

The Tibetan Book of Living and Dying: The Spiritual Classic & International Bestseller

A Walk with Four Spiritual Guides: Krishna, Buddha, Jesus, and Ramakrishna

The Way of Passion: A Celebration of Rumi

*Available from Hay House
Please visit:

Hay House USA: www.hayhouse.com®
Hay House Australia: www.hayhouse.com.au
Hay House UK: www.hayhouse.co.uk
Hay House India: www.hayhouse.co.in

The Magdalene Revolution

The Return of the SACRED FEMININE *and the Birth of* RADICAL EQUALITY

Andrew Harvey

HAY HOUSE LLC
Carlsbad, California • New York City
London • Sydney • New Delhi

Published in the United States by: Hay House LLC,
www.hayhouse.com® • P.O. Box 5100, Carlsbad, CA, 92018-5100

Indexer: J S Editorial LLC
Cover design: Barbara LeVan Fisher • *Interior design:* Bryn Starr Best

Cataloging-in-Publication Data is on file at the Library of Congress

Hardcover ISBN: 978-1-4019-6896-0
E-book ISBN: 978-1-4019-6898-4
Audiobook ISBN: 978-1-4019-6899-1

1st Printing

Printed in the United States of America

For Maria Callas

My guide into
the burning heart
of the Divine Feminine
and Mary Magdalene

Voce divina
di fiamma e di lagrime
innamorata eterna
della mia anima

Divine voice
of flame and tears
eternal beloved
of my soul

Contents

Preface

AS WE BEGIN our journey together into *The Magdalene Revolution*, let me invite you to find an image of Mary Magdalene that mysteriously thrills and moves you.

The Magdalene has haunted the artistic imagination of the West, and many of our greatest painters have celebrated her. Make sure you choose an image that truly and deeply speaks to your heart. Gaze into the Magdalene's eyes and ask her for the grace, strength, and courage to be receptive in your own unique way to the vision she has given me to give to you, and to everything she wants to reveal to you and in you, through it.

No vision of a being so vast and so multilayered could ever be definitive, just as not even the greatest Christian mystics could ever definitively define or describe Jesus. As you will come to see and experience, the revolution of love in action they birthed together is an endlessly expanding and unfolding one. Over years of hard and sometimes bewildering work, I have done what I can. Your sincerity, her grace, and the grace of the transcendent and embodied transfiguring love consciousness that she and Jesus lived and pioneered will do the rest.

This is a book not only for all Christians, but for all seekers, lovers of truth, and devotees of the Divine Feminine of every sex and sexuality, religion or no religion. The simple prayer I have used throughout my devotion to her and the labor of shaping and grounding the radical vision she has given me could be useful to you and enable you to stay open to all the demands and revelations she can offer us all: "Mary Magdalene, show me your true face and your true face in me."

If this does not inspire you, make up your own short prayer that expresses your desire to be in communion with her and the tender and fiery love force she incarnated and continues to transmit to all who honor and adore her from beyond time.

The image of Mary Magdalene that has burned in my whole being throughout the grueling and marvelous process of creating *The Magdalene Revolution* is one that I was given through a direct and life-changing experience of her over 20 years ago. I was a co-leader of a pilgrimage to the Divine Feminine in France. We visited Paris, Chartres, Vézelay, the mountain apparition site of La Salette, then came to a sun-drenched Saint Maximin, the town near the huge cave-womb of La Baume, where tradition maintains Mary Magdalene spent the last 30 years of her extraordinary and heroic life in meditation. On a cloudless Sunday, with 30 other pilgrims from all over the world, I climbed the winding and sometimes steep path up the mountain to the cave, now transformed into a church dedicated to her. I entered the cave: Immediately, a deep and glowing peace and blissful silence descended on me. I had visited caves in Ladakh and the Himalayas where great enlightened hermits had lived and experienced in them a similar silence and peace, but not so stunningly and richly as on that Sunday afternoon. I remember thinking, "Only a massive awakening could have left as its gift so profound a presence."

When at last I came out of the cave, I read the official description of what the cave and the Magdalene's sojourn in it symbolized. It rambled on about the Magdalene as a sinner who had devoted the last part of her life to fierce causes and penance, and at last—and only through the grace of Jesus—achieved salvation. I was thunderstruck and outraged; how could the woman who had been the first to see Jesus resurrected, whom even the most conservative and patriarchal parts of the Church had acknowledged as "the apostle to the apostles," have gone on to live a life of misery? She had witnessed, personally perhaps, the greatest single event in human history: How could she at the end of her astounding life be anything but ecstatic?

The immense silence that had drenched my whole being in the cave had no trace of anguish in it. Why was the Church perpetuating an old, sterile, degrading myth about the woman the Gospels clearly show us Jesus loved and honored so deeply?

Still disturbed, I walked down the mountain and across the plain beneath it to the restored old convent my ragtag group was lodged in. Something made me stop and turn around and gaze one last time at the cave entrance, now a small black dot in the distance. For a few eternal seconds, I saw with open eyes Mary Magdalene herself, tall as a tower, her arms outstretched, her face and body and dress pure burning gold, radiating and enclosed by a mandala of brilliant golden light.

Nothing could have prepared me for such a revelation and the awed and ecstatic astonishment it flooded me with. I did not speak of it to anyone. It took me two decades of meditation, prayer, and intense study to begin to understand a little of what I had seen, to find the courage to unpack what this vision might mean both for myself and potentially for others. It is this image of her I kept alive before me as I sculpted this book. It is the golden seed of the golden tree of life and freedom that I pray *The Magdalene Revolution* will be for you.

Through the grace of this vision and this image of her, I have come to know in the depths of myself what many other lovers of the Magdalene also know—that we are now living in the time of the Pentecost when the flames of the Magdalene's unmasked truth and glorious presence are descending to initiate, liberate, and irradiate all of us who are receptive. In the last 30 years, a plethora of brilliant, brave, pioneering books from distinguished male and female mystics, theologians, and visionaries has flooded the market, stirring passionate controversy and often exuberantly contradicting each other, opening up a myriad of approaches to her. Just as in the original Pentecost, after Jesus's Ascension, when the flames of divine wisdom and love descended to initiate the disciples gathered in an "upper room" in Jerusalem, so now the flames of the Divine Feminine as Mary Magdalene are torrentially descending all over the world to initiate and transform those who are ready.

There are two essential lessons I have learned for myself about this Pentecost of the Magdalene, that you who are reading this are potentially part of. The first is that the Pentecost of Mary Magdalene as incarnation of the passion, majesty, fierce and tender wisdom of the Divine Feminine does not erase, negate, or in any way challenge the original miracle: It fulfills and completes its initiation. As *The Magdalene Revolution* will, I hope, show you, it offers us for the first time and at a time when it is desperately needed, a comprehensive, all inclusive, all empowering and liberating vision, both transcendent and immanent of the authentic Christ consciousness, revealed in its golden radiance as a sacred marriage, mirrored and enacted in Jesus and Mary Magdalene's relationship, of the Divine Masculine and the Divine Feminine in the Godhead, in the creation, and in us. It is this vision that pervades and illumines *The Magdalene Revolution* in all of its astounding and constantly evolving applications, not only for our own personal spiritual journeys, but for the evolution of humanity as a whole, and of the world.

The second truth of this Pentecost that I have learned is that this Pentecost of the Magdalene's true human and divine nature is one that both inflames and necessitates all the different visions and approaches to her that are now being offered. Each of us who receives her fire, receives it in terms of our own gifts, sexuality, spiritual personality, and unique mission. Each of us who has heard her voice speak in fire from within our own souls and hearts will sing out what we receive in our own unique and transformed voices, empowering those whose nature and needs are akin to ours, and mixing our voices gladly and humbly with all the other unleashed voices in a divine mass of endlessly expanding celebration. *The Magdalene Revolution* is one of the singing flames of her great Pentecost and this celebration. May it inspire you too, dear friend, to become in your heart, life, and work, in your own unique and irreplaceable way, a singing flame of the sacred marriage.

When I first wrote those words on the morning of Friday, May 2, 2025, in what was my study in my small condo in Oak Park, Illinois, I was elated. I had been wondering whether I should dare to include this vision of her Pentecost that I and others have been receiving in a book that is, as you will see, already radical and provocative enough. That morning, my last fears disappeared, and I was graced the courage to sing out loud on the page the music that had long been sounding in my heart, and the joy I felt when I'd finished stunned me and confirmed viscerally the truth of what I had written.

It was a soft gray Chicago spring morning, and at about 11:00 A.M., I went out to do some shopping for me and my beloved cat, Jade, and to have a celebratory breakfast with *The New York Times*. When I returned at 11:45, there was a crowd milling, noisy and excited, outside my condominium building. Something dramatic had clearly happened. A young woman told me, "There's been a fire."

Still calm and elated and suspecting nothing, I went to the back of my building and saw that it was my condo that was in flames. Filthy black smoke was belching and spitting sparks of fire from its now shattered windows. Hardly able to stand or speak, I asked one of the firemen what had happened. "Unit four is destroyed, and the owner's cat is dead."

I do not need to go into the grisly details of what then unfolded, except to say that the single saving consolation I had that terrible morning was that Jade, who has been everything to me for 17 and a half years—my muse, my beloved, my tenderest friend, my teacher—was not burnt alive. I found her lying serenely, peacefully, in all her sumptuous calico beauty, on the floor in my bedroom, next to my study; the flames had not touched her. She had been asphyxiated by the smoke. There was no sign of fear or even suffering on her face.

All my manuscripts, books, all the small treasures I had accumulated over decades of pilgrimage and travel were destroyed. One whole life, I knew immediately, was over. I have been through, as many of you must have, many deaths, losses, and ordeals in my long life. This has been by far the most devastating. For several days, I did not know whether I could or wanted to survive it. Losing my possessions and facing potential financial disaster did not much disturb me. It was losing Jade, my cat-Magdalene, whom I had adored and been adored by, whose perfect beauty, wisdom, and tenderness had filled my life with joy for almost two decades, that almost drowned me in unbearable heartbreak and despair.

Weeks later, through the love of my friends, intense prayer, and spiritual practice with Jesus and the Magdalene and many messages from Jade in dreams and from an amazing animal communicator in Greece, I find myself a different person. I feel both posthumous and completely alive, shattered but not broken, more convinced than ever of the truth I'm trying to reveal to you in *The Magdalene Revolution* because I'm now raggedly living it, and more resolute than ever in my passion to serve you and the world with all I am and know, in whatever time is left to me.

The whole planet now is burning in the fires of a global dark night. Everyone who is even partially awake knows this. For decades I've been trying to warn everyone that what is here now was coming, and that for all its devastating reality, this unprecedented dark night is an inevitable purification and birth canal for a new embodied divine humanity. The fires of this night have now destroyed what was my life, but they have not destroyed the eternal love I lived with my beloved, and now I am realizing viscerally, they are freeing and expanding and liberating me, day by astonishing day, to become finally my naked, true free self.

In such a global dark night, no one at any spiritual or material level is immune to horror and sometimes intolerable grief and suffering. To pretend you are or might be is a dangerous illusion, because it will blind you to the necessity of doing the inner and outer work of uncovering your true human divine self and then working, creating, and serving from its calm passion the birth of a new humanity and a new world out of the ashes of the old, whether you live to see it fully realized or not. Only such intense, vulnerable, bewildering, dangerous, ecstatic work can begin to prepare you for what is already exploding, what is coming, and what is still even at this late hour in history possible. It is my deepest prayer that *The Magdalene Revolution* will inflame you to do this work in your own way, on your own path, as Mary Magdalene and Jesus did in their violent and terrible times to accompany us now as we come together to our own crucifixion and resurrection.

Never despair. Never give up. Never stop believing in the mercy and grandeur of the Divine and the miracles it will accomplish in you and through you, if you surrender to its demands in faith and trust.

Andrew Harvey
May 22, 2025
Oak Park, Illinois

Introduction

THE WHOLE OF MY WORK FOR 20 YEARS has been dedicated to trying to tell and embody the full story, with all of its transformative implications, of Mary Magdalene and her relationship with Jesus. I would not have been ready before to attempt such a difficult and radical enterprise. As a gay man and a devotee of the Divine Feminine in all its facets and powers, I have been for much of my life enraged by the churches erected in Jesus's name and their misogyny, homophobia, and exclusivism, as well as by the real crimes of the soul and heart these have indisputably led to. This rage, however, has never prevented me from continuing a passionate and reverent exploration of the Christ path and Christian mysticism.

I have come to discover for myself and in myself a more impersonal and balanced view of Christianity that can hold the great good that has persisted in it, while acknowledging the devastating betrayals of the authentic Christ that have characterized much of the Church's practice. This balance has led to the hope that permeates this book, the hope that telling the new story as best I can will inspire you, whatever path you are on in the churches and theologies infused by the Christ, to go through a joyful revolution, one that can break through and birth a new truth, the truth of Christ consciousness.

In this search, I have been constantly steadied and exalted by Mary Magdalene herself. Recently I was reading late at night the Gnostic Gospel of Mary. In it, Mary Magdalene presents a visionary teaching given her by Jesus only to be met by virulent skepticism and denial by the male disciples, especially Peter. On all the other occasions I had read this, I had been convulsed with anger, anger that her supreme realization and generosity had been met with such misogynistic violence. That night, however, something changed forever as I contemplated her reaction to this violence more deeply than I had ever done before. Mary Magdalene did not excoriate the male disciples. She did not humiliate them as a lesser adept might have done from the achieved heights of her own realization. She did not lambaste them as ignorant of the real Jesus, because she knew their love for him was as real as hers. Instead, she wept.

She wept, I saw clearly, for two interlinked reasons. She wept from cosmic anguish and disappointment that the men who so loved Jesus that they were prepared to give their lives for him could not hear a crucial transmission that came to them through a woman. And she wept, too, because she understood what that rejection would cost the men before her, how it would deform their understanding and the understanding of Jesus's life and teaching they would promulgate, and the tragic limitations of the faith they would establish. She was not only weeping for herself, she was weeping for them and for all the men and women who would be deprived of the Jesus she knew and loved so completely.

As this realization expanded in me, I understood viscerally that the time had come to dry those prophetic tears that Mary Magdalene shed, so her face in its full, humble, and confident radiance could stream its wisdom to us now, and the pain of the men who could not acknowledge who she was could at last be healed and transfigured.

It is in Mary Magdalene's great spirit of healing and transfiguration that this book is offered to all those who are open to its truth, to all those who know that the old story in all of its now obviously lethal ramifications is dying, and a new story with her and Jesus's love at the radiating center will be born because it completes and activates the full range of Christ consciousness. We are in the time of the Second Coming.

The Second Coming will not be, as many churches proclaim in different ways, the return of some movie-style Jesus avatar. Rather, the Second Coming will be, and is already for those with the eyes to see and the hearts to receive, the rise of the golden yeast of embodied divine love consciousness in action, in millions of beings of all faiths coming together to renew and regenerate our world. This rise is impossible without a full reclamation of the Divine Feminine, of the Motherhood of God, and without the recognition of Mary

Magdalene as the bride to Jesus's bridegroom, a co-equal and female Christ in her own right. The two of them are a complete, embodied love consciousness that unifies heart, mind, soul, and body and offers humanity a path of divine human love, whose power can engender miracles of inner and outer transformation.

The secret of the Second Coming will be the reception of the bride—the restoration of the full power of the feminine in union with the full power of the masculine in the celebration of their sacred marriage. The time has come for this secret to be shared with everyone who can receive it. Nothing less than the future of humanity depends on us learning and embodying this secret in our inner and outer lives—both in our private, spiritual practice *and* in our outer commitment to urgent, wise, sacred action on behalf of peace, compassion, and justice for all beings.

The Mary Magdalene that is being revealed to us after centuries of obscuration and denigration is not only the divinely chosen unique witness to the Resurrection. With Jesus, she is also the co-parent of the entire Christian mystical tradition and of its greatest and still largely obscured and unknown secret—the transfiguration process that was made possible and available to the whole human race through Jesus, his life, his message, and his Resurrection. It is this transfiguration process, I believe, which Jesus and Mary came to birth together in their sacred marriage, and *that* is the real Holy Grail, not any object. It is this transfiguration process that Mary Magdalene birthed in herself in the years after Jesus's Ascension, to ground it in the bones and cells of humanity. And it is this process—lived through and known with astonished awe by both male and female mystics in secret throughout Christian history—that her return is now inviting all beings to at this moment in human history, when everything depends on understanding it as much as we can and surrendering to its exacting but glorious laws.

These are vast, challenging, even deranging claims, because if they are taken seriously, they not only birth a new human story, but threaten and unravel the power structures of patriarchy. The return of the female Christ in her radiant equality with her beloved empowers a revolution in our understanding of the depth and glory of the Divine Feminine.

This revolution transforms our experience of both female and male identity. It dissolves the lies that support exclusively male priesthood and male-dominated hierarchy of all kinds. It drowns body hatred and sex hatred in a profound and glorious experience, the experience of authentic Christ consciousness, of the sacred unity of mind, heart, body, and soul. It offers to all beings a rugged but ecstatic path of divinization, the amazing process by which a human being becomes human and divine that fulfills both the mission of Jesus and the dream of the Divine recognized and celebrated by evolutionary mystics of all traditions.

The relationship Jesus and the Magdalene lived, that in marvelous ways we can experience but never codify, keeps leading us beyond anything we can imagine. May this journey we are on together inspire you to your own unique relationship with her and him, so you, too, wherever you find yourself on the path, can be inspired to open yourself to the great birth humanity is being offered; that you, too, will find in them sublime examples, transmitters, and teachers. But even more importantly and amazingly, may you come to see them as I do: as loving and compassionate friends who will never cease helping you, if you find in yourself the faith and the courage to keep opening to their help.

Such an opening is both the most glorious possible initiation and the most demanding. I know this from my own experience. Once you have even glimpsed the enormity of what the return of Mary Magdalene makes possible, you can never turn away, however much your old self wants to. This is true, in my experience, for men as well as for women, and for all those brought up in any patriarchal religion and system, even Hinduism and Buddhism, which often define enlightenment in dissociative and antifeminine ways.

Emily Dickinson said, "Tell all the truth, but tell it slant," and I have taken that great mystic's advice, often against my own masculine passion for immediate definition and clarity. I myself had to be prepared in stages to even begin to see the truth of the relationship of Mary Magdalene and Jesus—so strong is the resistance in all of us to the birth it makes possible. So I hope to prepare you in stages as well.

This is why this book begins with the vision I have been given and then proceeds to offer you what I have been offered—the crucial sacred information based on real texts and authentic mystical experience that allows us to integrate its ever-expanding revelation into our own unique relationship with Mary Magdalene.

Let these words from one of the greatest Gnostic texts, *The Thunder, Perfect Mind*, guide us as we take this journey into the glory of what Mary Magdalene and Jesus are offering us:

I was sent forth from the power,

and I have come to those who reflect upon me,

and I have been formed among those who seek after me.

Look upon me, you who reflect upon me,

and you hearers, hear me.

You who are waiting for me, take me to yourselves.

She and we, whether we know it yet or not, have been waiting 2,000 years for our all-transforming encounter with the female Christ she incarnates. May we all be worthy of such an encounter, and may we all be open to its urgent, radiant, always-evolving, ever-expanding teaching of divinization—the divinization its grace makes finally and astoundingly possible.

"I am returning to offer everyone who longs for it the great healing of all divisions—between body and soul, heart and mind, masculine and feminine, sexuality and sublime love, inner divinization and outer sacred action, in the Field of the true Christ Consciousness that is your birthright, the source of your being, the fire that ignites your transfiguration into your own unique unified Christ. I am returning to reveal to you the noble power of sacred soul-companionship of Beloved with Beloved, open to all sexes and sexualities that Jesus and I lived, to invite you to live it also and birth through it, with us as your brother and sister, a new divine humanity, a new world, and a new creation."

— MESSAGE FROM MARY MAGDALENE TO HER ADEPT MARY V IN A VISION ON HER FEAST DAY, JULY 22, 1991

Mary Magdalene in the Gospels

TO BEGIN OUR EXPLORATION OF MARY MAGDALENE in the Gospels and her relationship with Jesus, we must be crystal clear about three interlinked truths.

First, the Synoptic Gospels, while magnificent and foundational to the whole unfolding of Christianity in obvious and inspiring ways, cannot be said to paint a definitive or even comprehensive picture of who Jesus was. The last two centuries of biblical scholarship have proved beyond any reasonable doubt that each of them was written at different times for different audiences with different carefully sculpted agendas and perspectives. These Gospels have either added or subtracted material about Jesus's life or teachings, or both, that suit their governing purpose.

Jesus lived and taught and died and resurrected—that much those of us who know him inwardly come to be certain of. Yet to look to the Gospels for a complete awareness of his life and teaching is a fool's errand, although one enthusiastically pursued by many of the greatest figures of the Church. To my mind, there is a divine intention to allow for new knowledge and revelation to expand on what has been known and said.

Second, the Gospels were written by men in a patriarchal culture where the assumption of female inferiority, even inherent depravity, was a given. They continued to be interpreted and reinterpreted largely by men in other patriarchal cultures. By the 4th century, a master story had emerged in the circle around the emperor Constantine, who by a single edict in AD 313 transformed Christianity from a forbidden cult to the state religion. By AD 323 the Church had its official creed, the Nicene Creed, hammered out in the Council of Nicaea in southwestern Turkey.

It would be another 150 years before an official Bible appeared, but what was going to be included in it was already taking shape. In AD 367, Bishop Athanasius formulated a list of the 27 canonically acceptable apostolic writings that would prove identical with what became the official New Testament canon.

This master story concocted entirely by men asserted that, as Karen King writes in her final chapter of *The Gospel of Mary Magdalene*:

"An unbroken chain stretched from Jesus to the male apostles and on to their successors in the Church—elders, ministers, priests—and guaranteed the unity and uniformity of Christian belief and practice.

"In the drastically streamlined version of this story that most Christians accept, Jesus came to earth to found a religion called Christianity, called his male-only disciples to be its apostles and priests, and gave only them the sacrament of the Eucharist at the Last Supper."

And as Cynthia Bourgeault writes in her great book *The Meaning of Mary Magdalene*, "The obvious anomalies are overlooked why Mary Magdalene, who was specifically given the first apostolic charge by Jesus himself to announce the news of his Resurrection, was not included among the apostles and why Paul, who was not at the Last Supper and never met Jesus in his earthly life was. . . . The message being sent about the value of women and their full inclusion in the body of Christianity is only too obvious."

Third, this patriarchal distortion of the telling of the Jesus story, and its increasing orthodox streamlining in practice, entailed four interrelated, subtle disasters:

- The deliberate ignoring of the considerable role women played in Jesus's original mission as companions, supporters, and, yes, disciples who accompanied him in what some scholars now see as a deliberate and provocative statement of radical equality in the kingdom.
- The deliberate ignoring of the role that women played after Jesus's death in the early Church, where we know

from Paul's Epistle to the Romans and Philippians and from Pliny the Elder and Clement of Alexandria, that women could be deacons, priests, and even bishops.

- The suppression of texts, both Gnostic and otherwise, that in any way portrayed women as equal in visionary capacity to men and in any way presented Jesus as celebrating the motherhood of God and the Divine Feminine.
- The writing out of Mary Magdalene as the most crucially important of all his followers and perhaps even his consort or wife.

The consequences of these conscious attempts to suppress the feminine in all its forms were nothing less than the abortion of the birth of the divine human. Jesus had come to proclaim a birth that could only take place through the sacred marriage of all opposites—transcendence and immanence, male and female, body and soul. This tragic misinterpretation damaged the force and wholeness of the Christian mystical tradition which, for all its magnificence—and with the brave exception of certain women mystics such as Julian of Norwich, Hadewijch of Antwerp, and Hildegard of Bingen—could never fully embrace the body and sexuality. A message that Jesus intended to transfigure all of earth life became etherealized; centered largely on sin, guilt, and human depravity; deeply skeptical of visionary ecstasy and revelation; and inextricably wedded to patriarchal structures of authority.

The central task in the radical reformation of Christianity in the name of Jesus's original message is the reclamation of the full power of the sacred feminine in all its majesty and passionate compassion for all of life.

Now let us turn directly to Mary Magdalene as portrayed in the Gospels.

I am going to begin with what is to me the greatest key of all—the clue, in fact, to how to begin to restore Mary Magdalene in her full splendor and how to read what little the Gospels tell us of her in a revolutionary way.

Late one night some months ago, I was reading for the thousandth time the 20th chapter of Saint John's Gospel in the King James version that I love. This is the chapter in which Mary Magdalene meets the resurrected Jesus in the garden, and two verses suddenly became alive for me in a way they had never been before.

In verse 17 it is written:

> *Jesus saith unto her, touch me not, for I am not yet ascended to my father, but go to my brethren and say unto them, I ascend into my father and to my God and your God.*

Verse 18 reports:

> *Mary Magdalene came and told the disciples that she had seen the Lord and that he had spoken these things unto her.*

What broke upon me that night in wave after wave of recognition and joy was not anything in the words themselves. It was the fullness of what was *not* said in the gap between verse 17 and 18 that erupted in my soul.

Over the next days, what I had been graced to understand beyond thought and dogma unfolded in increasingly clear awareness: for in the hours between witnessing and being irradiated by the glory of the Resurrection and telling the astounding news to the male disciples, Mary Magdalene realized in her whole being the secret, miraculous meaning of her entire relationship with Jesus, a meaning even she, with all her passionate devotion and mystical awareness, could never have suspected—that she would be the one chosen by the Divine, in which the whole story of their union unfolded to be the first living flame of what Saint Paul called "the glorious liberty of the children of God."

In those hours, she was in her now increasingly divinized being. All the churches that would be created in Jesus's name, all the revelations to follow in the Christian tradition in both the male and female mystics, are alive and brilliant in her incandescent silence. All the sublime artistic achievements of Christianity, from its architectural to its artistic and musical marvels, were in her alone in embryo. All the discoveries made by Christianity's greatest mystics, from the Desert Fathers to Gregory Palamas to Saint Symeon the new Theologian to Teresa of Ávila and my own teacher, Father Bede Griffiths, of the transfiguration process that could birth the human being into embodied, divine humanity—all of these were vibrant in her as she walked from the garden to where the disciples were sequestered.

In those hours, she became something more extraordinary even than the mother of the Church or its glorious mystical and artistic traditions, or the guardian and guide to the transfiguration process. She became, with Jesus, co-parent of a new human race, the race that evolutionary mystics of all traditions have proclaimed as the goal of human evolution.

With this vision possessing me, I plunged into the Christian mystical tradition to try to find other witnesses to its splendor. After months of research, I found many exciting collaborations of what I had intuited, in the Desert Fathers, Clement of Rome, and Thomas Aquinas, among others.

Gratified as I was to discover these celebrations of Mary Magdalene at the heart of the patriarchal tradition, none of them seemed to me to go far enough. For weeks I was baffled as to where to look for what I was longing to find. Then I remembered Romanos Melodus, the passionate, prophetic mystic of the Orthodox Church and champion of the Divine Feminine, whom I first discovered 20 years ago when I was working on several books on Mary the Mother.

Romanos Melodus, probably of Jewish descent, was born in Emesus in Phoenecia toward the end of the 5th century. We know that he lived in Berytus (modern Beirut), where he was deacon before moving to Constantinople in the reign of Anastasius I, and that he died between AD 555 and 565. I had first met his thrilling ecstatic work 20 years ago when I discovered his Akathist hymn that celebrates Mary the Mother.

Hail you through whom we are clothed in glory.

Hail pillar of fire, guiding those in darkness.

Hail you through whom we gain our victories.

Hail healing of my body.

Hail healing of my soul.

I had realized all those years ago that in the Akathist hymn, Romanos Melodus had all but declared Mary as nothing less than the embodied Divine Mother, far more than the humble, surrendered, silent, obedient woman the Church adored. I understood Romanos Melodus had not only crystallized all the glory of the titles that the first four centuries of Christian mysticism bestowed on her, but without naming her as such, proclaimed her as Divine Mother, implying an even greater role in the Christ revelation than she had yet been given.

When I dived afresh into Romanos Melodus, especially into his great hymns of the Resurrection, I discovered two things that confirmed my intuition of his visionary prescience.

The first was a vision of Mary Magdalene herself. His Mary Magdalene is an inspired ecstatic of the highest visionary truth, the center and head of a group of women who, unlike the male disciples, neither denied Jesus nor fled the horror and danger of the Crucifixion. She was the already worthy witness of his Resurrection, a figure close to what is revealed to us in the Gnostic Gospels and especially in the Gospel of Mary. In hymn four, Romanos Melodus situates Mary Magdalene firmly in her mission of messenger.

Jesus says, "May your tongue proclaim these things, woman, and explain them to the sons of the kingdom who are waiting for me to awaken I who am, the living one. Go quickly, Mary. Assemble my disciples. In you I have a trumpet with a powerful voice. Sing a song of peace to the fearful ears of my hidden friends. Awaken them all as if from sleep, so they can run and meet me. Go say to them the spouse has awoken, leaving the tomb and leaving nothing within it. Chase away, apostles, your mortal grief because he is awoken, he who offers to all broken men the Resurrection."

When Jesus says to her, "Assemble my disciples," it is clear that Romanos is celebrating Mary not only as the first witness of the Resurrection, but also, and this is revolutionary, as the first and essential link of the assembly that in the end would create the Church. And then Romanos Melodus goes even further.

He has Mary Magdalene say, after she has seen Jesus resurrected: "I am filled with the transmissions of the Christ. I do not hesitate to say it. I have received the same glory as Moses. I have seen, yes.

I have seen not on the mountain, but in the tomb veiled not by a cloud, but by a body, the master of the light beings and the clouds. Their master yesterday, now and forever, says to me 'Mary, hurry. Go and reveal to those who love me that I am resurrected.'"

She, like Moses, Romanos Melodus shows us, knows herself to have been chosen as an intermediary between God and God's people. While Moses received his vision of utter transcendence on a mountain, Mount Sinai, Romanos Melodus makes clear the difference between his revelation and hers. Mary Magdalene receives her prophetic mandate not from transcendence alone, but through a personal relationship with her beloved, who fills her with the vision of him and his transmission. She has in a profound and mysterious way become one with him. He is, although resurrected and on his way to the Father, living inside her as her new essential identity from which she speaks. And it is this being possessed by him in heart, mind, soul, and body that gives her the courage to proclaim, "I have received the same glory as Moses," while making clear in what she says next that she is receiving this transcendent blessing in an utterly new way—in the tomb and in the darkest depths of matter, the very matter she witnessed transfigured in her beloved.

As the firstborn of the new creation, she shows us here what will happen to us if we dare to receive the full splendor of what she not only now knows, but what she is. We too will be like her, born into being filled with the Christ, and our flesh, our tomb, will be flooded with and transfigured by the divine light. We too will become the living grail.

Let us now plunge deeper into some profound parallels that Romanos Melodus undoubtedly intends between Mary Magdalene and Moses. In Leviticus 1, verses 1 and 2, we read of Moses, "Yahweh called Moses and spoke to him and told him, speak to the Israelites and say to them, 'When anyone brings an offering to Yahweh, bring as your offering an animal from either the herd or the flock.'" As for Mary Magdalene, in John 20:14, we read, "She did not know it was Jesus, and Jesus said to her, 'Do not touch me because I have not yet risen to the Father, but go and find my brethren and speak to them.'" In both cases, if you study the text, you see that the Divine is not at first clearly pinpointed.

In Leviticus, the Hebrew word *vahiqra* has no name subject. The one who calls is not identified, just as Mary does not know at first that she is in Jesus's presence.

In both accounts we see the Divine calling each of them by name. This calling by name establishes the foundation of the new relationship. The Divine is calling into a new task, the task of communicating God's astounding truth to the community.

In both cases, too, the message the chosen one is to give is in danger of not being believed because it rests on no tangible proof. In Moses's case, the tablets of the law were broken. In Mary's case, she was given the task of proclaiming the seemingly impossible: Jesus's Resurrection.

And there is another crucial similarity. Throughout biblical history, those whom the Divine summons to bear witness and transmit its message and word are never those who seem most qualified for this function. Moses proclaimed from the beginning his lack of eloquence, which made him run to Aaron for help. Aaron went on to betray him in the debacle of the golden calf; Jonah tried to flee as far as possible from the weight of the charge conferred on him; Jeremiah, when vision descended on him, was a young man, so young in fact that no one would think of inviting him to speak in public; Judith presented herself as God's last resort when all hope had been abandoned.

Now, in Mary Magdalene, the prophetic torch is passed to a woman, Jesus's beloved, who is asked to announce the Resurrection. Her witness would be both socially and legally null in the world of her time and would have to be relayed to the brethren if it was going to be heard. Because of the scandalous way the Divine chooses its messengers, they all find themselves in a precarious and profoundly unstable position, subject to skepticism, derision, and humiliation, as both Mary Magdalene and Moses were.

In Hymn Two of the Resurrection, Romanos Melodus continues, "When she had heard all the words of the Word, the young woman ran back to her female companions and said,

> O women, the marvels I have seen and will recount! I am filled with the vision and the words of the Christ. I have seen the master of the invisible realms and the clouds. Their master today, now, and always says to me, 'Mary, hurry, go. Reveal to those who love me that I am resurrected like an olive branch. Take me on your tongue to announce the good news to the descendants of Noah, showing them that death is destroyed and the beloved has been brought to life again, He who offers to broken men the Resurrection.'

Romanos Melodus, who as we have seen, compares Mary Magdalene to Moses, now compares the witness of Mary Magdalene to the olive branch the dove brought to Noah that signaled the end of the great flood. She and her witness are together, Melodus is implying, the sign of a wholly new creation that transcends the old, that announces the miracle of an unimaginable rebirth, not just of Jesus himself, but of the whole of humanity and the creation.

As Hadewijch of Antwerp wrote of her own mystical experience of the resurrected Christ 12 centuries later, echoing Mary Magdalene's ecstasy:

> *Oh this fury of love*
> *that explodes and transfigures me,*
> *this rapture of being all His,*
> *what wisdom in love's fury,*
> *what astounding victory*
> *in the fury of free love!*

With this vision of Mary Magdalene revealed by Romanos Melodus and Hadewijch ablaze in our hearts and minds, let us now take a deeper look at these representations not with the eyes of the past or even with eyes of the latest and best scholarship (although I will draw on that), but with the new eyes graced by what I call the "vision of the gap." If we do so, we will see the beginnings of a new story emerge that challenges the patriarchal formulation of who Mary Magdalene is and the continuing dismissal of the feminine and its authority in the Church. It also challenges all of us to rise to the radical grandeur of what it will make clear: the new path of evolutionary love that she and Jesus open for us together, the path that, if we dare to integrate its message into our lives, will change our vision of who we are—what consecrated and ecstatic relationship can engender, and what could still, even at this dangerous late stage of human evolution, be possible.

There are two dangers that I've come to see clearly in telling such a story.

The first danger is to trivialize the story in the attempt to make it immediately accessible to everyone. Evolutionary love is a quantum leap in our understanding of what love can be, and it requires mental and spiritual work to rise to its height, work we cannot avoid if we wish truly to be transformed.

The second danger is to tell the story of their love in such an idealized way that instead of inspiring us to do the inner work to emulate them and incarnate the truth of evolutionary love progressively into our lives, we give up, thinking that we are not capable of so amazing and rigorous an adventure. This is especially dangerous for those who have experienced great heartbreak and betrayal in love, or for those who have settled uneasily for comfortable and decent mediocrity. This second danger is hard to avoid because both Mary Magdalene and Jesus were such extraordinary beings, and the story of their love is suffused with miracle and an astounding heroism of heart, that not to tell the story in its magnificence is to betray both of them and the power of the path they open up for us.

This second danger is one we meet when we approach any of the great spiritual figures and prophetic transmissions of the past, and the courage we need both to recognize it and avoid it is hard won. This courage requires of us three things: (1) the willingness to forgive ourselves for the unillumined and compromised choices we have made, seeing clearly why we did so without shame or punishing self-judgment; (2) the determination to claim our own divine consciousness and nature in the face of a culture that denies it and in the face of our own continuing ignorance of its full beauty and power; and (3) the quiet passion to believe that whatever the griefs and mistakes of our past, we have within us as a divine blessing the capacity to change and be changed in ways we can hardly begin to imagine.

I have not found any of these three things easy, even after all I have been graced to experience on my mystical journey. My own search for a human and divine love has led me down many cul-de-sacs and threatened my heart with cynicism and despair. There have been many times in preparing and writing this book that I found myself saying to myself, I believe and honor Jesus and Mary's extraordinary love, but find it hard to believe that I could live and experience it in my own life. What I have learned is that these difficulties are to be expected, that variations of them will arise in anyone who risks confronting the glory of what Jesus and Mary lived.

What I have learned too is that with faith and the continuing grace of the Magdalene and the Christ, these difficulties are not insuperable. They have shown me with ruthless clarity all I continue to need to work on to clear myself of my old story to prepare for the revelation of the new one Jesus and Mary are birthing. These difficulties have also shown me in unmistakable ways that when I allow myself to experience and suffer them and then open them to healing grace, their authority begins to fade and a grounded hope for a new way of love starts to flourish, fragilely at first, but with increasing strength and joy.

As I have entered my 70s, I find myself freer than ever before, not only from the patriarchal messages about the body and sexuality, but also from my own sometimes painful past. I am aware that this freedom is just beginning and that it will need faith and persistence if I am to embody fully what I, through the grace of Jesus and Mary, am beginning to know. The journey into evolutionary love is a journey through the death of any of the old stories we have been told or have told ourselves about love. They die hard, but they do die, the more we allow the splendor of what Jesus and Mary lived to penetrate and irradiate us, as Mary Magdalene herself was penetrated and irradiated by the glory of the Resurrection.

Who Were Mary Magdalene and Jesus?

We are now going to approach together the first meeting of Mary Magdalene and Jesus. In order to open as fully as we can to what happened in one of the most momentous meetings of human divine lovers in mystical history, we will need to understand, as richly and complexly as we can, who they each were separately and what erupted in them both when they met. In order to do so, we will need to see them both in their humanity, sloughing off the myths that in both cases compromise or mask it, and in their divinity and in the divine archetypes their transformative meeting enshrine and activate.

What this entails is a careful, stage-by-stage winding journey toward their meeting, each stage of which gathers crucial and luminous information that will allow us to see and experience this meeting in its full revolutionary significance. Carl Jung wrote in *The Red Book*, "To give birth inside an age to the primordially ancient is creation. Salvation is the solution of the problem, the resolution of the task. The task is to give birth to the old in a new time."

Jung knew and exemplified in his writings and in his profound inner life what such a task entails—a sacred marriage of deep spiritual experience and discernment with exacting radical scholarship. Too much liberty of intuition leads to fantasy and illusion. Excessive reliance on scholarship, however brilliant, leads to the telling of an old story in interesting but not revelatory new ways. Only their rich, difficult, patient marriage can hope to midwife "the birth of the old in a new time."

This demands an abundance of my least favorite virtue—patience—the patience of a divine detective or archaeologist sorting through shards of clues and previous misinterpretations. It also demands, of course, exigent self-knowledge, an awareness of one's own limitations and shadows, as well as a capacity to unknow everything you learn.

So let me prepare you now for the spiraling journey toward experiencing fully the meeting of Mary and Jesus by giving you an overview of how I will unfold its stages in advance so you can trust and grasp where I'm hoping to take you and absorb the insights each stage offers you. Please, dear friend, read slowly and contemplatively. For the miracle at the marriage feast at Cana to reveal its richest and most empowering message to us, many different perspectives and often hidden or secret sources of revelation have to be brought together.

In the first stage of the journey, I attempt to remove from the portrait we have of Mary Magdalene the stains that competing stories of her have obscured it with, from both patriarchal distortion and the glamorous compensatory versions of some contemporary celebrators of the Magdalene. My aim is to reveal Mary in her ordinary extraordinariness, which makes her at once closer to us and more challenging and inspiring.

In the second stage, I invite us to turn to the man she went to meet in Capernaum, the 29-year-old Jesus. As I will show, we need to see Jesus both in his contemporary historical context, drawing on the best scholarship, and in the context of the continuing revelation of his divine mission, to begin to grasp what their meeting meant for both of them. In other words, we need to see him both as Rabbi Jesus at an important stage of his evolution and the evolution of his teaching and mission, and as the totally human and totally divine incarnation of Christ. Confronting the second, however, involves a radical cleaning of the portrait of Jesus that has come down to us both in the Gospels and in much of the Christian mystical tradition.

My aim here is not in any way to diminish the splendor of Jesus's mystical truth and identity, but to expand and ground our understanding of it by embracing at greater depths its marriage with his humanity. As with Mary Magdalene, this approach brings Jesus closer to us in our ragged humanness, while revealing new possibilities for our own human divine embodiment.

In the third stage, as we approach Jesus and Mary's meeting, I invite us to take a step back and envision it and its consequences by comparing it in some rich detail to the meeting of Shams and Rumi. Rumi, who lived in the 13th century, is Islam's and the world's greatest mystical poet, whose life was transformed by his meeting and relationship with a mysterious and wild older man, Shams of Tabriz. The profound parallels and differences between the meetings of Shams and Rumi and Jesus and Mary are explored to give us an overall sense of what happens when mystical revolutionaries meet and come into union. This stage ends with the vision I believe is most accurate of the inner crisis Mary Magdalene was in when she came to meet her ordained beloved.

In the fourth stage, we arrive together at the meeting again. I believe we need to clean it of all the competing and limiting versions of it, to begin to see it as it may really have been. This involves two reinterpretations—of Mary's so-called demon possession and of the traditional vision of Jesus as non-sexual. To debunk as helpfully and convincingly as possible all constricting visions of Jesus's sexuality and its potential transfiguring implications both for our understanding of Christ's consciousness and of the new path of love he and Mary together open for us, I then show what I believe to be the significance of his first miracle, the miracle of Cana at a marriage feast.

In order for this revelation to be as inspiring and empowering for us as possible, I invite you to contemplate in detail three different aspects of the tradition of what is called "sexual holiness" in Judaism. With the astonishing insights these explorations offer, we then return to the meeting of Jesus and Mary again and see it, I hope and trust, both in its extraordinary human depth and archetypal divine promise and birthing power.

It has taken me decades of inner and outer work to begin to be able to map such an approach to the radical richness of what the first meeting of these two sacred initiates of divine human love prepares for all of us.

I have tried to distill what I believe to be the most liberating and expansive information, in as clear and grounded a way as possible to reveal as much as possible to anyone willing to take this journey with me, of what Jesus and Mary's new kind of love offers us and invites us to embrace in the Divine, in them and in ourselves. May it amaze and hearten you as it continues to amaze and hearten me.

As we begin our experience together of this fugal unfolding of meanings and perspectives, I invite you to pause once again and remember the life-changing meetings you have yourself experienced, the mystery of how they occurred, how they affected and changed you. I suggest you choose three of them: a lover whose encounter transformed you; a spiritual teacher or wise, loving elder who revealed to you precious insights into the path of love; and an animal companion who, like my beloved cat Jade, initiated you into a realm of blissful, tender joy. When you have distilled in yourself the unique essence of each of these transformative meetings, mix the essences together in the core of your heart and allow yourself to feel as fully as you can the power of the sun of divine love, of which all sacred meetings are rays.

Who Was Mary Magdalene?

To begin to answer this question, we have to look first at the two versions of Mary Magdalene that are now predominant, both of them adamantly espoused, and both, I believe, limited.

In what I call the Master Dominator version, first codified by Pope Gregory I in the 6th century and endlessly repeated in different garish embellishments throughout Church history, Mary Magdalene is a rich, repentant prostitute, someone whose vicious excesses drove her to madness and into the presence of Jesus, whose all-forgiving love transformed her into the apostle of the apostles. It should go without saying that this version of her life is the concoction of a misogyny that has continued to wreak havoc with the message of Christ's consciousness.

While this version is limited, it nevertheless did paradoxically offer deep comfort to many men and women who felt their darkened lives excluded from grace. Countless Christians throughout history have been inspired by it, despite its now obvious fantasy, to believe in divine forgiveness's power of limitless transformation.

After all, if a degraded, crazy prostitute could be transfigured by the love of Christ into the first witness of the Resurrection, then believers could feel that no sin, however scandalous or outrageous, could prevent them from being resurrected by God's mercy. The price for this inspiration, however, was the obscuration of Mary Magdalene's real status and importance, and through that, the continuing mutilation and degradation of women, the body, and sexuality. Armed with this version, the patriarchal Church could continue in its celebration of exclusive male authority and in its championship, in the name of Jesus, of an etherealized, bodiless, purely transcendent love that negated or imprisoned the splendor of Eros and offered no path to Eros's divinization.

In the second version, which radiates through the work of some feminist theologians, both male and female, and a host of channelers of what is claimed to be Mary Magdalene unadulterated, Mary Magdalene is presented in various resplendent roles—as the daughter of a royal line, as an initiate into the Egyptian mysteries, priestess of Isis, steeped in sex-magic and esoteric law of bewildering complexity. This version exaggerates in the opposite direction from the patriarchal one and is clearly and perhaps inevitably compensatory, a reaction born out of age-long trauma and not necessarily out of considered wisdom.

This second version has the advantage of celebrating Mary Magdalene as an adept in her own right, as Jesus's equal and teacher, as a woman of divine dignity, brilliance, realization, and passion. Its disadvantage is that, like the first version, its more fanciful claims are unsubstantiated by any of the traditional or Gnostic texts or by the Gospel of Mary Magdalene herself (*The Gospel of the Beloved Companion*) and can too easily be refuted by those theologians who continue to consciously or unconsciously want Mary Magdalene enclosed in the old patriarchal box. The channeled information about her that ballasts this version is frequently contradictory and can easily be dismissed.

There is, however, a third version of who Mary Magdalene was and is, which fuses the richest and most resplendent truths of both the patriarchal and exaggeratedly feminist versions without being trapped in the limitations of either. In this third version, which informs this book, Mary Magdalene is neither a wealthy, repentant prostitute nor a priestess of Isis. She is, as Jesus was, a marginalized, ordinary, extraordinary woman, probably from Magdala, of exceptional spiritual abilities, a passionate seeker of truth, whom Jesus loved and was loved by and who taught him as he taught her in their sacred union.

Jesus, after all, was a carpenter's son. Why could Mary Magdalene not have been a farmer's or artisan's daughter? The central and revolutionary message of Jesus's lowly birth is that all human beings have within them divine consciousness and so the potential of becoming divine themselves. Why couldn't the woman who was destined for him also have been from the lower marginalized classes he so loved, and whose courage, dignity, and humility his message celebrated again and again?

Jesus did not have to travel to Egypt and India to become fully enlightened, as some versions of his life have improbably claimed, and Mary Magdalene did not have to be schooled in the mysteries of Isis to be awoken to her divine nature while she was in her home or walking down the street in Magdala. An educated glance at human mystical history would show us that the Divine is quite capable of waking people up to the radiance of their divinity wherever they are and in whatever circumstances they find themselves.

Let us turn now and look at what the best contemporary scholarship reveals of who Mary Magdalene was. Mary Magdalene was a Jewish woman from the city of Magdala on the western shore of the Sea of Galilee, and her nickname "Magdalene" was almost certainly given her by Jesus himself, who liked giving those close to him nicknames. Bruce Chilton writes in his magisterial *Mary Magdalene, a Biography*:

"Although Simon was a fisherman, Jesus dubbed him Rock (*Kepha* in Aramaic, *Petros* in Greek). This name made fun of the instability of Simon's boat, when Jesus used it as a platform to preach to crowds on the shore. (Given Simon Peter's sluggishness in understanding what Jesus said on several occasions, *Rock* might allude to some mental density as well.) The two other leading apostles, James and John, were obviously a noisy pair; Jesus called them *boanerges,* sons of thunder (Mark 3:16–17).

"The Gospels don't report that Jesus personally gave Mary the name Magdalene. No one can prove he called her that, but by inferring that he identified one Mary among the several other Marys the Gospels mention by calling her Magdalene, we can explain why that name appears so consistently."

Bruce Chilton adds, "How much less romantic might later legends of Mary's wealth, elegance, and seductiveness have been, had scholars and fabulous alike remembered that Magdala was a fishing town known throughout the region for its fish."

The name Magdala derived from the term *migdal,* a low stone tower for keeping fish. Again, Bruce Chilton writes, "Holding facilities were part of a complex of stone breakwaters docks and reservoirs that distinguished this town of about 3,000 residents. Local fishermen netted fish from the Sea of Galilee, especially trying for the plentiful sprat, a small bony fish about six inches long that could be dried for export. They dragged loads of live fish into stone holding tanks and then stockpiled them for drying and salting."

Magdala was also three miles southeast of Tiberias, the city Herod Antipas built to be a new capital city to replace inland Sepphoris, named after the ruling emperor Tiberias.

This proximity to Tiberias of Magdalene is important for an understanding of her nickname because Tiberias for the contemporary Jews was a monument to idolatry and impurity. The historian Josephus tells us that the Jews who moved to the city were the flotsam of Galilee, trash washed up on the shore. As Chilton writes, "These settlers became vehicles of the uncleanness that Herod Antipas had released throughout the Galilean region." And it is this uncleanness and its force of impurity that also clings to Mary Magdalene's nickname.

Since Magdala was so close to Tiberias and dominated by it both politically and economically, it's important to note here that this does not mean Mary Magdalene herself was impure, as the patriarchal version would have it. Jesus's nickname for the woman he loved and recognized as his equal could well have been ironic.

Complex irony, as anyone might note who reads his parables carefully, was one of his favorite weapons of truth.

Another myth that many reputable modern scholars, both male and female, have made clear needs to be expunged from the Mary Magdalene story: that she was fabulously wealthy. Both the patriarchal and feminist versions of Mary Magdalene are, I believe, compromised by this fantasy.

Let's take the patriarchal version first. Here's how Pope Gregory I spawned a legion of corroborating fantasies, when on September 21, 591, he preached a homily in the basilica of San Clemente in Rome on Luke's story of the sinful woman who anointed Jesus's feet with her tears and with expensive ointment from an alabaster jar. The implication throughout his homily is that Mary Magdalene had grown wealthy from her exploitation of male lust and now repented. "It is clear, brothers, that the woman previously used the unguent to perfume her flesh in forbidden acts. What she therefore displayed more scandalously, she was now offering to God in a more praiseworthy manner. . . . She had displayed her hair to set off her face, but now her hair dries her tears. She had spoken proud things with her mouth, but in kissing the Lord's feet she now planted her mouth on the redeemer's feet. For every delight therefore she had had in herself, she now immolated herself. She turned the mass of her crimes to virtues in order to serve God entirely in penance."

This long-lived fantasy has unfortunately not died out. In one recent scholarly reconstruction of her life that derives its exuberant authority from Luke's association of Mary with Johanna, who had married Khuza in Herod Antipas's household, Mary and the powerful Johanna were business buddies, and Mary used Johanna's connections and her own wealth to host extravagant dinner parties in which she employed Jesus as a stand-up comic. You cannot make this stuff up.

In the version of certain feminist scholars, as well as the great majority of the woman channelers who claim to have received messages from the real Mary Magdalene, her wealth is also emphasized, and for an opposite reason—to give her sovereignty and dignity and sometimes even royal status, and also to explain how she could have lived for long periods in Egypt and become an initiate in the

Isis mysteries. In our squalid contemporary New Age so obsessed with using spirituality to gain financial power, such a picture could seem not only convincing but inspirational. Perhaps, too, presenting Mary Magdalene in such a lavish way was subconsciously designed to make her seem special and unique. Sadly, however, the obsession with her wealth and royalty simply mimics part of the patriarchal story it is meant to detonate.

It cannot be said too often that the real problem with both these versions is that they have nothing to do with how Mary Magdalene is presented in any of the texts that she appears in.

Let us look now at Luke, Chapter 8, where we meet Mary Magdalene for the first time as part of a group of both men and women who accompanied Jesus:

"And there were some women who had been healed from evil spirits and ailments: Mary, who was called Magdalene, from whom seven demons had gone out, and Johanna, Khuza's wife, Herod, Stewart and Susannah, and many others who provided for them from their belongings."

Careless reading of this crucial verse has boosted the fantasy of Mary's wealth. The reality, though, is that it simply does not say that Mary shared Johanna's wealthy status. In fact, if you read this verse carefully, it contrasts the two women.

As Bruce Chilton writes crisply: "Among the women Luke mentions, Johanna is aristocratic, perhaps wealthy and well connected. Mary, on the other hand, doesn't have Johanna's status or connections. What she has are demons."

No ancient text nor any reasonable speculation suggests that Jesus ever moved to Magdala to appear at her dinner parties as a spiritual Stephen Colbert or that Mary owned property there that she put at Jesus's disposal.

The Mary Magdalene that Jesus met in their first encounter was a humble Jewish woman, probably unmarried, probably rejected by her family as unclean because of the agonizing and deranging crisis she was consumed by (a crisis we will explore in stages to come), and in her early 20s.

And now we must ask another question: Why did Mary Magdalene in her agony choose to come to Jesus? There were many healers and wannabe prophets in the Judea of her time whom she could have gone to in her desperation. What drew her to him? Had she prayed to meet one of God's hidden ones, knowing that only a being of ultimate knowledge could heal her? Had she received an unmistakable sign in a dream or vision that it was Jesus who would redeem her from herself?

When Mary Magdalene first met Jesus, he was in his late 20s and had moved from Nazareth to Capernaum. A near stoning (Luke 4:16–30) had shown him brutally that the small town he had known since his childhood would never embrace him as a teacher. As Bruce Chilton writes, "In Capernaum Jesus hit his stride. This fishing town of a couple of thousand people provided him with a secure haven and his reputation as an exorcist grew."

Chilton goes on, "Jesus settled in with two brothers named Simon and Andrew who had originally come from Bethsaida (John 1:44) and had married into a fishing family in Capernaum. Accommodating Rabbi Jesus was not a routine act of hospitality. His own needs were modest enough. . . . The strain came from the eager crowds that thronged around him. Venues where Jesus practiced exorcism and healing could become so crowded that people were unable to move. The Gospels describe a scene in the house that was so crowded that four men had to break a hole through the roof and lower their paralyzed friend to Jesus on a litter to be healed (Matthew 9:1–8, Mark 2:1–12, Luke 5:17–26)."

That scene suggests the environment in which Mary Magdalene first met the young rabbi. Capernaum was abuzz with Jesus's reputation. You had to fight your way in to see him. The Jesus then that Mary met was a famous healer, exorcist, and preacher of a new divine supremacy and power that the Aramaic scriptures had promised: the *malkuta delahah*. The kingdom of God.

The Jesus that Mary met was like Mary Magdalene herself, from the marginalized class. He was a *tekton*, an artisan maker of wooden products like doors and frames, at the lower end of the peasant class, who may have had on occasion to beg for his living and who came from a family that most likely owned no land. Like Mary Magdalene herself, he knew the sting of poverty and suffered both the subtle and obvious outrages of social, economic, and political humiliation.

Jesus had been a disciple of a famous ascetic teacher, John the Baptist, who had proclaimed him as something like the messiah the Jewish tradition had been awaiting. His first sermon in Nazareth after his definitive awakening to his divine identity, and the temptation in the desert that followed and integrated it, had announced a new order—one in which all beings, especially the poor and afflicted, would be honored and celebrated in a victory of love over inequality, justice over systemic religious and political oppression. This sermon had so scandalized Jesus's listeners that they had tried to kill him; he only narrowly escaped with his life. He decamped to Capernaum where he, in Chilton's words, "hit his stride" and became widely known all over Galilee as a radically unconventional healer exorcism teacher who surrounded himself—as Mary Magdalene would have known—with a devoted band of women as well as men, and lived in a freewheeling, convivial, all-inclusive way that was already arousing the ire and condemnation of religious purists.

What would have drawn Mary Magdalene the most to Jesus, however, was what she undoubtedly heard of his teachings of the Kingdom—the *malkuta delahah*, the divine supremacy promised in scripture.

Mary, through her own mystical awakening, had had direct, dazzling, disturbing glimpses into this divine reality and perhaps knew something too of the oral tradition of the *malkuta delahah*. As Chilton writes so memorably of the power that that oral tradition held: "Jesus taught that God's kingdom was the revolutionary principle behind the whole cosmos. One day, all of life would shimmer with divine fullness and energy. Caesar's might would dissolve and the kingdom would push away any resistance with its force as natural and mysterious as a sprouting seed, as inexorable as rivers in flood."

Mary Magdalene would have heard, too, that Rabbi Jesus was also able, through the mysterious and galvanizing power of his own realization, to give those who came to him the direct and naked experience of the *malkuta delahah*. It was this undeniable experience that Mary needed to ground in her whole being—mind, heart, soul, and body—to be able to end and transcend the horrifying inner war that was laying waste to her sanity and her being.

Mary Magdalene came to Jesus then both shattered and completely open, despairingly trusting in the presence of this man who had known, as she had, poverty, exclusion, derision, and extreme controversy, and who was living in the freedom of his life and the radical majesty of his teachings. This was the truth that she herself had glimpsed but not known completely how to interpret or integrate—that she might be graced to receive the all-healing and all-grounding revelation she knew she needed, not only for her future spiritual progress but for her very survival.

This is as far as wise contemporary scholarship can take us. In order to enter the fullness and revolutionary significance of the meeting that could potentially transform our whole understanding and practice of Christ consciousness and of Jesus and his mission, we have to dare to go further.

Just as I have argued we have to interpret Mary Magdalene's role in the Gospels, inspired by what she became in the Resurrection Garden, so we have to see the Jesus she met on that all-transforming day in the small, crowded house in Capernaum, not only in the context of his contemporary world, but also from everything we have learned and continue to learn of the extraordinary divine love force incarnated in him. This is the love force that would lead to the Resurrection and Ascension, as well as to the whole Christian mystical tradition of Transfiguration born from it.

In order to begin to imagine the effect of this meeting not only on Mary Magdalene but on Jesus, we have to confront two interlinked catastrophes of misinterpretation that have radically limited, narrowed, and even aborted the true reception and embodiment of the revolutionary love consciousness Jesus came to seed in human experience. Confronting these catastrophes, and there is no other suitable word for what happened, is in my experience both agonizing and revelatory.

It is agonizing because such a confrontation reviews the depths of the betrayal of the embodied evolutionary power of Christ consciousness that has tragically disfigured not only the practice of the churches erected in Jesus's name, but also the emphasis and discoveries of a significant part of their mystical traditions. It is revelatory because even beginning to glimpse the truth of what was born through the destined meeting of Mary Magdalene and Jesus and unfolded in their unique relationship offers us a vision that not only revolutionizes what we have come to know as Christianity, but offers all those who dare to embrace it a path that could still, even at this tragic moment of human history when everything is at stake, change everything.

The first catastrophe of misinterpretation has proved to be of Jesus himself. Modern scholarship has mostly presented Jesus as a Jewish rabbi wisdom teacher of radical brilliance and disturbing originality and largely debunked later claims that he was or claimed to be the unique Son of God. While such scholarship has greatly advanced both our knowledge of the Jewish religious and mystical background that partly shaped Jesus and deepened our awe at and respect for his humanity and courage in the appalling conditions of his time, it cannot begin to address or "explain" the grandeur and majesty of the divine consciousness that we can now see from its effect on human history was incarnated in him.

The Jesus that was and is the living Christ appeared to and permanently transformed Paul on the road to Damascus, also appeared to and permanently transformed a long and momentous list of great male and female mystics, from the Desert Fathers to Teresa of Ávila, Hildegard of Bingen, Meister Eckhart, Hadewijch of Antwerp, Seraphim of Sarov, and countless others. That Jesus appeared to me in my middle 40s in a church in Coimbatore, South India, flooding me with love fire and printing in fire on my soul the mission of sacred activism that has consumed and ennobled my life. This Jesus that is the living Christ cannot be circumscribed or even imagined by a scholarly approach that sees Jesus as just one more wisdom teacher, however original or illumined.

Just as modern scholarship limits the mystery of who Jesus was and is, so tragically does the official tradition of the churches erected in his name and professing to teach truth by his authority. Modern scholarship in a largely skeptical and secular age has stressed Jesus's humanity and limited—either through spiritual arrogance, mystical ignorance, or a subtly toxic marriage of both—any unabashed embrace of his divinity. The tradition of the churches has done the exact opposite in its partly understandable but still dangerously exaggerated obsession with Jesus's divinity.

This tradition has engendered an etherealized disembodied Jesus separated from the humanity he incarnated into to transfigure. It has over centuries of accumulated and now fossilized dogma created a Jesus who demands worship as the unique Son of God, the supreme Lord Savior-Redeemer-Messiah separated through and in glory from the very humanity his incarnation came to reveal as inherently divine and so capable of infinite transformation. This tradition clearly believed it was honoring the Christ event in Jesus by separating Jesus in his sinless purity and magnificence of divine power from the rest of us. But now those with eyes to see know that this creation of an etherealized Jesus falsified the all-inclusiveness of his life and message, distorted the radical challenge of his teaching and example, created a damaging, inflated adoration of celibacy as the one true way to Christ consciousness, engendered a set of indisputable teachings that promoted misogyny, body hatred, and sex hatred, and denied drastically the role of the Divine Feminine in life and creation, the very Divine Feminine that Jesus himself identified with and celebrated as Hochmah or Sophia.

The result is a world that has been vastly distorted and deformed by this tradition, one that privileges male power, denigrates the sacredness of human life and the creation, continues to demonize the body and its potentially divinizable energies and desires, and continues to split apart, inwardly and outwardly, humanity and divinity in ways that keep humanity abject, paralyzed, self-disgusted, depressed, obsessed with sin and imperfection, unaware and disempowered of its true nature and boundless potential and so, unable to rise to the challenges our now global dark night imposes.

There are two great keys to deconstructing and unraveling the dangerous etherealization of Jesus's humanity that has had such disastrous consequences. The first great key is to understand that the conflation of Jesus with God that led to the tragic separation of Jesus from the very humanity he came to transfigure was a comparatively late form of theology, crystallized only at the Council of Nicaea in AD 325. Father Bede Griffiths, with Thomas Merton, one of the two greatest Christian mystics of the 20th century, wrote in his masterpiece *A New Vision of Reality*:

"This theology, though perfectly correct and legitimate in itself, is a particular kind of theological language which was developed over many centuries in the West and certainly corresponded with the people's needs at the time, but today presents for most an insuperable difficulty. Examples of this language are God became man, he came down from heaven and God appeared on earth. These images, which were quite natural to people in the past, now appear as essentially mythological and make the gospel message appear totally unreal and irrelevant."

Bede Griffiths goes on to make clear, however, that "This language is not the language of the New Testament itself. . . . The New Testament has a completely different perspective. It does not start at all from Jesus as God, but from Jesus as man. Jesus himself never speaks of himself as God. His favorite designation of himself is as Son of Man, which in Hebrew and Aramaic is practically equivalent to human. . . . The Son of Man is the most meaningful of all the titles of Jesus."

What this means is that Jesus himself, while proclaiming his inner unity with God, never proclaimed himself the unique Son of God, and knew himself as human, intimately one with all humanity.

"Seen in this perspective, Jesus does not appear as an isolated phenomenon, a sudden appearance of God on earth. He is the fulfilment of the whole plan of creation, drawing the manifold of creation back to unity, drawing all humanity back to God, *to that fullness of being for which it was created*." (The italics are mine.)

If Jesus's humanity is not embraced in its own complete, poignant richness, vulnerability, and archetypal complexity, how could our humanity be revealed to itself as inherently divine and so divinizable, capable of being drawn back to God, to that fullness of being for which it was created?

Adoration of Jesus as God without recognizing Jesus as also Son of Man and primordial human condemns us to remain untransformed in the depths of our own humanity. Reduced to begging a fictive fantasy of Jesus for our redemption instead of truly daring to follow his human and divine example, to birth with the grace of the Divine that progressively divinized him our own divine humanity, our own unique Christhood. It was to make this scandalous and astounding birth available to all of us, whatever our past failures and derelictions, and whatever our cruelly inadequate assumptions of who we are, that Jesus's whole life example and teaching was dedicated.

And now we must confront subtly a nuanced second catastrophe of misinterpretation that has prevented the full force of the Jesus event from transforming human experience. The concentration in the tradition obsessively on Jesus and Jesus alone on a unique divine manifestation in Him has led to the writing out of the most sacred feminine aspects of the sacred feminine aspect of this manifestation—the relational. This writing out of the feminine and relational has led to a disastrous transcendentalization of Jesus himself because it is completely misunderstood or fails even to try to understand that the Gospels do not record only the experience of an astounding man. They also speak to those who can hear of the revelation that authentic Christ consciousness is one of intimate human and divine relationship to all things—to the Divine itself, to the creation, to all sentient beings, and to all the small and large events of life, a relationship that mirrors the intercommunion of energies that mystics of all kinds recognize as the reality of the universe and modern physics has uncovered in all its sweep and cosmic reach.

What the Gospels reveal is an intensely human Jesus, compassionate to all beings, but loving a few with particularly personal love, utterly unconventional in his embrace of the poor, the wayward, the disinherited, the abandoned, whose presence and the healing and revelatory actions that flow from it manifest and make manifest the living reality of the Kingdom.

The Gospels, when read with this growing and amazed understanding, reveal that kingdom consciousness is immediate, fearless, direct communion on all levels of the human being with all levels of divine manifestation, a communion both intensely personal and impersonal, that establishes effortlessly and is itself a field of potential for transformation. This subtle miracle of transfiguring relationship is reenacted again and again in all of Jesus's relationships—with his disciples, male and female, with his family, with those he healed and preached to, and, of course, with Mary Magdalene.

Jesus is a divine and human being, yes, but even more astonishingly, a field of inter-communing love energy, whose organic power expands in the great story of his evolution until its cosmic completion in the Resurrection and beyond.

This field of love energy is, as Jesus—in his constant proclamation of identity with Sophia, or *Hochmah*—makes clear, a Divine Feminine energy that embraces the whole of life as sacred and accepts human beings in all their desires and frailties and longing. Nothing is foreign to it; nothing and no one is excluded from its tender, burning embrace. If we fail to try to understand the unconditional comprehensiveness of this Divine Feminine energy, we miss not only the teaching of Jesus as love field; we miss also the evolutionary power that such a love field emanates. We miss, in fact, that Jesus's presence and actions are a birthing field.

It was this love, this birthing field of a presence, that Mary Magdalene met on that day in Capernaum. The whirlwind of acute psychic misery and equally acute and fierce glimpses of revelation that had driven Mary Magdalene into his presence also made her the one who could see immediately who Jesus really was. She was far too desperate and undone to be remade and resurrected by anything less than unmistakable divine intervention. The depth of her agony and the sincerity and passion of her search for truth had drawn to her and earned for her the supreme grace of meeting him and knowing him as he really was, as fully human and fully divine, as Son of Man and as primordial man, as God man and human, divine male, beloved, the one destined for her, seeing and knowing her both in her agony and her glory from within herself, with a love beyond judgment that blessed all she had been through and understood and reflected back to her blindingly the truth of who she really was and what she would become.

With these visions of who Mary Magdalene and Jesus were separately fresh in our mind and heart, and as we journey toward their meeting, let us again pause and breathe and contemplate as broadly as possible what a meeting between two such extraordinary beings signifies.

When two beings meet, like Shams and Rumi, like Jesus and Mary Magdalene, to enact divine revelation, they have, as Rumi wrote, "been in each other all along." And the timing of their meeting is central to everything that then unfolds. Nothing is by chance in such a meeting. It is preordained. Both are destined to be forever transformed by the other. Nothing in either of their lives will ever be known or experienced in the same way again, because the love that blossoms in fire between them is total, all-consuming, and all-renewing, a love that jets from the source of divine love itself in divine reality to embrace and embolden them both in the way that they then live out the overwhelming mystery they were born to embody and transmit.

The similarities between the two greatest mystical love stories we know, that of Shams and Rumi, Jesus and Mary Magdalene, are profound and revelatory. Shams and Rumi birthed from their sublime nonsexual friendship what Rumi recognized and celebrated as "a new kind of love, neither above nor below," a love neither transcendent alone, nor merely physical, but a radical new force born from the electric fusion of both, a love at once totally human and totally divine.

"A new kind of love, neither above nor below," but also sexual, flowered, as we will see, between Jesus and Mary Magdalene, who ends her appearance in the Gospels in the way we have witnessed as the transfigured mother of the Church and its deepest mystical traditions, a resurrected beloved alive in every cell of her body.

Shams, in his towering but isolated realization, knew he needed someone into whom he could pour the molten lava of the revelation of love and wisdom that had been poured into him and divinized him. He knew that the love that had transfigured him was innately relational and needed to be transmitted completely to one other being, so its mystery could be spread to all those with eyes to see and ears to hear. He prayed for long, lonely years to be given the grace of a human beloved who would not be afraid to pay the price for so vast a gift, and at the preordained time met his beloved in Rumi.

When you read what Shams wrote about Rumi in his *Maqamat*, a series of jagged notes and divine reflections, you understand that the relationship that then erupted was far more than a master-disciple union or even the deepest human love affair of the heart. It was a relationship as new, as radical, as revolutionary as the force of love it was destined to birth, and from its beginnings, it transcended all categories that could explain or codify it. The *Maqamat* makes it diamond clear that Shams was as amazed and stunned by Rumi's inner beauty and capacity for visionary adventurousness as Rumi was amazed and stunned by Shams's unshrinking majesty of being.

What Rumi gave Shams was far more than an obedient, empty vessel into which he could pour the burning wine of his revelation. The relationship between them was itself the revelation, a relationship of profound sacred equality: a beloved-beloved friendship in which Shams was as transformed in his way as Rumi was in his, a friendship that revealed the evolutionary power of authentic, naked, visionary love relationship itself and prepared for humanity a new kind of love.

This was, we can now begin to understand, the relationship also between Jesus and Mary Magdalene, with the difference that in Jesus and Mary Magdalene's case, it was a complete male-female love lived from the illumined, ecstatic heart in every realm of the mind, heart, soul, and loving body.

Just as Shams and Rumi's love was perceived by their hidebound contemporaries as something dangerous and even scandalous, and just as both separately and together endured horrible opposition, sometimes from those closest to them, so the love that Jesus and Mary Magdalene—as we see in the writing out of Mary Magdalene from the Gospels and in the revelations of her real dignity in the Gnostic Gospels—caused tremendous division among the male disciples who shared none of Jesus's astonishing openness, whether to Divine Feminineness or to the actual women in his wandering group or to the sacred feminine in himself.

Both evolutionary, transformative loves were birthing something wholly new, and the forces that did not want this birth to occur of "a new kind of love, neither above nor below," that could empower the whole human race, attempted to destroy it in a way that only made it more adamantine. Nothing, even Shams's murder by a group organized by Rumi's eldest son, could prevent Rumi from the realization, after a long agony and madness, that Shams lived eternally in him as him.

Nothing the male disciples said or did and nothing the male witnesses of the Gospels or the male authorities that followed them could say or do, nothing—even the full wrath of the Romans and Jewish religious authorities could enact in the horror of crucifixion—could annihilate the evolutionary splendor of what Mary Magdalene and Jesus lived, or prevent Mary Magdalene from the realization that the Resurrection birthed in her: that she was now, through the miraculous power of the love she had lived with Jesus, the first born of a new creation that love itself had helped to engender, a realization that would expand in passion, power, and glory through the rest of her life, one forever both with her beloved and divine love itself.

And just as we are now beginning to understand the transformative depths of Shams and Rumi's friendship, so only now are we beginning to receive the full impact of the love between Jesus and Mary Magdalene. It is not a coincidence that both great mystical love stories are now being revealed to us in their fullest implications. They belong together. They inter-illuminate each other. They offer, in their different but divinely interrelated ways, the astounding guidance humanity both needs and is now at last able to receive. They are both revelations of the evolutionary power of total love to transform the world. Rumi and Shams's Islamic world, Rumi knew, could not receive the full truth of their love in their time. But he also knew that the time would come, as he wrote, "Those tender words we spoke to one another, which are stored in the secret heart of heaven, one day they will rain, fall and spread, and the whole world will grow green with our love."

After all they went through together, Jesus and Mary Magdalene must have known also that the mystery they were living could arrive only in luminous stages in the humanity it was destined to transform—a humanity made at last able, through the agony and yearning of a global dark night that is revealing the bankruptcy of all patriarchal systems of power, to begin to imagine and embody the beloved–beloved relationship and realize its power to effect miraculous change in extreme circumstances. There is no more exposed and searing a meeting in mystical history. When Rumi met Shams, he fell off his horse and crawled to embrace him. When Mary Magdalene met Jesus, she was already almost annihilated by the agony of a dark life she could not bear.

No meeting we know of has been so searing or transformative, and no meeting has been so misunderstood both by the patriarchy and by some of those who understandably want to exalt and honor Mary Magdalene, but both either claim the meeting did not happen in this way, because it seems to privilege Jesus as healer and savior and deny Mary Magdalene's equality with him, or that what Luke calls her demon possession was a divine madness contemporaries with limited psychology could not understand.

The patriarchal narrative consciously or unconsciously made of the story a convenient and devastating way of defining Mary Magdalene as a prostitute whose possession was the dark reward for having shamelessly indulged her carnal desires (and getting paid for doing so) and used this narrative to demean not only her but all women and the feminine through her. The exaggeratedly feminist version, in its honorable passion to divinize Mary Magdalene from the beginning, has also in its own way failed, I believe, to comprehend the full terror and beauty of the story of their meeting.

I once spent a weekend with well-known women mystics of Mary Magdalene. It was in many ways a thrilling and sacred experience because of the passion and wisdom each presenter was on fire with as she spoke of the woman who so inspired her. When it came to broaching the subject of Jesus and Mary's first meeting, however, nearly all the women present—in a way that shocked me—either dismissed the story altogether as a patriarchal add-on or glamorized it as revealing Mary Magdalene's divine status in a way no one around her could begin to comprehend, except perhaps Jesus himself. One of the presenters thumped the table and proclaimed, "Mary Magdalene was not mad, not possessed. She was blazing with mother glory, and Jesus was the only one just capable of being overwhelmed by her truth."

Neither the patriarchal nor the feminist version is accurate. The patriarchal narrative is maimed from within by its misogyny and more subtly by its assumption that in their meeting, Jesus is clearly the superior, the Son of God, meeting a crazy woman and healing her, unchanged in any way by the extraordinary being he encountered. The feminist version, while eloquently and rightly honoring Mary Magdalene, misses crucial, fierce revelations of the transformative love between the two of them that distorts the alchemy of the revelation itself that they birthed. We can no longer afford any of either version's distortions if we are going to meet Mary Magdalene both in her fully human and fully divine reality, and if we're going to begin to understand both the personal and archetypal radical depths of the love she lived with Jesus and Jesus lived with her.

Only by reentering the story of their first meeting, with all our human and mystical senses open in unknowing, can we begin to discover a third version, or have it unveiled to us.

Beyond both versions of this all-transforming meeting between Mary Magdalene and Jesus, there is thankfully another version emerging in brave and pioneering scholarship. This one honors both the spiritual dignity of the woman destined to witness and embody the glory of the Resurrection and the transfiguring effect the meeting had on both Mary Magdalene and Jesus himself.

In this third version, the young woman, probably in her early 20s, who had walked alone the 10 miles from Magdala to Capernaum, certainly abandoned by friends and family, was not demon-possessed. The conception of her as possessed is a patriarchal demeaning of her.

In this version, which I have come to believe, Mary Magdalene was neither demon-possessed nor a prostitute maddened by her vices. Rather, she was a woman who had undergone a series of massive awakenings, both to the glory of divine love and to the horror of the world of brutal patriarchal power into which she had been born. She had been plunged into an excruciating and terrifying dark night, torn apart by the revelation of truth that simultaneously exposed her both to the splendor of the divine presence and the agony of the world, especially the agony of what that world was inflicting on the Divine Feminine power being born in her.

Nothing and no one in her world could heal or help her, because what she was destined to incarnate was a vision and a power dedicated to the subversion and reconstruction of all inherited structures that suppressed or degraded the Divine Feminine and a new kind of love with the man who stood before her.

Radical awakening, such as the one that prepared Mary Magdalene to meet her divine human consort, is always both ecstatic and horrifying: ecstatic because it reveals the Divine in both its transcendent and immanent magnificence; horrifying because it exposes one without mask or protection to the multiple betrayals of that splendor in human society, betrayals all the more terrifying because of the divine truth revelation has made unforgettable.

Imagine what Mary Magdalene must have experienced, not only as a soul but as a woman, awakened both to her inherent divinity and to the overwhelming dark powers in religion and society. In her time in Jewish society, women were treated mostly as inferior chattels, subject in every way to the whim of fathers, husbands, and brothers-in-law. With no legal rights of their own and confined to domestic servitude, women were prohibited from divorcing their husbands, although a husband could get rid of his wife for a whole slew of violations, including leaving her hair unbound. Divorce for a woman would be a life sentence. She would be left with no support, and if accused of adultery, she could be stoned, with no legal consequences for either the men who stoned her or her adulterous lover.

The religious practices of the time reinforced this comprehensive degradation of the feminine. There would be no safe harbor in the Judaism of Mary's day for a woman awakening tumultuously to the truth of her feminine divinity. In the synagogue, women sat apart from men in a small gallery and were considered unclean during menstruation. They were allowed to read the Torah, but were largely prohibited from preaching.

Who could Mary have possibly turned to for confirmation of sacred guidance in a world where the very possibility of being an awakened, empowered woman was dismissed and denied?

As if these constrictions were not savage enough, Mary Magdalene's awakening took place in a world dominated by a Roman occupation that was corrupt and brutal, routinely using torture, crucifixion, and rape to terrorize the Jewish population. As I previously mentioned, Mary came from Magdala, only a few miles from the city of Tiberias, famous for its depravity and the luxurious buildings and villas where the Roman conquerors indulged their vices and flaunted their wealth and power over a cowed and increasingly impoverished Jewish people. From the study of colonial occupations throughout history, we know that imperialism with its unfettered and brutal power corrupts not only the colonizers, but also the colonized, driven either into seething, helpless, secret hatred and outrage or into a collusion that erodes their integrity and identity. All this would have been icily clear to Mary Magdalene and a source of agonized sacred anger.

The woman who stood before Jesus in Capernaum was at once ablaze with revelation and burning in the fires of an aghast clarity about the multiple oppressions and injustices both of her Jewish world and the Roman power that corrupted it, initiated at once into divine presence and human obscenity, unable in her loneliness and lack of awakened guidance to begin to hold such extreme opposites, and so in real danger of being annihilated by them both.

Later women mystics who followed the path pioneered by Mary Magdalene knew the paradoxically exalted and tortured state that drove Mary to seek out and meet Jesus, because they experienced it themselves on their lonely, unsupported, dangerous journey to female Christhood. The most eloquent of these witnesses was Hadewijch of Antwerp, the 13th-century Beguine who experienced in her time what Mary Magdalene had in hers—the extremity of an immense awakening to divine love, coupled with the terrifying experience of patriarchal power that sought at every turn to demean, degrade, and destroy her because of the majesty and depth of her realization that threatened not only Church dogma, but also the Church's age-long dismissal of women as inferior and incapable of awakening.

It is to Hadewijch then that we can turn for illuminating words on the dark night that descended on Mary Magdalene and menaced not only her sanity but also her survival.

Humiliation and brutal adventures
year after year.
All things are bitter to me
that my eyes have seen . . .
Living like this disgusts me.

———

Love led me to such dazzling knowledge,
now all I do is reel from her savagery.
Who do I turn to in this mad universe?
Where love herself is victim, judge executioner.
My senses shrivel in the madness of love.

———

O tenderest love,
Arise in me fully in your highest being,
So my senses may resurrect from death.

Mary Magdalene sought out in Jesus, then, the highest being who could resurrect her senses from death. For her, crucified by reality, the meeting with her beloved would be more even than a rebirth. Her crucifixion and Resurrection preceded Jesus's and prepared her to be the one who could work with him in surrender and adoration to prepare the miracle she would witness and begin to embody in the garden.

Again, we can turn to Hadewijch to initiate us into what Mary Magdalene experienced in direct communion with the Christ. Please, dear friend, read Hadewijch's momentously passionate and all-embracing description of her union with Christ twice and slowly, daring to put yourself in her place, whatever sex you are.

"He came in the form and clothing of a man, as he was on the day he gave us his body for the first time. He looked like a human being, a tender and beautiful man with a face radiating light. He came towards me as humbly as someone would who belonged to another totally. He gave himself to me in the shape and form of the sacrament, as is the custom. Then, as is the custom too, he gave me to drink under the appearance and with the taste of wine.

"After that he himself came to me. He took me entirely in his arms. He pressed me against him in such a way that all my limbs felt his as he filled them with the bliss my heart and humanity longed for. . . .

"He was in me without separation and I could not tell myself from him.

"After that I remained in a dying into him and melted away until nothing any longer remained to me of myself . . ."

Hadewijch's sublime and comprehensive vision of the Christ's transcendent sensuality brings us directly into the presence of the 29-year-old Jesus in that crowded, noisy room in Capernaum.

Jesus's Sexuality

NOW IT IS TIME TO CONFRONT HEAD-ON one of the greatest mysteries surrounding Jesus: his sexuality. The patriarchal version that has dominated the churches is clear. Jesus may have been human, but he was sinless, pure, and celibate. This version was promoted for nearly two millennia in what Karen King calls "the Master story" with its denigration of the body, its profound unease with and distaste for sexuality, its denigration of the feminine, and its relentless promotion of the hegemony of male and female celibacy. The institutional power of this "Master story" has largely gone unchallenged, and even in the progressive churches, it still casts a strong and life-denying spell, ensuring that the Divine Feminine—with its revelatory truth, passion for creation, mystical splendor, and hunger for transformation of all human life—remains drastically confined.

The time has come for this story to die. The misery it has caused, the dysfunction it has bred, the lovelessness and secret hatred of life it has engendered, the paranoia at differences of all kinds, especially sexual, it has promoted—all in the name of the Being whose message of all-inclusive, all-transfiguring love remains the most potent ever given to humanity—shows that it cannot be the story either of the man Jesus or of the authentic Christ consciousness.

The great Christian mystic poet and revolutionary, William Blake, said it most clearly and unequivocally when he wrote, "The Bible must be shaken upside down before it will yield all its secrets. The priests have censored and clipped and mangled. They give us a celibate Jesus born of a virgin, without the 'slightest stain' of sexual content, which is blasphemous nonsense."

The brilliant key word here—the word that changes everything—is *blasphemous*. For centuries the patriarchy has told us that it is a blasphemy to imagine Jesus as sexual, and that the only finally real path to Christ's consciousness lies in obeying and following its "censored, clipped, and mangled" version of it. Blake dares to reverse this insanity and proclaim it is precisely this master story that is blasphemous for three interlinked reasons: It denies the mystery of Jesus's incarnation as both divine and human; it denies the fullness and richness of Jesus's humanity by overemphasizing his divinity; it distorts and radically degrades the central thrust of his mission to reveal and empower the divinity in our humanity; in distorting and degrading this core of his message, it aborts the birth he came to midwife, of a new humanity.

Blake knew from his own Christ consciousness that "The treasures of heaven are not negations of passion, but Realities of Intellect [his word for direct gnosis of eternal reality], from which all the passions emanate uncurbed in their eternal glory."

Blake knew, too, that what the divine human Jesus had come to awaken in humanity in his own divine human image was, in Blake's marvelous and awestruck words, "the head sublime, the heart pathos, the genitals beauty, the hands and feet proportion." And that without the transformed and exuberant tender eros Jesus himself exhibited in his relationships both with men and women, such an abundant, creative, free-hearted, both passionately and wisely loving divine human being simply could not be birthed. In *The Everlasting Gospel*, Blake writes of the censoring, clipping, mangling masters of the old story:

They call a shame and sin
love's temple that God dwelleth in
and hide in secret hidden shrine
the naked human form divine
and render that a lawless thing
on which the soul expands its wing.

Or as Jean-Yves Leloup, a great contemporary Orthodox mystic who has done pioneering work on the Gnostic Gospels, writes in his *The Sacred Embrace of Jesus and Mary*, "If Yeshua did not live his sexuality, then sexuality is unredeemed."

Like Blake, Leloup knows that "What is at stake here is total salvation, the liberation of the whole of the human being by imbuing all of the dimensions of this being with consciousness and love." Leloup adds more calmly than Blake, but with the same heartbroken clarity, "Religion has failed in its duty by neglecting the spiritual discipline of physical ecstasy. In its unwillingness to establish the link between theophany—the revelation of divinity—and sexuality, it has allowed this connection to fall into oblivion." For Leloup as for Blake, this obliteration of the link between theophany and sexuality is nothing less than a dangerous blasphemy that conspires with the degradation of humanity that now threatens its very survival.

What Blake and Leloup and many other brave, modern mystics made clear is that the real question about Jesus's sexuality is not "Was he sexual?" (if he was human, as he was, he was sexual), but far more challengingly, what kind of sexuality would the beloved in human form live and express?

I once had the following conversation with Father Bede Griffiths, perhaps the greatest Christian mystic of the 20th century. Bede said:

"We just cannot go on arguing in more or less convoluted ways whether Jesus was sexual or not. The arguments on both sides can sound convincing, depending on your training or prejudices. Both sides miss the point.

"If Jesus was a sexual being, and I believe he was, as human beings in an age when the sacred beauty of Eros, of sexuality has been degraded both by the churches and religions and by the modern world's pornographication of everything, can we still summon a profound enough sacred imagination to imagine a sublime sexuality? That, my dear Andrew, is the real, difficult, amazing question."

I asked Bede: "What, at this time of your life, in your middle eighties, do you now understand as sublime sexuality?"

He gave me a definition that began to transfigure my life. He paused a long time and then said softly, "Eros and agape, desire and selfless love fused together, transfigured by adoration of the other in God as a manifestation of God."

What more complete and gorgeous definition of Jesus and the Magdalene's love, and potentially our own, could we have?

If you want to, pause and reread slowly the quotations of Blake I have offered and Bede's words together, and contemplate, as deeply as you can, the healing unified love-field they will begin to initiate you into. Then contemplate how your own emotional and sexual life might have been if you had been brought up with a vision of "sublime sexuality" as natural and possible for you. This will not be comfortable at first, but will lead, if you persist, to new understanding and great joy.

Let's ask the question about Jesus's sexuality in a different way: If his mission, and the mission of Christ consciousness incarnate in him, is to divinize the whole of human life in all of its transcendent and immanent relationships, how could he *not* have been sexual? And how could he not have lived out in his sexuality a path for us to divinize ours?

The greatest wound in humanity, as both Blake and Leloup make clear, is the split all of the orthodox religions have promulgated in different ways and widened and deepened—between body and soul, the earthly and the heavenly, human erotic desire and divine enlightenment. The entire mission of Jesus was to heal that split forever by revealing the Divine at the primordial core of the human in a way that birthed life more abundantly, a new and divine human race living consciously with passionate compassion in kingdom consciousness.

In his love for Mary Magdalene, Jesus lived out this conscious and passionate kingdom consciousness in a way that not only transformed her, but also fulfilled and transformed him and his teaching. His human evolution in the divine consciousness he was born with had guided him also to the sacred meeting with the divine woman, destined to be his consort, his wife, and his most illumined disciple. Yet even more wonderfully, she was also destined to be his co-pioneer in birthing a new path of embodied, divine, evolutionary love for all of human relationship, especially the erotic and sexual. Daring to see and celebrate this clearly changes forever our vision of what Christ consciousness is, of what sexuality can be, and what its most loving, tender, and ecstatic expression can work in us and for us.

Before we look deeply into all that the meeting between Jesus and Mary Magdalene meant, let's look first at Jesus's first miracle at the marriage feast at Cana, where essential mysteries and secrets await us.

The Miracle at the Marriage Feast at Cana

It is essential if we are truly to embrace and be transformed by the revolutionary implications of the miracle at Cana to place it in the context where Saint John's Gospel places it—immediately after the great prologue of Chapter 1 that announces Jesus's identity with the *logos*. If we do so carefully and as richly as possible, great healing truths will be revealed that will illuminate the whole meaning of the marriage feast.

Everything depends for our deepest understanding of Jesus's incarnation on how we interpret "in the beginning was the Word" and how we interpret "and the Word was made flesh."

In John 1:14, the prologue proclaims of Jesus, "and the Word was made flesh and dwelt among us and we beheld his glory." "The Word was made flesh" in Greek is *kai o logos sarx egeneto.*

The Greek word for "beginning" is *rkche* (pronounced *ar-kay*) and the phrase "in the beginning" echoes the first verse of Genesis, "In the beginning, God created the heaven and the earth," where the Hebrew word for "beginning" is *bereshit*. Rabbinical tradition reveals that although *bet,* the first letter of *bereshit,* is the beginning of the Bible, the letter *aleph* comes before *bet* in the Hebrew alphabet. What this implies is momentous, nothing less but that the unsounded implied *aleph* signifies the primordial origin of divine unity from which all duality, *bet,* not only arises, but is permeated by on all levels.

In other words, utter unknowable transcendence in a mystery of sacred marriage unites with, permeates, and lives in every conceivable realm of immanence.

This all-pervading, all-sanctifying original divine essence, then, is what the "word"—*logos*—is one with and an expression of.

In order to understand what Saint John's Gospel is really saying, however, we first have to admit that translating *logos* as "word" drastically reduces its implications. *Logos* does not signify "word," at least not in any normally comprehensible sense of the term. The word for "logos" in Hebrew is *dabar.* That means not only "word," but also, astonishingly, "infusing intelligence" and "creative information." In Semitic thought, *word* and *event* are in no way separate concepts. A true word is also simultaneously an act. What this means is that *logos* would be far more accurately translated as "creative word," the informing intelligence and creative information of the original source that holds together, shapes, sustains, and evolves all existing things in all realms.

In Greek, *logos* is masculine. But when we dive deeper into its multifoliate meanings, we discover it also as the perpetual dynamic, feminine birthing force of all things, a birthing power that Jesus incarnated fully to reveal to us and in us the creative power that flows through our whole being when we are aligned with the source, the beginning, and the illumined actions that emanate from it.

The second phrase of the first verse of Saint John's Prologue is translated as "and the word was with God." This, too, unfortunately, is an inadequate and far too heady and static translation of the original Greek: *kai o lógos en pros ton theón.*

The key word here is *pros,* which means "toward" and implies orientation, movement, and evolution all at once. So this phrase in Saint John's Prologue, crucial for our understanding of how the creative word expresses itself in the universe, in the creation, in Jesus, and in ourselves should read, the logos is *toward* God.

If the creative word is *toward* God, then its essential work is one of what Gregory of Nyssa called *epektasis,* "endless expansion," an endless expansion of evolutionary possibilities in all realms from within the divine core of life.

It is this Father/Mother logos, at once infinitely peaceful and infinitely creative, that Saint John's Prologue says in verse 14, *is made flesh in Jesus.* Here again, we need to pay careful attention to the Greek if we are going to be initiated into the depths of what is meant. The phrase *the word is made flesh* is in Greek, *o lógos sárx egéneto.* As in the other statements we have examined, flesh is too limited and narrow a translation for *sárx. Sárx* itself is a translation of the Hebrew word *basar.* In Hebrew, *basar* is always traditionally associated both with *nephesh* (soul) and *adam*, made of clay.

In Hebrew, *basar* means and refers to the whole living human being. A more accurate and illuminating translation then of "and the word was made flesh" would be "the word manifests in the human."

This far richer vision of Incarnation itself as a marriage of the Divine with the whole of the human being was glimpsed by a few early Church fathers. Epiphanius used the Greek word *enanthropesen* when writing of the Incarnation, which means that the Incarnation becomes *anthropos*, human. Jean-Yves Leloup writes, "These exegetes clearly perceive the original Hebrew meaning behind the Greek invention of *sarx*, a meaning which must imply *anthropos*, fully human," and goes on to quote an early pope, Damasus, who grounded himself in this truth when he wrote in AD 374, "for if an incomplete man was incarnated, then the gift of God is incomplete and our salvation is incomplete, for it is not the *whole man* who has been saved . . . "

Had the Christian tradition listened to Pope Damasus and Epiphanius, it would have been impossible for it to preach contempt for the body or deny that Jesus was sexual, or that the path to divinized sexuality he was to open with and through Mary Magdalene is one of his and their most transformative gifts to us. What this inspired message from Pope Damasus makes clear is that the deepest meaning of the *logos* being made flesh is that the whole of the human being in Jesus was wholly divinized, without in any way diminishing, demeaning, or degrading his humanity.

The path of Christ consciousness, then, is not one of dualistic repression or separation of soul and flesh, but of their progressive divinization together in the word through this inextricable marriage of word and flesh, in the logos field. This process of the human becoming God does not entail a denial of the body or sexuality, but a transfiguration of both. As Irenaeus, a Christian bishop and theologian living only a few generations after Christ, wrote before the flesh/soul split had become commonplace in Christian theology, "The glory of God is the living human person; the life of the human person is the vision of God."

In Jesus's being and in his unfolding evolution, this greatest of all secrets is progressively unveiled, so that we who love him and follow him can have a map, an unforgettable, precise, and infinitely inspiring map of how it can unveil in us and through us. When and if Christian tradition embraces the all-inclusiveness of this truth, it will begin to give birth to the real Christ consciousness, fully embodied and fully divine.

With this grounded and expansive vision of the opening prologue vibrant in our minds and hearts, let us look now to Chapter 2 of Saint John's Gospel, in which the first miracle of Jesus at a marriage feast is described. Please read the words of Saint John's Gospel slowly, and imagine yourself, with all you now know of Jesus, actually present yourself, an awed witness to everything that unfolds.

> *2:1 And the third day there was a marriage in Cana of Galilee, and the mother of Jesus was there.*
>
> *2:2 And both Jesus was called and his disciples to the marriage.*
>
> *2:3 And when they wanted wine, the mother of Jesus sayeth unto him, "They have no wine."*
>
> *2:4 Jesus sayeth unto her, "Woman, what have I to do with thee? Mine hour is not yet come."*
>
> *2:5 His mother sayeth unto the servants, "Whatsoever he sayeth unto you, do it."*
>
> *2:6 And there was set there six water pots of stone after the manner of the purifying of the Jews, containing two or three firkins apiece.*
>
> *2:7 Jesus sayeth unto them, "Fill the water pots with water," and they filled them up to the brim.*
>
> *2:8 And he sayeth unto them, "Draw out now, and bear unto the governor of the feast." And they bear it.*

2:9 When the ruler of the feast had tasted the water that was made wine and knew not whence it was, but the servants which drew the water knew the governor of the feast called the bridegroom.

2:10 And sayeth unto him, "Every man at the beginning doth set forth good wine, and when men have well drunk, then, that which is worse, but thou hast kept a good wine until now."

2:11 This beginning of miracles did Jesus in Cana of Galilee and manifested forth his glory and his disciples believed on him.

Three linked questions arise in the mind of anyone who embraces the truth of Jesus's full human sexuality as inseparable and inextricable from his full divinity:

1. How could Jesus and his message have ever been conscripted to serve a misogynistic body and sex-despising vision when *his very first miracle was at a marriage*?
2. How in the name of the Son of Man can most Christians continue to ignore the truth this miracle proclaims—that human sexuality is holy and worthy of celebration, especially when consecrated in sacred union?
3. Why would something so momentous as Jesus's first miracle, a miracle that is the sun of which all his other miracles are rays—have taken place at a human marriage feast to honor it and increase its joy if there was not a transformative secret at its heart, one indispensable to the transformation of humanity?

I have spent 30 years ferreting about in dusty libraries to read as much as I can find of the Christian tradition's treatment of this miracle, and I have never found these questions asked. Whenever I have asked them of my Christian friends, I have been met either with a wary condescension or angry resistance, as if just my asking them was a blasphemy.

So let me try to offer here as comprehensive and revelatory an unpacking of the significance of the marriage of Cana as I can, rooted in 30 years in and initiation into many of the world's mystical traditions as well as the Christian.

Jesus, a Son of Man and primordial human, enacts his first miracle at a marriage feast to make clear four things:

1. That the fundamental nature of the Divine and so of the universe is the sacred marriage in the One of transcendence and immanence, "father" and "mother," the absolute godhead and the embodied godhead;
2. That the fundamental truth of Jesus's own nature that both mirrors and embodies this truth of divine reality and the miraculous powers it emanates is a marriage of masculine and feminine, a father identity (the "I am" awareness) with creative, radical mother compassion (the "I love, serve, nourish all beings as myself" consciousness);
3. That the goal of the human search for God that he himself has come to enact and reveal is the realization in heart, mind, soul, and body altogether in the awe of the sacred marriage, a realization that births and keeps birthing the divinization process in ever subtler expressions—to make us, in Irenaus's words, "fully alive";
4. That matter itself, formed by the lovemaking and interpenetration of transcendence and immanence, is capable—as Jesus's own journey from Resurrection to ascension and beyond unveils—of endless and astonishing permutations of refinement.

I realize that what I am saying here might seem either impossibly grandiose or impenetrable to many, but these four interlinked truths and revelations, though lived by Jesus with unique intensity, are known in all of the world's mystical traditions by the handful of mystics in each who have realized them. These truths are known and lived by Kabir, by Abhinavagupta of the Kashmiri Shaivite lineage, by the Vajrayana masters of Mahayana Buddhism, by the Shaivites of the lineage of Tirumular in South India, by the Iranian mystics celebrated by Henry Corbin who cultivated in themselves the being of light, by the Taoist alchemists, and by certain Christian mystics such as Hadewijch and Saint Symeon the New Theologian and Angelus Silesius, who were taken into and transfigured in what the Gnostic Gospel of Philip calls "the bridal chamber."

These truths have also been known and witnessed by humanity's great evolutionary mystics, such as Teilhard de Chardin, Sri Aurobindo, and the Mother, all of whom know both from inmost personal experience and revelation that the nature of the universe as a marriage of transcendence and immanence makes possible an endless and progressively more potent insemination of the immanent by the transcendent that births, in turn, endless new creations.

The next secret the marriage of Cana story makes evident is that for this sacred marriage to be fully grounded and realized in all of its potency, the Divine Feminine must be recognized in all her divine authority and loved and obeyed in all her laws of compassion, interconnection, and celebration of her creation. Jesus, after all, performs the miracle of Cana at the behest of his mother.

The significance of this has been almost completely missed by a long succession of Christian mystics who grapple, sometimes absurdly and always limitedly, with why Mary's role in compelling the Son of Man to manifest his miraculous power is so essential. Some of them condemn her as a typical pushy, nagging Jewish mother; others mock her as a mother trying to show off her brilliant son. Still others acknowledge Mother Mary as saint and prophet and apostle and martyr, but are still limited in the powers they ascribe to her, limited as all Christian mystics have been since the early Gnostics, by unconscious inherited misogyny, obsession with Mary's virginity, and by virginity and celibacy in general.

They all miss what the marriage of Cana makes clear: that Mary, as the living embodiment of the divine mother, is the instigator of Jesus's first miracle. But she's also the living symbol of the force of the Divine Feminine that activates and permeates all of Jesus's being and messages, along with the miracles that stream from his embodiment of the sacred marriage.

What recognizing this reveals is what all the mystics of the sacred marriage in all traditions know—that without the full return of the majesty, passion, life, wisdom, and compassion of the Divine Feminine being restored in its fullest dignity and power, the all-divinizing potential of the sacred marriage, and its potential to transform the whole of life into its marriage feast, cannot be realized.

Turning Water into Wine

NOW WE CAN BEGIN TO APPROACH the many interlinked revelations contained in the central act of the miracle at the marriage of Cana, the turning of the water into wine.

The first revelation is of the nature of Jesus and the mission of his incarnation. Jesus himself, the Son of Man and primordial human, is in his nature a sacred marriage of all conceivable opposites, mirroring the nature of the Divine itself. The deepest and most radical fact of his presence and the powers that stream from it is to manifest in human reality the essential truth of reality itself—that transcendence permeates, suffuses, and evolves all of immanent creation.

This unity is manifest to those initiated into what Jesus called "kingdom consciousness"—in other words, drunk on the wine of true perception and embodied bliss that the sacred marriage is always pouring out to those daring to drink it. As the second letter of Peter I, verse 14, proclaims, "The word became flesh to make us partakers of the divine nature." To partake of the divine nature means to drink constantly of the wine of the sacred marriage so as to be progressively intoxicated and transformed by both the ecstatic peace and the dynamic evolutionary power of divine nature itself.

This understanding of wine as a symbol of the bliss and expansive empowerment that comes from direct experience of the sacred marriage is not unique to Jesus. It permeates the mysticisms of the Middle East, of both the Jewish and Islamic Sufi mystics; it is also employed with dizzying variations by the Buddhist, Taoist, and Hindu tantric masters.

In kabbalistic mysticism, what is called "protected" wine is nothing less than a symbol of messianic redemption. *Protected wine* refers to wine fermented long enough to be purified of dregs and symbolizes both the transformation of evil and the sefirot of Binah, the great mother, also known as the higher shekinah, through whose grace both what we call evil and what we call good are united in the mystery of unitive consciousness. In many kabbalistic texts, the Messiah himself is described as being "adorned in higher wine."

As Mordechai Leiner of Izbica wrote, "Since the day the world was created, he, the Messiah, has been washing his garments in the higher wine"—the wine of the sober ecstasy of the highest knowledge in which all opposites are reconciled and united—Eros and agape, body and soul, luminous mind and aroused, enflamed heart, masculine and feminine, the dark and the light.

For many kabbalists the purpose of the mystical path is to prepare your whole being to drink this "higher wine" so its perfect, dregless joy can transfigure you into becoming its humble and royal embodiment. As Leiner wrote, "Drink and become drunk lovers, for seedlings need to be watered from the deepest river, the supernal mother, for she first gives them to drink from that wine" (Song of Songs, Chapter 5, Verse 1). The correspondences between this vision and the miracle at the marriage of Cana are obvious: Jesus as Messiah as Christ at the behest of the supernal mother, turns the water into this higher best wine so that those who struggle to embody what he is enacting and making available realize through his grace his own undivided fully human and fully divine being.

The fullest expression, however, of this understanding of wine is found in Rumi's poetry, where all of the linked meanings of wine are alluded to and celebrated most comprehensively in these six lines from *The Mathnawi*:

The wine of divine grace is limitless.

All faults come only from the faults of the cup.

Moonlight floods the whole sky from horizon to horizon.

How much it can fill your room depends on its windows.

Grant a great dignity my friend to the cup of your life;

Love has designed it to hold His eternal wine.

These six lines encapsulate the central message of the miracle of the marriage of Cana, that the divine grace that streams to us from the essential fact of the sacred marriage of transcendence and immanence is limitless as the Divine itself is limitless both in presence and evolutionary power.

In the third line, Rumi reveals the truth of what drinking the limitless wine of divine grace will reveal to us when we are ready: "Moonlight floods the whole sky from horizon to horizon." This refers to the experience that is acknowledged by all mystics of the sacred marriage as the key to our increasingly conscious "partaking of the divine nature"—the experience of the eternal light as being both the ground and the substance of everything that exists. As is known by all realized mystics, this light is a diamond white light—moonlight—and it floods the whole sky of our illumined knowing to reveal finally and unforgettably its presence in and as everything including, of course, ourselves.

Rumi's fourth line, "How much it can fill your room depends on its windows," reveals, however, that while this experience of the divine wine ends one life, it begins another, one that keeps unfolding ever fresher, ever-deeper realizations of oneness. In many traditions such an experience is heralded as definitive enlightenment. Mystics of the sacred marriage know that while this experience permanently alters our whole perception and knowledge of what reality is, it is only the beginning of another grueling and amazing journey through which we "marry" what has been revealed to us and in us to all the different aspects and facets of our incarnation—heart, mind, soul, increasingly divined body.

In the last two lines, Rumi writes: "Grant a great dignity my friend to the cup of your life; love has designed it to hold His eternal wine." Rumi does not write "cup of your mind" or even "cup of your heart." With Jesus-like daring he writes "cup of your life." What this shows us is that as your whole being, mind, heart, soul, body becomes a window, becomes transparent to grace, we realize just what limitless divine grace is offering us is nothing less than the life at the core of our own life, the divine nature itself. This realization goes far beyond normal understanding of what enlightenment is.

If you make enlightenment, as all the patriarchal traditions have drastically tended to do, into only an affair of awakened consciousness and not also a transmutation of all emotion, desire, and physical life itself, then you will not even know, unless grace directly instructs you, that awakened divine perception is only the beginning of what you are offered through the infinite generosity of divine love. You will never know what Jesus and Rumi and the other mystics of the sacred marriage come to know, that the deepest meaning of the miracle of the marriage of Cana is that you yourself are a sacred marriage of light and matter, capable of being born into ever more powerful fusions of both when you drink and keep drinking the best wine—the wine of the Divine Feminine wisdom and bliss that creates and permeates the whole of reality, both uncreated and created.

Any body shame or body hatred, then, is a form of blasphemy and is a result not of an honoring of the spirit but of an ignorance that the body itself is a creation of the light, permeated and activated by the spirit through its subtle centers, called chakras in the Hindu system but known in all mystical traditions in only slightly differing descriptions. The fact that this sublime and joyful knowledge has not permeated our global human consciousness is a dark tribute to the patriarchal orthodoxy that has disfigured in different ways all the world's religions.

This brings us to potentially the most radical meaning of Jesus's miracle of turning water into wine at the marriage of Cana. In turning the water into wine at a marriage, Jesus was symbolically transforming the water of ordinary unillumined sexuality into the wine of the revelatory ecstasy of a sexuality suffused by adoration and divine consciousness. His knowledge of himself as a divine incarnation gave him direct knowledge of *all* human beings as divine incarnations, gifted with infinite evolutionary potential. His experience of his own physical impulses and desires being radiations of the divine love he was one with gave him direct awareness of what human sexuality could be if it was lived in the increasingly grounded experience of the sacred marriage of transcendence and immanence—nothing less than the site of the direct and transfiguring encounter with the creative sacred energies of the father/mother itself.

It is by the light of Father Bede Griffith's vision and his presence, then, that I understand that in the miracle at the marriage of Cana, Jesus's turning of the water into wine was showing the way for human beings to bless sexuality as an expression in human life of the ecstatic divine marriage and to experience sexuality through its consecration as an initiation into the creative bliss energies of the universe.

As I navigate my 70s, I know that my body and sexuality are holy—that everyone's body and sexuality like mine are capable of being subtly, magically, progressively divinized, and that this divinization process is one with full Christ consciousness. In fact, this is its greatest blessing, since through its grace, the whole of the human becomes inseparably interconnected with the Divine normally in the heart core of life.

For 30 years I have plunged into a study of the Buddhist and Tantric systems. I found in both a celebration of the power of the Divine Feminine to illumine consecrated sexuality and reveal it as a door into oneness, into all-pervading divine consciousness. At Cana, I now see Mary as mother is asking for a revelation of this power and its potential for healing and transformation.

I also plunged into a detailed study of the sources of Jewish mysticism that Jesus could have himself been inspired by. What I discovered would take a long book to celebrate comprehensively. But for our purposes here, let's try to understand the consciousness and purpose of the man who met his ordained consort in that crowded room in Capernaum. Three interlinked streams of mystical Judaism confirm and expand the analysis of what I have offered here, of what I have come to call the sacrament of Cana. These three streams are:

- The mysticism of the sacred marriage of the masculine and the feminine in the first temple.
- The profound mystical revelations that sprang from the honoring by certain Jewish mystics contemporaneous of Jesus of the Song of Songs.

- The glowing understanding of consecrated sexuality that flowed from both these streams that was crystalized by the marriage mystics of the later kabbala into a vision of how the reverent practice of what one of them, Nachmanides, called "sexual holiness," could transform both the substance and the evolution of the human race.

What Jesus had come to see, both in his first miracle at Cana and in his recognition of and full human and divine love for Mary Magdalene, reflects not only the tantric wisdom traditions of the east but the richest wisdom of the tradition he was born into and nourished by.

Before I present to you, in a precise, brief, potent form, these three streams of what I call "the Jewish tradition of sexual holiness," I invite you to integrate what I have offered you up to now of the mystery of the wine of the miracle of Cana.

Imagine the "wine" Jesus manifests at Cana as a stream of all-transforming golden light entering your whole being through the top of your head. Allow that light to enter your mind and transform it into a mind radiant with divine knowledge. Let it pour down from your mind into your heart, and expand it into a sun that radiates its light throughout your body. Take the golden light pouring down into all the bones, muscles, and cells of your entire body and imagine it radiating golden light to all creation, as Mary Magdalene did in her astounding appearance to me in the south of France.

You are now saturated with the golden wine-light in every part of your body, and radiating from your body throughout the universe, feel how you are now fully alive, in your full divinized humanity. If you want to, do this practice twice, slowly, with relaxed but intense focus, and you will begin to taste deeply the sacred marriage of transcendence and immanence in your genitals and bones and feet as well as your enlightened heart and mind.

Imagine now how your whole life would change if this taste became a steady, normal knowing irradiating all you are and do, from cooking to shopping to talking with your friends, making love, and serving others. You are now ready to enter the three streams of revelation of the Jewish tradition of sexual holiness.

One word of advice as you read the next few pages: Keep an image of Mary Magdalene and Jesus meeting for the first time in that noisy, bustling room in Capernaum alive in your heart. In the pages to follow, allow the sacred information they offer to make that image ever more beautiful, holy, and incandescent.

Let's begin with the mysticism of the sacred marriage in first temple spirituality. Brilliant modern research by Margaret Barker and others has revealed that in the most ancient tradition of Israel, Yahweh was conceived as both male and female. It was they who created, sustained, and evolved the world.

As Betty Kovacs writes in *Merchants of Light*, "Yahweh was both male and female. The feminine side of Yahweh was called Wisdom, consort of Yahweh, the Queen of Heaven, the bright and radiant one whose teaching was like the light of the dawn. She was the great lady, virgin, lamp of the gods, holy Spirit, nursing mother, and consort of the human king, the anointing oil for the high priests, winged sun, and the great tree of life in the garden of the gods called Eden. She was the water of life flowing from the fountains in heaven, like four rivers flowing from Eden. And it was she who brought all pairs of opposites into harmonious balance. We are told that the spirit of Yahweh was the spirit of Wisdom."

Further support for this ancient tradition can be found in the biblical book of Jeremiah. In it, Yahweh asks the prophet Jeremiah, "Do you not see what they are doing in the towns of Judah and in the streets of Jerusalem? The children gather wood, fathers kindle fire, and the women need dough to make cakes for the Queen of Heaven." From this we see that the Bible itself bears witness to the importance of the worship of the goddess Asherah in the lives of the people of ancient Israel and Judah.

This ancient tradition of Yahweh as both male and female was almost obliterated in 621 BC by the Deuteronomists at the time of Josiah, King of Judah. During a renovation of the temple, Josiah's high priest Hilkiah claimed to have unearthed a scroll that purported to be Book of the Law of Yahweh by Moses. Most scholars now believe this scroll was a forgery written either by Josiah or Hilkiah or as a collaboration between them both. Using this "miraculous" scroll as indisputable authority, Josiah then began his own set of revolutionary reforms that were designed to return Israel to the invented past religion of Moses and their ancestors. What this entailed was a ruthless and methodical erasure of everything to do with Yahweh's feminine consort, Hochmah/Asherah.

All objects associated with her were removed from the temple. Her sacred groves were cut down, her altars destroyed, her sacred images burned, her wisdom literature excluded from the sacred writings. All her stories were also drastically rewritten under the direction of the Deuteronomists. The cosmic tree of life sacred to her became, in the "new Genesis" myth of the Garden of Eden, the tree of the knowledge of good and evil that an exclusively male Yahweh forbade Adam and Eve to eat from. The divine mother herself was morphed into this new story, into Eve portrayed as a dangerous, devious woman who allowed herself to be seduced by the serpent into cajoling her man to eat the forbidden fruit and so plunged humanity into death and exile from Eden.

The cosmic tree that in the ancient tradition glowed with the golden mother fruits of enlightened wisdom and immortality became the vehicle for the fall of humanity, and the majesty and blessing of Asherah was distorted through the Deuteronomist's shrinking of her role into the figure of Eve, and into becoming a source not of abundant and fertile life but death and devastation.

For all Josiah and his henchmen's (the Deuteronomists) violent and fanatical efforts, however, memories of the First Temple celebration of the sacred marriage were never completely effaced. Rabbinic tradition tells us that the ark in the Holy of Holies of the Second Temple built by Solomon contained not only the law but "a man and a woman locked in intimacy in the form of a hexagram that was the marriage of two triangles—the masculine fire facing upward, feminine water facing downward and into the earth."

Modern scholarship has made it clear also that although Josiah's reforms drastically reshaped the sacred writings and so Orthodox Jewish practice, many Jews continued secretly to believe that the First Temple was the true temple and preserved in various secret forms the ancient worship of wisdom as Queen of Heaven. A large number of priests even fought with the Babylonian forces against Jerusalem in 586 BC because of Josiah's purge of the Queen of Heaven and the traditions of the First Temple. The refugees who fled to Egypt after the Babylonian destruction of Jerusalem insisted that the disaster was as a result of divine retribution for the abandonment of wisdom. In their own temple at Elephantine, they continued to worship Yahweh along with his consort, now called Anath.

In Jesus's own time, the memories of the ancient tradition of the First Temple were still alive in the many mystical Jewish groups that accepted neither Roman nor Orthodox Jewish authority and damned them both as corrupt. These included the Essenes, whom Jesus almost certainly visited in their settlement in the desert near Qumran. They were committed to what they believed to be the true covenant between God and Israel and sought to renew in their desert settlement this ancient truth.

Jesus quotes extensively from Essene sources, both in the Sermon on the Mount and throughout his teachings. It is unlikely he was an Essene himself, as some scholars have claimed, since they largely consisted of monastic older men living in simple austerity, and Jesus was emphatically not monastic and lived deliberately among all kinds of people. There is no doubt he respected many of their tenets (their sharing of property, for example), their radical new democratic order, their distribution of work and food and clothing and shelter, their respect for freedom, and the way they lived in peace, allowing no weapons. He respected and learned from them.

There were other groups he could have learned of this ancient First Temple tradition from as well. During the Hellenistic period, scholars have shown there were several groups of Jews who kept this tradition alive—some in Jerusalem, others in surrounding areas. Still others were in Egypt, like the Therapeutae, whom Philo of Alexandria commended for their holy way of life. Besides, as E. R. Goodenough makes clear in *By Light, Light: the Mystic Gospel of Hellenistic Judaism*, many of these Jewish groups were also open to the sacred marriage mysticism of the Greek mystery tradition:

"Judaism in the Greek-speaking world, especially in Egypt, had been transformed into a mystery."

It was this "mystery" of the sacred marriage Jesus may well have been initiated into. Asherah was alive in him as well as Yahweh. Even before he met Mary Magdalene, he knew himself as much the child of the embodied divine mother as well as of the transcendent father, the absolute.

The Tradition of the Song of Songs

THE SONG OF SONGS, called in Jesus's day the Song of Solomon, is a compilation made in the 4th or 5th century BC, possibly by a single editor of Hebrew, Syriac, Egyptian, or Moabite love songs and wedding hymns that were sung at marriage ceremonies and feasts.

The song was probably taken into the Hebrew canon as a result of the allegorical interpretation—still dominant in Orthodox Judaism—which equates the "bridegroom" in the Song with God and the "Beloved," or "Shulamite," with Israel. This identification was taken over and adapted by a long list of brilliant Christian mystics—from Origen and Gregory of Nyssa, William of Saint-Thierry and Bernard of Clairvaux—for whom the relationship between "bridegroom" and "beloved" passionately and magically represented the intimate bond between Christ and his Church or between Christ and the searching human soul or between Christ and the soul in the union of the Eucharist.

This exclusively mystical and transcendental interpretation of the ecstatic eroticism of the Song of Songs, both in Orthodox Judaism and the Christian mystical tradition, was not the only one Jesus could have been acquainted with and inspired by. In many of the Jewish spiritual groups active in his time, the Song of Songs was celebrated and explored as a mysterious revelation of the beauty, force, and power that could be unveiled, released, and activated by human sexuality when married to and suffused by divine love and ecstasy. These groups did not know what scholars now know, that the Song of Songs is a compilation of profane marriage songs. They would have accepted the traditional belief that it had been composed by King Solomon. As part of this traditional belief, its composition was linked either to Solomon's famous meeting with the Queen of Sheba or to his marriage to Pharaoh's daughter, and its glorious eroticism was not merely symbolic of mystical ecstasy, but as earthy and real as it was exalted and divine, the lived revelation of a man who had combined a holy love of women with unsurpassed divine wisdom.

Drawing on this vision of Solomon as a complete human and divine being, certain groups in Jesus's time that worked intimately with and celebrated the Song of Songs interpreted the rapturous exchanges between bridegroom and beloved as being simultaneously between Solomon and the human beloved, and Solomon with the Divine Feminine incarnated in his human beloved. For them, and perhaps for Jesus too, the Song of Solomon sang of the divine mystery and revelation at the heart of human sexual love, how when human sexuality was lived in adoration and worship, it could lead in both partners to the unveiling of divine identity, to the drinking of the wine Jesus manifested at the marriage of Cana, whose taste made ecstatically evident the marriage of immanent and transcendent in all things.

Twenty years ago, I met with a group of boisterous and illumined young Israeli kabbalists in Safed to share their wisdom on this aspect of the Song of Songs tradition. There were two mysteries they kept returning to and elaborating with ever more exuberant intensity that are relevant to our understanding of Jesus and his turning of the water into wine at Cana and of his meeting with his "bride" in Capernaum.

The first mystery arises from contemplating the richness of the innumerable comparisons with which the Song of Songs tries to describe the physical beauty of the lovers. The body of the female beloved is a garden, a city with its towers, an army of banners. Her lips are like threads of honey, her breasts like bunches of grapes or twin fawns of a gazelle. Her belly a stack of wheat, her belly button a wine cup. The male bridegroom is a bouquet of myrrh, an apple tree among the trees of the wood or a gazelle.

One of my kabbalist friends told me:

"For us this means that when sexuality is experienced as directly divine by being offered up to the Divine in prayer, the ecstasy that is engendered is recognized as the creative love force of the whole universe. The beauty the lovers celebrate in each other is a beauty that links them through this recognition to the beauty of the whole creation. If you read the Song of Songs with this awareness, you notice that the extravagant profusion of sensual imagery has the magical effect of making the images of the creation more vividly present than the human bodies of the lovers themselves that become shadowy, mysterious, and vanishing, vanishing into a field of rapturous union with the cosmos. The more the metaphors are heaped up, the more they become interchangeable, and the more the desire that sings so passionately in the Song of Songs becomes a polymorphous celebration of everything that exists."

The second mystery concerns Solomon himself as the archetypal sage king, as Jesus is for Christian mystics.

My closest friend in the group brought a text from the Zohar Hadash Shir Hashirim to our breakfast table in the small golden stone square we had been meeting in every day.

"I have kept the best for last," he said, and then he read very slowly:

"When the temple [the second temple] was built below and the sanctuary was firmly established, then the Song of Songs could be revealed, as sanctuary needed to be joined with sanctuary."

He read this sentence twice to make sure that I understood how radical it was to link the building of the second temple to the giving out of the Song of Songs.

"The text," he went on, "goes on to say that when Israel was in the wilderness, their sins and doubts caused the erotic coupling of Yahweh with the Shekhinah to be *ahor be ahor*—back to back."

When the Israelites crossed the river Jordan and entered the Promised Land, male and female were separated. As the text says, "When Israel crossed the Jordan River and Moses died, the Holy One set her, the female, the Shekinah, apart and installed her in the tabernacle of Shiloh."

This began a new process of gradual merging of male and female after separation that climaxed with the completion of the temple where the text says, "She joined with King Solomon and the worlds were face to face."

The relation between male and female became face to face, a new ecstatic and revelatory encounter that mirrored and emanated the power and joy of divine reality. The text says that at the moment when the worlds were face to face again, "All evil offspring and all evil spirits were then gone from the world and had no dominion."

He paused and, his voice shaking a little, read the next lines from the Zohar Hadash Shir Hashirim: "And at that time, when evil was removed from the world and the Woman and her Man were left face to face, it was then that the Song of Songs was revealed."

When the "woman" in Mary Magdalene and the "man" in Jesus met in Capernaum, as you will understand soon, a fresh and prophetic revelation of the Song of Songs tradition was unleashed.

The Jewish Tradition of Sexual Holiness

AFTER THAT WEEK OF CONVERSATION in Safed, several of the friends I had made kept in correspondence with me. They fed me poems and book lists and encouraged me passionately into exploring what they called the divine sanity of the kabbalistic system that they characterized as bringing to their richest unfolding essential themes already latent in ancient Judaism. Over and over again, the letters and e-mails stressed three interlinked themes: (1) that Yahweh is both male and female; (2) that Yahweh's creation was and is an extension of God encountered directly in time and space, the infinite in the dress of the finite; and (3) that the human body itself is a hologram of the Sephirotic tree of life, and with all its energies and desires potentially divinizable by conscious, sacred intention.

One of these friends, whom I shall call Eliezer, as he wishes to remain anonymous, took it upon himself to educate me in what he called the tradition of sexual holiness. Two 30-page letters he so generously and fervently wrote me remain among my most precious possessions.

In his first letter, he sent me this quotation from Spanish kabbalist Moses de León.

Please, dear friend, read this slowly, twice, and register in your whole being how its radical teaching overturns and expands what the patriarchal esoteric traditions of both Judaism and Christianity have taught:

"The purpose of the soul entering this body is to display her powers and actions in this world, for she needs an instrument. By descending to this world, she increases the flow of her power to guide the human being through the world. Thereby, she perfects herself above and below, attaining a higher state by being fulfilled in all dimensions. If she is not fulfilled both above and below, she is not complete.

"Before descending to this world, the soul is emanated from the mystery of the highest level. While in this world she is completed and fulfilled by this lower world. Departing this world, she is filled with the fullness of all the worlds, the world above and the world below.

"At first, before descending to this world, the soul is imperfect; she is lacking something.

"By descending to this world, she is perfected in every dimension."

In the long commentary Eliezer then wrote out for me, he said, "This passage celebrates more precisely and eloquently than any other in the kabbalah what this tradition knows: that the purpose of the soul entering the body is to divinize the body and all its energies and desires. The soul is not damaged or constricted by entering the body, as the ascetic formulations of other Western and Eastern systems maintain, to the terrible detriment of the innate holiness of all life. On the contrary, the soul enters the body rapturously, gratefully, because it knows that through the body its wisdom and reach will be immeasurably expanded. Through its marriage with the body, the soul 'perfects herself above and below, attaining a higher state by being fulfilled in all dimensions.'"

At the end of his letter, he said, "Meditate on all this. In two weeks, I will send you something else that will change your life." Two weeks later, Eliezer did indeed send me something that has changed my life. He sent me the following five paragraphs from the Iggeret ha-Qodesh letter on "Sexual Holiness" from the 13th century, attributed to Rabbi Moses Ben Nachman, also known as Nahmanides, a Spanish rabbi who emigrated to Palestine. I shall never forget the joy that flooded my being as I first read these paragraphs slowly, phrase by phrase, as if drinking the best wine of the miracle of the marriage feast of Cana. I remember thinking also, "I wish I had always known this secret. The whole of my emotional, spiritual, sexual life would have been different." Again, dear friend, I invite you to read Nahmanides' words twice, slowly, allowing them to awaken you yourself, directly.

Here is the quotation that he sent me:

"Sexual union is holy and pure when performed in the right way at the right time and with the right intention. Let no one think there is anything shameful or ugly in such union. God forbid! The right kind of union is called *knowing*. It isn't called that for nothing. Unless it were very holy, it would not be called knowing. . . .

"We who possess the Holy Torah believe that God created everything as divine wisdom decreed. God created nothing shameful or ugly.

"If sexual union is shameful, then the genitals are too. Yet God created them. How could God create something blemished, disgraceful, or deficient? After all, the Torah states, God saw everything that he had made. And behold, it was very good.

"The evidence is clear in the account of creation we read: the two of them were naked, the man and his wife. Yet they felt no shame. Before they ate from the Tree of Knowledge, they were contemplating the pure forms, and their intention was entirely holy. To them, the genitals were like eyes or hands in other parts of the body.

"When sexual union is for the sake of heaven, there is nothing as holy or pure. The union of man and woman, when it is right, is the secret of civilization. Thereby one becomes a partner with God in the act of creation. This is the secret meaning of the saying of the sages when a man unites with his wife in holiness, the divine presence is between them.

"Human thought has the power to expand and ascend to its origin. Joining the source, she is joined with the upper light from which she emanated; she and he become one. Then when thought emanates once again, all becomes a single ray. The upper light is drawn down by the power of thought. In this way, the Divine presence appears on Earth. A bright light shines and spreads around the place where the meditator is sitting. Similarly, when a man and a woman unite and their thought joins the beyond, that thought draws down the upper light.

"You should welcome her with words that draw her heart, calm her mind, and bring her joy. Then her mind will be linked with yours and your intention with hers. Speak with her in words that arouse desire, love, and passionate union, and in words that draw her to the awe of God."

And then on another piece of paper, Eliezer wrote:

"Cannot refrain from adding just one more kabbalistic quotation. After this one, you, dearest friend, will have everything you need to make your own sexuality as holy and transfiguring as I know you so deeply yearn for it to be.

"Baruch Ben Abraham tells us that for years he believed that saying one should hallow oneself during sexual union meant that one should sanctify one's thought by eliminating any intention of feeling physical pleasure. 'Sometime later, God favored me,' he writes, 'with a gift of grace, granting me understanding of the essence of sexual holiness. The holiness derives precisely from feeling the pleasure. This secret is *wondrous, deep, and awesome*.'" (The italics are mine.)

It was this wondrous, deep, and awesome secret I now realize, decades later, that Jesus wanted to make available to all humanity in his turning of the water into the best wine of the miracle of Cana. It was this wondrous, deep, and awesome secret Jesus was to live with Mary Magdalene in ways that progressively transfigured them both.

In the last part of his letter, Eliezer wrote, "There is one more secret the kabbalists have known since the time of Solomon. It will blow your whole being open.

"When a man and a woman live their sexual love in a consecrated, consciously divine way, the children born from such a concentrated rapture will be born on another evolutionary level, their whole being, heart and mind and soul and body seeded with the light code of divinization. Not only will the people who practice this divine sexuality be increasingly transformed themselves by the light energies that descend on them and irrigate them, waking up the muscles and bones and cells in them to their divine light origin, but the children born from them, from this transfiguration, in the process will themselves be seeded with all they will need to activate this process and live it, so potentially taking the whole of humanity to another evolutionary level of divine embodiment. Jesus turned the water into wine as his first miracle, to announce this most amazing of evolutionary possibilities and sacred technologies offered by the sacred marriage of immanence and transcendence."

What I understand too now is that this evolutionary possibility is open to everyone of any gender and sexuality who is graced with a beloved and pursues consecrated love in a beloved–beloved relationship. The "children" born from consecrated sexuality can be works of transforming sacred passion and wisdom in any of the arts and sciences as well as works of sacred activism and justice, any works in fact of any realm that build the lineaments of the birth that is arising in the death of our current global dark night. Nothing is impossible to the lovers infused with the sacred energies divine lovemaking invokes and releases. Nothing is impossible to those separately and together who are fused in sexual holiness.

Please read the above two paragraphs again slowly, allowing their glorious revolutionary message, which my research over 30 years has found echoed in Kashmiri Saivism, secret Saivite and Vajrayana tantra, and in Taoist alchemy, to galvanize you with amazement and hope.

In the miracle of the marriage feast of Cana, Jesus is opening up a transfiguring path of evolutionary love. In his relationship with Mary Magdalene, he lived that path out in all its splendor and power, as did the great holy woman who was his consort.

Now at last we can see from all that we have explored together that the meeting between Jesus and Mary Magdalene is the realization and activation in the core of both of their lives of the multiple interlinked revelations of the miracle of Cana. It is at once the meeting of a 29-year-old man and a woman in her early 20s in the full vigor and passion of their youth, and the divinely scripted coming together of two evolved, embodied souls destined with unique intensity and courage to experience and live out together a radical new path of evolutionary love. This is a path that has been obscured for millennia by a Church that privileged celibacy and demonized the body and sexuality, but which is essential for us now to reclaim as richly as we can in all its archetypal and actual power.

On an archetypal level, the meeting of Jesus and Mary Magdalene mirrors the coincidence of opposites of Divine Masculine and Divine Feminine in a primordial vision of the sacred marriage that permeates and illumines in different but related ways all the great mystical revelations of humanity. In their meeting in that crowded, noisy room in Capernaum and in the noble, divine, human passion that flowed from it, transcendent father and embodied mother reunite with the Asherah-Shekinah force—banished since the destruction of the first temple—and redeem Yahweh. The passionate longings of the "bride" and "bridegroom" in the Song of Songs are at last consummated.

What these archetypal reunions make available to all those who begin to comprehend through grace the miracle of what is happening in Jesus's and Mary's meeting is what it made available to them—an endless river of the best wine of Cana, that higher wine that both drenches us with embodied divine consciousness and activates within it possibilities of "endless expansion" and helps us become parents of a new and increasingly divinized human race.

Tempting though it may be to rest in the glory of such archetypal recognitions, the full revelation of what Jesus and Mary realized through their love can only be approached through trying to understand what living such a revolutionary passion meant for and cost both of them in gritty human terms. Beginning to understand the constellation of archetypal reunions that powered the sacred passion between them is just the beginning. We then have to explore how they, as human beings and human bodies in a terrible and brutal time, came to live out these reunions—so that we too can begin to find the wisdom and courage to live them radically in our own terrible and brutal time.

Contemplating the beauty of Jesus and the Magdalene's meeting only in its archetypal dimensions can be a way of avoiding the fierce, rigorous, transformative work we need to do to incarnate its evolutionary splendor in our own deepest relationships and in a time when time itself is running out for the human race.

The Meeting and the Glance

IN THE LATER TRADITIONS OF GNOSTIC CHRISTIANITY, in what is known as the Sophianic Gospel as described in Tau Malachi's brilliant *Living Gnosis*, we can find a story that describes Jesus and Mary's first meeting. It is most likely apocryphal, but as Cynthia Bourgeault writes, "At both the psychological and spiritual levels, it seems to ring true."

In this story, a beautiful and mystically advanced Mary Magdalene is promised in marriage by her greedy, worldly father to a wealthy Babylonian merchant. On the way to Babylon, however, her caravan is attacked by robbers and Mary Magdalene is sold into slavery and prostitution. After a period of brutal degradation, she regains her freedom but remains imprisoned in hatred and outrage.

Then in a dream the Magdalene receives the message that she must return to the land of her birth and search for the Anointed One, who will liberate her from her agony. Awakened by this dream that she recognizes as divinely inspired, she leaves immediately for the Holy Land. The story tells us that at the precise moment that Mary Magdalene crosses the Jordan, Jesus is rising up from the waters of the baptism in which the Voice announced him as "my beloved son." And even more astonishingly, given what we have been exploring, the story then tells us that on the day that Mary Magdalene first enters the Holy Land, Jesus performs the miracle at the marriage feast of Cana. As Tau Malachi writes in *Living Gnosis*, "The great mystery of the gospel was already transpiring between them before they ever met in this world."

Mary Magdalene finds her way to where Jesus is teaching. A crowd is clustered around him, and she hides herself in the back, hoping to stay unseen. But while he is speaking, the Sophianic Gospel tells us:

> At one point he glanced at her, caught her gaze and something passed between them. She was thunderstruck. An energy and vibration filled her whole body. A sight opened and she saw his true form "as light and fire and truth" and a love such as she had never known welled up in her.

This sublime paragraph guides us in the most profound and holy way into the truth of what transpired between Jesus and Mary when they met. In the Eastern religious systems the "glance or gaze" of an enlightened master has for millennia been recognized as perhaps the most effective form of initiation.

In Advaita Vedanta, for example, the four most powerful forms of initiation by an enlightened being are said to be, in ascending order, teaching, touch, silence, and then gaze. The great Hindu sage Ramana Maharshi, for example, rarely spoke, rarely touched anyone except for the animals he loved so deeply and taught in and through silence, and, as you will see, through his direct transforming "gaze."

My father, at 25, was the head of police in the South Arcot district where Ramana's ashram was situated and knew Ramana well and loved and was loved by him. When I asked him what Ramana's silence was like, he answered in one word, "deafening." And then he said, "His silence was momentous, unlike anything I have experienced before or since, but it was nothing compared to his gaze. Very occasionally, when I was with him, he would turn and look at me without blinking for a few long, long minutes. My whole being would fill with what I can only describe as a great peace. I was and am, as you know, a diehard old-school Christian. And at first I was frightened, but I knew Ramana, trusted him, and used what I experienced with him to help me begin to imagine what it must have been like to be around Jesus."

And then he told me the following story.

"One day I had come to present to Ramana one of the big-shot dignitaries of Madras, the state finance minister, whom I knew to be a crook, an elegant Eton-educated brahmin, but a crook nevertheless. Ramana hardly gave him the time of day, which secretly amused me and made me revere him even more. The minister wanted to be seen meditating at the feet of the Divine One, so we sat in silence. A few minutes passed, then suddenly the peaceful room filled with shouting. A disheveled beggar, clearly drunk, had run into the room and started shouting. 'Stop all this rubbish. God does not exist. This old fraud is just fooling you. Why doesn't he get a job? My wife and children died of cholera last month, and my hut burned down last week, and yesterday the doctor told me I have lung cancer.'

"Ramana's attendants grabbed him and wanted to throw him out. Ramana signaled them to stop and said, 'Bring my friend to me.' The man, still muttering drunkenly, came and stood before him. Then Ramana said with deep tenderness, 'I am sad you have suffered. I understand your anger. Come and sit down and look into my eyes.'

"In the two years I had known him, I had never heard him speak so much. The beggar, who had been so furious, calmed down and sat and lifted his eyes to Ramana's. The beggar and the sage sat gazing at each other, and tears started streaming down the beggar's face. I could see his face clearly. I was only a few feet away. These weren't tears of grief or rage. They were tears of joy. When Ramana lowered his gaze, the beggar wiped his eyes with his filthy sleeve, stood up, and left the room. On my next visit, I saw him working in the ashram garden. Ramana had accepted him as his disciple."

"What do you think happened in that gaze?" I asked my father.

My father smiled. "He saw God, and all his questions were answered. He saw and experienced God, just as Job does after all his miseries. It was that experience that healed him. Ramana gave him that experience. It was the one time I can say I witnessed a miracle. Please don't now ask me how Ramana's gaze transformed him. I had and have no idea. Nothing I had ever known prepared me for what I saw, and I will remember it until I die."

In one of his greatest odes, Rumi remembers the revelatory power of Shams's gaze and how it forever changed him.

The thought of a final beauty leaps like a deer in my heart
like the moon racing up the sky, like a lily
lifting its head suddenly from the river grass.
See, all the world's images are running to your image.
Scraps of iron drawn by a magnet of light.
Diamond becomes stone before you lions, small flowers.
The sun before you shrinks tinier than any atom.
In you this whole world blazes now like Mount Sinai.
Each of its atoms foams over with fire-water.

In that noisy room in Capernaum then, the man God and God man gazed at the woman ordained for him and "the something" that passed between them left her "thunderstruck." Her whole *body* filled with "an energy and a vibration." But it was not only her body that felt itself in a wholly new way. Her sight opened, the visionary center the Hindus called the Ajna chakra, and Mary saw the young man standing in the noisy room at Capernaum in a way that would mark her forever—with the vast and burning love that would possess and continue to transform her for the rest of her life and beyond.

She saw him in that moment as none of the disciples—and perhaps only his mother—had seen him as he was in his essential Christ nature, "light and fire and truth." Her own mystical and visionary experiences had prepared her for this revelation, one that has been repeated in the inmost experience of countless Christian mystics after her. And her agony had incinerated her and hollowed her out so completely that the wonder she was receiving could burst in the depths of her body, then in the depths of her sacred being, then, unifying everything, in the depths of her permanently shattered open "sacred heart."

And it was then that a love such as she had never known welled up in her. Her visionary openings had given her the first tastes of such a love. But these tastes had been abstract flashes of the lightning of the divine love, the light and fire of truth. Such flashes had not been enough to prevent the horror and suffering that had engulfed her and lashed her to the edge of suicidal insanity. Now, that lightning stood before her in and around the body and presence of a man only a few years older than she was.

Mary Magdalene was not exorcised of seven demons. How could such a grim, flat sentence describe what the words of these Gnostic texts stammer to relate? Mary Magdalene was transfigured by the already transfigured one, Jesus the Christ. It was that transfiguration that healed her.

But that was not all that happened in that shared gaze.

Jesus, too, was forever transformed.

I believe what transpired between them in that shared gaze astounded, shook, and transformed everything he already knew, just as it astounded, shook, and transformed Mary Magdalene and everything she had ever known.

When Shams met Rumi on November 29, 1243, at the intersection of two roads near the main square in Konya, he had been told by a vision of Allah to go to Konya and even given the name of his destined beloved. Nothing, however, prepared him for the ecstasy that flooded him when Rumi fell off his horse and staggered and ran into his arms. Again and again in his writings about that time in the *Maqamat*, Shams cries out, "I never imagined such a beautiful being could exist." Shams prayed for a decade to meet a beloved friend brave enough to love and receive all he was and all he had been given to give. Allah had shown him that his desire had been granted. But nothing prepared him, or could have prepared him for the divine joy of the fulfillment of that desire or the incandescent passion that flowed from him, and from the man whose inner beauty dazzled and amazed him just as much as his own majesty of being dazzled and amazed Rumi.

However divinized anyone, even Shams, even Jesus, may be, the Divine has astounding secrets up its light sleeve, secrets that take those who have already traveled further perhaps into the mystery of love than anyone else, ever and always further.

For such a miracle of recognition to occur in the first place, it cannot but be mutual, for the simple and life-changing reason that such a miracle cannot take place when any trace of separation remains in either beloved, whether they are intimate friends as in Shams and Rumi's case, or sexual partners also, as in the case, I believe, of Jesus and the Magdalene.

You do not have to be Shams or Rumi or Jesus and Mary Magdalene to know the truth of this. Anyone who has ever loved someone else with their whole being, whether human or animal—heart, mind, body, soul—has tasted this revelation. My father in his last conversation on his deathbed told me, his usually grandly British voice shaking:

"Your mother and I have been married for forty-six years, and I will tell you that I love her more this morning than I have ever loved her, than I have ever imagined I could love anyone, even her. When she comes to see me every morning, I just gaze at her and all that goes through my mind is, how could I ever be so graced? Such an amazing, mysterious, brave, beautiful woman, and for forty-six years, through everything life has thrown at us. God knows I know she can be maddening, especially when she sails into one of those stories we have all heard a thousand times—and when she drinks too much, God, especially when she drinks too much and starts raging against the socialists or the Russians or whatever else is swirling through her wild mind—but those are all just minor details now. Funny little flea bites. Nothing more."

And then he added, "It is so strange, Andrew. I cannot think of myself anymore, of Bernard Alexander Fortescue McLeod Harvey, without her in me and with me. I do not exist without her in me and with me. And the only thing I regret about dying is leaving your mother and our love."

We fell silent. And then I saw his face brighten and he smiled his wonderful, regal smile, the smile my mother called his "Clark Gable." And he said, very quietly, "I know too, you know, I can never leave her. Once true love comes, it stays. Saint John's gospel tells us God is love. So where would God go?"

It was the longest speech I ever heard my father give, and every word all the more precious and holy from my father being like

Ramana, a man of few words, is imprinted always on my soul as the truth of sacred marriage and sacred relationship. The last thing he said to me as I stood in the door, gazing one last time into his eyes was, "Never forget the love that made you. May it always give you confidence and courage."

And my body and being, like Mary Magdalene's, filled with joy.

The Gaze as an Annunciation

WHAT THE CHURCH HAS MISSED, and even most Christian mystics apart from a handful of women like Hadewijch and Elizabeth of the Trinity, is what Cynthia Bourgeault, commenting on this Gnostic story in her majestic book on Mary Magdalene, writes so delicately and wisely: "Can such a gaze ever pass in one direction only? The story makes clear that the impact of that something which passes between them is as compelling for him as it is for her." She goes on: "He (Jesus) sends for her immediately. . . . Later, according to this legend, after a time of seclusion in the wilderness in which he gives her teaching and initiates her, they are married and work together as mystically conjoined partners."

Then Cynthia Bourgeault writes something quietly revelatory: "In real life if something of this sort ever actually took place, it was probably a great deal messier, a good deal more ambivalent. For an emerging young spiritual master at the time self-identified as a Nazirite, in other words, as an austere ascetic, one can only imagine that his first encounter with that eternal gaze through which true love announces itself must have been a replay of his mother's story some thirty years earlier, when that sudden visitation of an angel announces solemnly that one's life is not going to be like what one thought it was. While he, too, ultimately made his way to that same 'let it be,' I suspect he did not come to it without a good deal of interior struggle."

Only an illumined woman mystic who knows the subtle resistance of even the most illumined man to being flooded and irradiated by the volcanic power of the Divine Feminine could have written that. Jesus was the incarnate Christ, but he was also a man, one whose human religious identity had been formed at least in large part around the Essene Nazarites and John the Baptist—around, in other words, visionaries of transcendence and ascesis. While he spoke searingly and movingly of feminine wisdom, and in a way that shows he was already attuned to the feminine archetype of God, to actually encounter that feminine archetype in a living, breathing, visionary woman must have shaken him to his core. And in a way, as Cynthia Bourgeault says, that cost him a good deal of interior struggle.

The work of the eruption of unmistakable and unavoidable love in the life of any human being, even one who is an incarnation of God, threatens not only any previous identity you may have formed, but also all its concepts and theories, however convincing and magnificent. The encounter with the Divine Feminine in another incarnation could only have been for Jesus initially deranging, even at times disturbing. In order to fully embrace and integrate what the gaze at and from the woman he was face-to-face with awakened in him, he would have to surrender in ways even he could not have imagined. The encounter with the authentic Divine Feminine in all her agony and authenticity and beauty and naked passion is always a revolution—for women, yes, but especially for men, whatever their sexuality. This is because of all the unconscious entitlements and secret and largely unacknowledged, baseless superiorities any male ego, even the most enlightened, has been fortified by.

While it is easy to imagine why a woman of Mary Magdalene's inner stature and crucifying outer experience would have been overwhelmed by meeting Jesus in all the divine beauty of his presence, it is essential to dare to imagine why Jesus also was overwhelmed by her—by the depth of her soul, by the agony she had been through, and by the capacity for initiation, revelation, and wisdom it had carved out in her. She saw him as he was, all "light and fire and truth." He saw *her* in that moment as she had been, was, and would be all at once, and his embodied soul fell before hers in amazement and astounded adoration.

The reunion of the two halves of eternal and embodied reality, of all the archetypes that we have seen swirl around their meeting, could only be equal and mutual. How else could such a reunion, with its momentous consequences for humanity, possibly occur, than in the ecstasy of recognition and adoration in which both were transfigured? She by him, he by her.

When two divine lovers meet, a third, the One, is birthed, and both are not only changed but transfigured. As Moses de León wrote in the Zohar, "All spirits of the world are made up of male and female. When they come forth in the world, they come forth as male and female. After that, they split up in their own ways. If a person is worthy, then they will unite together. That is, he will find his soul partner and unite with her *in one unity, affecting everything spirit and body.*"

Cynthia Bourgeault's sublime commentary on the story of Mary Madgalene and Jesus's meeting implies another great secret of their love. She compares its impact on Jesus to the impact the Annunciation had on his mother. Just as the angel's message to Mother Mary and her surrender to it inaugurated a new era, so the coming together of Jesus and Mary Magdalene began for both of them—and through them for all of us—a new path of embodied, divine, human, evolutionary love. It has its roots, as we have seen, in the inspired depths of the Jewish tradition, but also, as we will see, transcends those roots in urgent, dynamic, transformatory ways that had to be carved and lived afresh in terrifying and agonizing circumstances.

The Jewish tradition, for all its knowledge and celebration of the Divine Feminine's brave and radical sanctification of consecrated sexuality, remained subtly imprisoned in patriarchy. It was this subtle imprisonment of the Divine Feminine within a masculine-dominated tradition that the love, the real and equal and mutual human and divine love of Jesus and Mary, was destined to rubble—in ways that profoundly challenge not only the Jewish tradition, but also the Hindu and Buddhist tantric systems that also often tilted toward masculine empowerment and liberation.

What the churches have never been able to face, mired as they are still in patriarchal forms and dogmas, is that the love that erupted on that day in Capernaum between Jesus and Mary is the love not only of master and disciple, but far more importantly and radically, of equals, of beloved and beloved. Even those in the progressive churches who claim to honor the fullness of this love and embrace its totality shrink from the revolutionary implications of the equality and mutual adoration that it entails: the challenge to transform Jesus's message and the dogmas and institutions that claim and transmit to guard that message.

In Jesus and Mary's own time, this equal love created such a disturbance in the male disciples around the Christ and in the writers of the Gospels that it was either minimized or, as we have seen, perverted and written out altogether. This disturbance remains a potent force of limitation and obscuration, and a source of resistance that is subtler perhaps than in previous centuries, but still dangerous.

Uncovering this resistance in its secret recesses in myself and working doggedly with its sabotaging voices has been one of the main revelations of writing this book, and a sobering and humbling one. Although in many ways our time is the one destined to receive the full transmission of the Christ's and the Magdalene's sacred passion, truly to receive it will still involve for women and men a tremendous inner struggle. It will mean a meticulous and grueling unwriting in the depths of ourselves of many scripts, both secular and sacred, that we have accepted as timeless truth. Both Mary Magdalene and Jesus had to die into the love that united them and continued to transform and rebirth them, and we will also.

The rewards of that death are incalculable and glorious, but the process it entails can be bewildering and even harrowing, and involves repeated leaps of courage and faith in the Father/Mother's hunger to birth us all at last into our own whole, humble, radiant magnificence. It is far easier to be the lover of the beloved than to claim in awe and amazement the status of the beloved in mind and heart, soul and body. Because when you begin to dare to, a thousand manicured and authoritative inner voices mock you; call you mad, vain, and deluded; and repeat in ever subtler and more ferocious ways the messages of body hatred and sex shame and inevitably limited realization that keep you enslaved to the patriarchal past and its limited visions of "salvation" and "enlightenment."

What has helped me most in my own journey is understanding that Jesus and Mary also must have struggled to face and embrace and live and integrate the splendor of what love offered them. This has allowed me to call on them, as every new difficulty appeared, to expose increasingly fearlessly to them my doubts and inhibitions and insecurities. I have received from them the grace to continue to try to break through, whatever the cost, into the transfiguring birthing field their love establishes, transmits, and radiates.

Mother Mary must have received inwardly, along with the message that she was destined to birth the Anointed One, the revelation of everything that that would cost her and him. In that room in Capernaum, Jesus must have experienced in one divine moment both the new spring that love was offering him and the Magdalene (and us)—as well as the difficulties, oppositions, even terrors, that living it out would inevitably attract and entail.

Mother Mary, at age 12 or 13 in her small room in Nazareth, had to dive into the radiant depths of her being to fetch the courage to pronounce the fiat that changed human history. Similarly, her son, thrilled and aghast at what was being revealed to him, in him, through the woman that stood before him, had to dive into the depths of his own divine consciousness to speak the fiat that accepted and honored the new path of embodied divine human love—that love opened up for him as part of the mission to transform all the terms of Earth life he had been given. Perhaps he had not known that this, too, would be asked of him as it had never been asked before of any prophet or avatar. He must have sensed immediately that he did not and could not know all that this new kind of love would demand of him, and that there was no possibility now of evading either its rigors or its revelations.

The yes that flamed out in that glance between him and Mary Magdalene would have to be repeated in them again and again, at ever greater depths of truth and surrender, until its work was completed. Knowing this does not diminish who Jesus was and is, as some patriarchal critics continue to claim through lack of mystical imagination. It increases, in fact, our wonder at what his heroic soul was prepared to take on and live and endure and labor to reveal. It also offers the key to what *we* must be willing to surrender to bravely and progressively be receptive to what Mary Magdalene and Jesus are trying to initiate us into.

The Beloved–Beloved Relationship of Sri Aurobindo and the Mother

THE ONLY COMPARABLE RELATIONSHIP between an enlightened man and woman in mystical history, one that unfolded almost two millennia later, is that of Sri Aurobindo, the greatest evolutionary philosopher and mystic, and his sacred consort and equal, the Mother Mirra Alfassa. When Sri Aurobindo in 1912 met the woman who would transform his work and life in countless and extraordinary ways, he had already realized himself as a divine incarnation. And Mirra Alfassa also had matured into an astonishing and many-faceted realization of her own destiny as a living embodiment of the Divine Feminine.

From both Aurobindo's and the Mother's accounts of their coming together, we know that they both recognized that it was divinely scripted, that it revolutionized both of their spiritual paths, and that together, infusing, informing, sustaining, witnessing, and constantly saluting and encouraging each other, their union would be dedicated to a constantly expanding and deepening work of evolutionary revolution. From Mirra Alfassa, later called simply "the Mother," Aurobindo learned the crucial role of the Mother's descending supramental light in the birth of an embodied divine humanity he already knew he was to pursue. From her time with Aurobindo, Mirra then confirmed and grounded in herself the path of the birth of a new humanity both her early childhood visions and later explorations of the occult and various mystical traditions had led her to.

While we know a great deal about the spiritual evolution of their relationship and the Mother's continued evolution after Aurobindo's death, inspired by this and taking it even further into working directly in a new yoga of her own—the yoga of the transmutation of cells—we know little about what personally and humanly transpired between them. Recent biographies have suggested that they did initially have a sexual relationship. When Aurobindo met Mirra, she had had a number of profound liaisons with gifted men, two marriages, and birthed a son, and was clearly not on a body-denying path. Aurobindo had also been briefly married, but was when he met her a celibate yogi utterly dedicated to his own awakening.

Biographies that suggest a period of sexual passion between them served to deepen their intimacy and intensify their mutual dedication to the work they were both committed to were met predictably by howls of outrage and derision, both from the ashram in Puducherry and from the Hindu religious establishment that privileges celibacy as indefatigably as the Catholic Church. For many of us who revere and learn from them both, however, although nothing can be proved, this suggestion and possibility only increase our awe at the great and sublime love they lived in such continually mutually transformative ways and deepen our contemplation of the finality and completeness of the union they so clearly knew and enacted. Whether they were physical lovers for an initial period or not, they were undoubtedly as Jesus and Mary were, in a beloved-beloved relationship, recognizing and honoring each other as equals and equally enmeshed in the details and intricacy of the evolutionary adventure they pursued together and could not have continued to pursue without each other's constant support, witness, and fearless encouragement.

They, too, as Jesus and Mary did, enacted in their own unique, radical way the dynamic potential of sacred marriage, and through that enactment offer us an evolutionary path of sacred partnership at the highest and deepest levels, which, as we shall see, offers us keys and clues to what Jesus and Mary Magdalene's must have been.

In the late 1970s, when I began to explore Aurobindo's and the Mother's work, I met the French Canadian poet and mystic Guy

Lafond, who had known the Mother well and been one of the few who were able to see her in the last period of her life, when she was working on her yoga of the transmutation of the cells. One day, he told me he had asked her what had been the main difficulties of her life with Aurobindo and the work they had undertaken as mystical partners. He smiled, paused, and then said, "You know, Mother's first response was a long, dry, ironic cough."

Then she continued, "Difficulty is too small a word. A math theorem is difficult. Playing the Bach *Toccata in D* is very, very difficult. Perfecting your serve in tennis takes years of difficult practice. The work Aurobindo and I did together was made more than difficult. It was bewildering, baffling, agonizing, hilarious, frightening, boring, impossible, only just possible, altogether all at once.

"You would think from the majestic clarity of his books that Sri Aurobindo always knew where he was going and that I always knew, after all the work I had done in so many, many fields, but you would be wrong. Sometimes for weeks and months, we found ourselves in mysteries where neither of us knew anything or could know. And yet we knew we had to go on like children in a thick forest with no paths in the middle of the night. Difficult, my dear Guy, would have been easy.

"And then there were the so called disciples. You think they're crazy now, pretending to worship me, but really thinking I've lost my marbles, trying to stop anything I am up to from getting out and thinking that if it does, my reputation will be shredded. What they mean is, of course, that their tidy little lazy ashram world will crumble or that they, as I have done continually, will have to give up what little they know and have to keep starting again and again, which none of them as far as I can see even begin to want to.

"Yes, they are crazy now, but they have always been crazy, entitled, spoiled, demanding, vampirical, jealous of each other's visions and so-called progress. The ashram was always, even in the early days, a mixture of a kindergarten for refugees from reality and an insane asylum with all the amenities, of course: good food, tennis courts, my little talks and music recitals, but still an insane asylum. How they harried Aurobindo with their demands, their repetitive, idiotic questions. Sometimes he would spend eight hours a day writing his marvelous letters, trying to answer their questions, their narrow little kindergarten questions, when he could have been dedicating that time to the work. His patience and compassion were astounding, but sometimes I could see he was exhausted, and I would beg him to stop, but he wouldn't. Sometimes I think he would have lived ten more years at least, if it hadn't been for the disciples eating him alive, always demanding more and more of him, as if they'd even begun to absorb the treasures he had already laid at their feet.

"And then there were the forces, the dark, destructive forces that would do anything to stop the work being accomplished or trivialized and perverted. They knew and they know, that if we succeeded, their reign over humanity would end, and they did everything—they do everything—to stop us. You get used to them, you know; you expect them. They become almost like annoying acquaintances you cannot shake. But you always have to stay sober, stay vigilant, watching all the corners to try and anticipate where they are going to leap from next. Difficult would be easy, my friend.

"If we had not loved and revered each other completely and not surrendered again and again to the demands of the work, whatever the cost, nothing at all could have been accomplished. We were pioneers, and this is the way things go for pioneers. If we had just given the disciples what they wanted, an old-fashioned Indian yoga, everything would have been easy as baking a lemon cake, and the forces would have slunk away. But that wasn't and isn't our way, and it isn't my way."

I was a young, idealistic seeker, drunk on my first mystical experiences, and a part of me was aghast at what he was telling me. I did not want my spiritual icons to be either human or in any way self-doubting and bewildered, as I of course continued and continue to be. But I knew I was hearing truth, a truth that I would need to absorb as deeply as I could if I was ever going to be authentic. I wrote down that night in my journal everything that Guy had told me about the Mother, and 20 years later, when I read Satprem's 13 volumes of Mother's Agenda, the staggering and heartrending account of her last yoga of the cells, everything that Guy had told me was confirmed.

I have shared all of this here for what I hope by now are obvious reasons: to imagine either Jesus or Mary Magdalene or the unfolding of their love in glamorous or serenely idealistic ways is to betray them and keep us safe, cocooned from both the inevitable human cost and from the brave divine splendor of what they lived. If we are going to follow them as pioneers of a new path of transfiguring evolutionary love, we will need to follow Jesus's own matchless advice to the disciples to ask for the grace to be able to combine in ever deeper depths the "wisdom of the serpent" and the "innocence of the dove." In other words, we must ask for the grace to imagine and experience both ultimate divine possibility and all the inner and outer shadows that conspire, sometimes subtly, sometimes with breathtaking viciousness, to unnerve and rubble it. Only by daring to live and fuse together such exigent opposites will we have any hope of either being instructed by their love or daring to live its truth in their name and through their example.

Into the Desert

RETURNING NOW TO THE GNOSTIC STORY about their meeting, afterward, Jesus and Mary Madgalene went together into the desert, where "Jesus initiated and taught her."

One thing I think we can be sure of, however, is that the Gnostic story gets it slightly wrong: It claims only Jesus taught Mary, when the woman he found himself face to face with in that room in Capernaum taught and initiated him also. Mary would have her own mysteries to pour into her beloved. Their marriage would be the best wine made from both their profoundest joys and griefs; the moments of tension, fear, exhaustion, or bewilderment at both what was offered them and what it would entail; their shared tendernesses and ecstasies, and their mutual revelation.

Jesus had first begun to become the Christ in the desert after his baptism, where he had met his dark double and both rejected that double's seductions and integrated his lacerating and nihilistic wisdom into his expanded consciousness. Only in the absolute bareness of the desert could such a marriage of the extremes of his divinity and humanity have begun to crystallize. Now again, another path had opened up in him, had been announced for him in his meeting with Mary Magdalene—the path of divine human love, a path he knew he had to live completely to be able to open it for all of us. He also knew that he could not open it alone, because it was a path that could only be forged in the furnace of a mutual, equal, total love with the woman destined for him.

Mary Magdalene had also known the desert—the inner desert of the dark night. It had incinerated her identity and reduced her to a cry, and its unforgiving mirror had reflected all the horror of a world gone mad and brutal with power. She had experienced this desert as a living death, but it had brought her, as she staggered through it bewilderedly, to him, to them. And now she was ready to return to it.

Mary had crossed one desert losing all hope, only to meet all hope—and light and fire and truth—in Jesus, and with him she would go back, but differently this time. She would go into the desert with him to be undone and remade in herself and in him, and with him, and in the One in both of them and beyond both of them. There she would be taught and initiated, and she would teach and initiate. She would discover, as he would, that all teachings and initiations flow from the One and back to the One beyond and through both of them. She would come to know what her mystical daughter Hadewijch came to know. In three interlinked quotes from Hadewijch's glorious work, we can begin to glimpse the map of the transformation Mary would live with Jesus, and he with her.

Please contemplate them slowly, savoringly, integrating their revelations into your own path.

You drive the sages and wise crazy.
Throw them in boiling chaos.
And when they despair
drown them in your super abundance.
malicious villain, radiant with mercy
tender as a lamb, pitiless
like a wild beast, utterly free
In your desert without mode.

The comings and goings
assaults and caresses
Of the beloved
are designed
with sublime ruthlessness
to purify the soul
of every passion and lead it
into the desert of the Godhead

where it is dragged
beyond itself, as that desert
absorbs it into itself
and loses itself utterly
so it is no longer named "soul"
but God with God.

Efface yourselves
before the desert splendor of Truth's Face,
and follow in all things
in awe and trembling, with unshakable passion,
its fierce and noble demands.

Of course, we can never know everything that transpired between Mary and Jesus in the wilderness. What our most profound and reverent sacred imagination and our own experiences of revelation in love can, however, reveal to us is our four interlinked realities:

First, the desert would deepen and ground the lightning glance that had married them by rooting its radiance in its unborn, undying source, the One Light.

Second, in the desert, in lovemaking, in unmasked intimacy, in silence, they would come to know each other completely, merge, and fuse and separate in the wonder of being two in the One.

Third, in the desert, both their sacred masculine and sacred feminine would flow into and irrigate and begin to transmute each other into each being both sacred masculine and sacred feminine in their own unique yet eternally intertwined androgynous truth.

Fourth, in the desert, Jesus would receive from Mary Magdalene the blessing of the awakened woman embodying the passion of the Mother for the Father, and Mary would receive from Jesus the great peace of ultimate surrender to transcendent father being. And this exchange would alchemically "engolden" them both.

When Jesus and Mary came out of the desert, each would have in each other what the Gnostic story calls "a mystically conjoined partner united to each other in heart, mind, soul, and body."

The two of them would be in union with the One forever, now the unchanging Third in their every detail and movement of love. Both Jesus and Mary knew that whatever then unfolded would be both as glorious and terrible as the desert was, the desert that dissolved and rebirthed them. And they would both be steadied to meet together with unshakable passion the "fierce and noble demands" of the life they would lead.

What had been born between them in the desert, and the marriage on all levels it had alchemized, would now continue to birth both of them through everything. They would now live in a mystery we are still deciphering and will never completely understand—but miraculously, through their grace, we can begin to imagine and even more critically, with their help, live.

Now, with all we have begun to know, let us return to the Gospels. They seem and are so chary in their depiction of the woman who changed everything for the man they celebrate with such beauty. Yet, if we read with the eyes of a divine detective sharpened by desert light, we can find in the Gospels what we are looking for. We can find signs of the ways the written-out woman helped, inspired, instructed, invigorated, and sustained the man she loved and who loved her; signs of the ways she helped birth in him new ways that without her would not be open; signs of how their love prepared both for growing and astounding transmutation.

Even in a text scoured nearly clean of Mary Magdalene, we find jewels to string around her neck or to fix in a light crown on her head. This is the crown of the beloved of the beloved, the one who loved and knew him as no one else loved and knew him, the one he would show himself first to in his miraculous new body at the Resurrection. He did so for the simple reason that her adoration, wisdom, tenderness, and passion had helped him bless his body—had helped his light marry each of his muscles and bones and cells, and so prepared the ground for such a revelation that she had helped birth in him.

You cannot resurrect what you have not completely blessed, and it was through their love that Jesus learned to bless the flesh he also was, and the uncurbed glory of its passions.

The Warrior of Light

If you speak frankly about evil and the demonic forces of what Saint Paul calls the principalities and powers in contemporary spiritually correct Christian or New Age circles, you are greeted by outrage or condescended to as an evangelical wannabe or secret dualist—the ultimate condemnation! The very moment when evil and the demonic forces at its command are having a worldwide orgy of inner and outer destruction, threatening the very survival of humanity and a great deal of nature, the very existence of evil in the demonic is denied by liberal humanists and atheists and also by those claiming to be enlightened nondual mystics.

What this means in practice is that evil goes unacknowledged, unreacted to, unchallenged, both in ourselves and in the viciously manipulated, unequal, oppressive economic, political, and religious structures that dominate our world and are not only hopelessly inadequate to deal with the multiple crises of our global dark night but are consciously or unconsciously driving, fueling, and manipulating these crises for money and power and so hurtling the human race toward oblivion.

At the heart of the Christ's mission, as the Gospels—especially Mark's Gospel—make almost terrifyingly clear is the unillusioned and fierce confrontation with and rugged transformation of evil and the demonic forces it commands both in the individual self and in the world. This is not, as a prominent Buddhist once said to me with a superior smile, because Jesus was insufficiently enlightened and a dualist, and that had he had the awakening of the Buddha or Nagarjuna, he would have "done things differently."

It was because Jesus had an ultimate knowledge of the One through his divine identity with the logos and knew that the One is beyond both what we know as good and what we know as evil and employs both in its desert without mode for its own mysterious redemptive ends. It was because Jesus lived in the heart of a mad, cruel, brutal world of Roman power and, as a marginalized tekton, saw and felt acutely its savagery at work and knew that he had been sent to initiate human beings into kingdom consciousness by living out its power and splendor and humility in everything he said and did.

Jesus knew that the path that he'd been sent to forge could potentially transform all forms and habits of human life by divinizing it. Through the law of the dance of opposites in the One, it would inevitably draw to it the fiercest, most vicious possible opposition both from the principalities and powers for whom the birth of an embodied, divine human race would be an unmitigated disaster and from the human beings these forces manipulated through narcissism, greed, addiction, and lust for power.

Jesus was not a secret dualist or only partially awake. As an emanation of the Real, he was a supreme realist, illusionless both about the destructiveness of the darkness and the addiction to power that have taken over the world. He knew the price that would have to be paid to resist, overcome, and transmute that darkness, and the price of the evolutionary wisdom that overcoming and transmuting darkness in ourselves and in the world would demand of us as it was demanded of him.

In Mary Magdalene he had a mystical partner whose past of violation and suffering had also broken her open to evil and the power of dark forces, and whose awakening with him in the desert had alerted her to the titanic struggle that the transformation of humanity and its structures of cold evil into the kingdom must inevitably entail. She was a woman whose soul had been forged in the fires of atrocious trauma that would have driven someone of lesser mettle mad or nihilistic. She had, in her dark night, seen evil on every level unmasked, but she had also seen the Light and him irradiated by it, as he had seen her.

With Mary, Jesus would never have to soften anything about the work they now shared, neither its precariousness nor its vulnerability to malice and sabotage of all kinds, nor the exhaustion and heartbreak and agony and hours of naked despair that it would entail that he had veiled from his followers and disciples, but did not need to veil from her because he knew she alone was brave enough to accept them and strong enough to steady and comfort him in them as he would steady and comfort her.

Only a warrior could have endured what Mary Magdalene had had to endure before she met Jesus and not be rubbled completely. Only the warrior in her could love the warrior in him with such abandoned awe. Only a warrior could accept the devastating cost that being Jesus's consort would exact: the cost of the disciples' incomprehension, envy, and malice; the cost of suffering what he had to suffer without any possibility of self-detection; the cost of being inevitably sidelined, marginalized, and forgotten in a patriarchal society that would, they both knew, never accept her sublimity or honor her splendor.

Only a warrior born of the same desert that he was could face unflinchingly with him love's revolutionary fierce and noble demands. After meeting Mary, Jesus had taken her immediately into the desert, not only to be alone with her, but also to show her in the desert's mirror the fires she would have to walk through with him. She had chosen these fires out of the full divine passion of her human love for him, and out of her own fierce and unbounded hunger for a new world remade by love. None of the male disciples, as their behavior throughout the Gospels and especially during the Passion makes clear, would accompany him as she would through everything. In Saint Paul's words, "bearing all things, believing all things, hoping all things, enduring all things," accepting the ultimate martyrdom too out of love for him, of never until in our time being recognized for what she was and is.

Mary Magdalene, after her sacred union with Jesus was sealed in the desert, became his co-warrior in the Christ's relentless combat against the dark powers that worked to abort the birth of a new humanity. She worked with him by his side, with her own strength and majesty of realization one with his, in the trenches of darkness.

This we can see clearly in the role she played in Jesus's work as an exorcist, a work for which he was already famous when he met her and continued with her. Modern scholars have also revealed her as a meticulous, precise source of the stories of exorcism that thread the Gospels, especially those in the Gospel of Mark.

Jesus says in Matthew 12:28, "If I throw out demons by God's spirit, then the kingdom of God has arrived on you." We know from the Gospel of Luke that Mary's transformation was considered an exorcism, and that must have given her a privileged, if constantly disputed position among Jesus's disciples as one in whom the kingdom of God had arrived. Yet, as Bruce Chilton points out, "Mary's role as a teacher who related Jesus's exorcisms and their significance remains unacknowledged in the Gospels and in scholarship."

Thanks to Chilton, this crucial aspect of Mary's work with and for Jesus can now be seen in its full significance. Just as scholars have revealed that Peter was the source of stories related to baptism, Chilton makes clear that Mary is "the single most important conduit of stories concerning Jesus's exorcisms." And he analyzes brilliantly three stories from Mark of Jesus's exorcisms.

The first arises from the beginning of Jesus's time in Capernaum, circa AD 25 (Mark 1:21–28). The second is set in the period that begins with Jesus's flight from Herod Antipas in AD 27—the story of Legion, a man possessed of innumerable demons that Jesus exorcised and sent into a herd of pigs that then ran off a cliff. The third is a story of exorcism after Jesus's Transfiguration in AD 30.

Chilton's analysis reveals the essential truth: What marks Mary's realistic signature in these stories is that Mark's narratives show the demons violently resisting Jesus. Mary knew from her inmost experience of him that the battle Jesus was engaged in on the subtle levels was a cosmic war of worlds, a war against the dark forces that manipulated human beings into creating and sustaining systems of cruel, degrading power, like the power of Rome that was pulverizing their world. The coming of the kingdom, they both understood, demanded the overcoming through the power of the spirit of God of those forces that kept brutal old order in place. Mary's own dark night journey, and the impact that Jesus's holiness had had on her, helped her to understand viscerally because she had lived it, the power of his presence. But she also understood why the forces of evil would be arranged against that presence to prevent it birthing a new world, the world he had opened for her and that their love was now living in, in sacred union.

It is astonishing that Mary knew the most terrible weapon the demons would have in their hunger to resist Jesus was their unique knowledge of his identity. Her own journey to the edge of nihilistic madness had in some mysterious way given her the ability to see him as he really was in his light and fire and truth. The nameless, possessed man in the first story in Capernaum calls Jesus "the Holy One of God," and the man called Legion in the second story calls him "son of Highest God."

Mary knew from her own experience how when dark forces were confronted with the power of his purity, they would dissolve. As Bruce Chilton writes, "The spiritual combat between Jesus and the forces of impurity was resolved because the unclean spirits recognized purity when they experienced it. Violent though their rebellion seemed, the demons ultimately recognized their own nonexistence."

Mary Magdalene knew not only the horror of being ravaged by the dark forces, but also the power of the Christ presence, of its holy love and adamantine purity—to reveal to those forces their nothing, their nullity, and to dissolve and transform them. And as she lived and worked with Jesus, she knew how ferocious and costly the Christ's struggle with the dark is to those who engage it fearlessly and without illusion. As the supreme realist she also had become, she wanted every detail of the work of Christ's consciousness in the fight against evil to be transmitted with illusionless clarity to all those who, like her and him, take up the cross of love, so that all of them can be steadied, informed, and emboldened.

In my early 30s I was on a train going to from Oxford to London on a gray winter morning. There was no one else in my compartment but a man, probably in his early 70s, short, pudgy, red cheeked in a crumply, stained black suit and dirt-scuffed black shoes. He kept trying to catch my eye, his own eyes twinkling with an unmistakable, almost brazen cheerfulness. Although I had intuitively warmed to him, I was too lost in my own self-involved misery to engage him in the conversation he obviously wanted. Eventually, he broke the silence himself with the line I still chuckle at.

"You know, dear boy, I am an exorcist."

"An exorcist," I found myself replying. "A real one? Like in the film?"

"Well, not quite like in the film, although it did have some accurate details. Yes, I am an exorcist. An Anglican exorcist."

He said the word *Anglican* with a slight tremor at amusement.

He went on, "You didn't know, did you, that there *are* Anglican exorcists? There are three of us—one in York, one in Kent, and me. Not enough to go around, given what is going on, but we try. And, God are we kept busy. Sometimes I want to retire and play with my old dog, Pops, and grow country roses, but I can't. Jesus didn't retire, did he?"

I gulped and there was a long silence. I had a decision to make: to flee the compartment and find another one or engage him. I decided to engage him.

I said, "It is a little strange to think of an Anglican exorcist. All the Anglicans I know seem to know is how to cut cucumber sandwiches."

He added, giggling a little, "And arrange flowers and organize bingo bonanzas to raise money for the new church carpet. Yes, dear boy, we can be a most uninspiring lot. Not hot on passion and adoration, much too infra-dig, much too con-tin-ental."

He drew the syllables out in such a way, we both laughed. I relaxed and forgot whatever it was that was darkening my heart.

"No Anglican I have ever known," I said, "has breathed a word to me about the Devil."

He said, "The lukewarm miss everything. The Devil is real, you know. Not just the big Kahuna, but a seemingly endless host of minor but very nasty ones. I've met quite a few of them in my time."

"How did you begin your career as an exorcist?"

"Good God, dear boy, it's not a career. I'm eccentric, I suppose, but not mad. Who would want exorcism as a career? For me, it's an inescapable vocation, one I never even dreamed of but couldn't not embrace."

"Why?"

"Because when I was a young priest, having visions and being filled with strange ecstasies, saying Holy Communion and living a frightfully and perhaps a rather self-righteously purer-than-pure life, the Devil came to me."

"Came to you?"

"He appeared in my bedroom, just as he does in the medieval stories, as a huge, stinking goat with flame eyes, and started to walk toward me. Sometimes he's a lot subtler. But that first time, I knew he wanted to kill me, and I was terrified."

"What did you do?"

"I grabbed a crucifix on my dresser and shouted the first thing that came into my mind, *The Lord is my shepherd*, and brandished the crucifix at him. He laughed a horrible, ugly laugh and disappeared. A week later I was going to see the bishop on parish matters. The bishop was a good old soul, not like some of them, and a bit of a secret mystic. And he heard me out and at the end said quietly but firmly, 'I think you are destined to be an exorcist. I'm going to send you off to Larry in York for a few weekends of training. You seem to have got the basic hang of it all, but perhaps a little more will be required.' I went to see Larry in York, got trained, and here I am, forty years later. I have done one hundred and forty-three exorcisms, and I am off to my one hundred and forty-fourth in Camden, of all places. A young Jamaican girl, barely out of kindergarten."

Then he grew serious.

"When you came in," he said, "I saw you were both unhappy and a true lover of God. I wanted to tell you you're going to be fine. Your heart will take you to Christ through many detours that will all be necessary and blessed. And when you find Christ, you will find your true self, and he will show you the truth of what I am about to say. Just remember this conversation when that time comes. Evil exists. Principalities and powers exist. Demons exist. Black magicians in conscious league with them exist. Demons work on many in many different ways and take over either the wholly unprotected or those who have already, through their wounds or innate propensities, become open to dark impulses.

"Demons have sworn perpetual enmity to the truth, to love, to the kingdom of Christ. And they are brilliant and subtle and lethal. They are everywhere now, given free license, because no one, not even those in the Church, really believe in them.

"If you go on a profound mystical journey, as you will, you will meet them. So you had better start knowing now what to expect. To turn up for God in a world running from God is to invite the dark to try and destroy you. Jesus knew this better than anyone. And those he draws most intimately to him will meet the dark in its unmasked form, just as he did."

There was a long silence. His sincerity had profoundly shaken me. Then, seeing my face, he smiled.

"But do not worry. Be advised, be alert, but don't be scared. Just stand secure and strong in the Christ force, just like Mary Magdalene, that great warrior of love, did. And nothing in this world or any other can defeat you."

"Mary Magdalene?" I had not heard her name for years.

"Yes," he said, "she's my girl. When I feel too small and useless to go to him, he can be a little intimidating, you know? I go to her, and she helps me more than any words of mine can describe. The demons can't stand her, but they'll just have to put up with her. She's been doing her work for two thousand years, and she isn't going anywhere. In fact, in my humble opinion, it's rather amping up. Not a lot of my colleagues really believe me when I speak of Mary Magdalene. But I'm too old and I have seen too much. And I know her too well not to say—excuse my language—what the hell do they know?"

The Sign

BEFORE WE PLUNGE back into the Gospels and Mary Magdalene's role as anointer-beloved, there is one more graced experience I feel compelled to share with you. Even conservative scholars recognize Mary Magdalene as the initiatrix and master of the tradition of anointing and the teacher of Jesus himself for the sacred power and blessing, a tradition she may have been instructed into in Magdala.

What their chosen constriction of vision prevents them from is what we will be exploring together, that her anointing of him was a sublime act of adoration from wife to husband, from one divine human beloved to another, from one increasingly divinized body to another. This was done not only to sanctify him, but to empower him on the devastating and amazing journey that would birth the Resurrection. This expansive vision, as we will see, revolutionizes our understanding of what the tradition of anointing could be in Christianity. As Cynthia Bourgeault writes, "To reclaim anointing in its original context would make it the sacramental centerpiece of a whole new vision of Christ based on spiritual transformation and the alchemy of love."

It is this original context and alchemy of love that the experience I will share with you illuminates. As you read what happened to me and my friend in Mary Magdalene's cave in France, please realize, as I do now, with awe, gratitude, and amazement that what we were given was not given for us alone, but to give you hope, wonder, and joy, and to empower you with the vision I have been offering throughout this book.

Before I began to write this book, I knew I had to revisit the places in France where I and many others believe Mary Magdalene ended her life. I asked my dearest friend, Sheryl, to accompany me, knowing her passion both for Christ and the Magdalene. Of course, I knew that I could not only unabashedly share everything I was receiving, but also learn from what she, too, was experiencing.

Ours is a 20-year-old sacred friendship, and Sheryl's unique marriage of worldly discernment, generous power, and mystical profundity—and her own lived experience of a sacred marriage with her partner, Howard—have been for me a constant fountain of blessing and delight. We had met in Paris before making our way to Vézelay, and then to Saint-Maximin, near Mary Magdalene's cave. In Paris, Sheryl gave me a colored Xerox copy of a painting of Jesus I had never seen before, but which moved me by its fusion of human beauty and divine majesty. As she handed me the picture and my eyes filled with tears, she told me that she had rung a mutual friend of ours, a divinely gifted psychic and guide we had both turned to, and he had told her that we would both be given what he called a conclusive sign in the cave of Mary Magdalene. He had not been specific, but had said that this sign would bring us both miraculous joy.

Seven days later, Sheryl and I found ourselves alone in the middle of a soft gray afternoon in the vast cave, now transformed into a church, where Mary Magdalene is said to have spent her last 30 years in solitude. We wandered reverently through the cave, not talking but drinking in its grounding peace. Then we sat together staring at the altar and started to pray.

I prayed to the Magdalene that I be adequate to the task of this book, to guide and help me be both as brave and judicious as I knew I would have to be if its revolutionary message was to be transmitted as clearly as possible, and to save me from any of my own unconscious shadows that could in any way dim the outflowing of her great light. I pledged to her that I would do whatever I could and go through whatever was necessary to honor her as she was revealing herself to be.

Almost immediately after both Sheryl and I had finished praying and were sitting together, a young man in his late 20s entered with his slightly younger beloved companion. They were both tall, about six feet, nobly beautiful: He was lean and athletic in his black jeans and brown jacket, with the seared face of a philosopher or poet; she was in dark-blue silk slacks and a dark-blue silk-and-wool sweater that clung to her and subtly accentuated the perfect compactness of her torso. Even more startling and inspiring than their physical presence was the palpable soft passion that flowed between them. They were not holding hands or hugging, as many loving couples might do. They moved separately, entirely sufficient in themselves but guided, it was strangely clear, by a dignified and harmonious profound mutual respect and adoration. They did not seem to see us at all, even though we could not help but stare at them, however discreetly. They never acknowledged us, but moved as if to an invisible music.

First, they went up to the shrine above the altar and stood there in silence, then they separated. She went to pray to Mary Magdalene, kneeling to the large baroque white sculpture of her to the right of the shrine at the back of the cave, her head bowed and the blue river of her back illumined by flickering candlelight. He walked to the back of the church and sat down in the pews across the aisle from us, his face in profile, staring fixedly in front of him, his hands folded in his lap. As they both prayed in their different places and ways, it seemed to both Sheryl and myself, as we said to each other later, that through their prayer and the subtle but unmistakably potent and holy link between them, the cave filled with the sacred power both of us felt. We felt it not only in our awed minds and hearts but in the depths of our bodies, as a subtle, fiery energy dancing in our cells and bones.

Sheryl saw the promised sign before I did. She whispered to me, "Look at his face," her voice shaking a little. "What do you see?"

Until that moment I had been drinking in the blessing of their love and presence, and the expansion their devotion had seemed to activate in the power of the cave. Then, at Sheryl's insistence, I turned to look at the profile of the man sitting about 10 yards from us. I had noticed his beauty and been moved by his dignity and natural authority, but nothing in my previous perception prepared me for what I then saw.

"Oh my God," I stammered.

"Yes," Sheryl smiled. "Oh my God."

His face was exactly the face of the Jesus on the paper Sheryl had given me. I had prayed to that face in my bedroom secretly at night throughout my trip, and there he was in that cave with her.

"It is them," I said, "the sign. Him and her, separate, together, the marriage."

Sheryl nodded.

The only thing I can remember of the long moments that followed is that my mind was plunged into a silence of amazement and a gratitude that drowned all thought. Looking back, as I have done every day since, I realize that I had expected whatever sign to be given would be given in the terms of all my previous mystical education, in dreams or sudden grace to intellections, or in the divine illumination of an ancient text, or in momentary, unforgettable experiences of being irrigated in mind and body by divine love fire.

Nothing could have prepared me for this sign, this grace, of being with my best friend in the Magdalene's cave, experiencing this miracle with me, and so confirming that I was not lost in fantasy.

Sheryl said to me, "I feel we should leave. We have been given more than we could ever have imagined. To stay any longer seems irreverent. Let us go outside and wait for them to exit so we can see them one last time."

We went out and stood on the stone square balcony outside of the cave, overlooking the now sun-speckled plane stretching before us in its majesty to Saint Maxima. Twenty minutes passed and the couple had still not come out.

Sheryl looked at her watch. "The cave closes at six. That's twenty minutes from now. Let's walk down the path we took. It's the only path down. We could wait to watch them there."

We walked down the path, found a large smooth rock, and sat on it, waiting and praying silently. We waited for an hour. Evening started to fall. They never came.

The sign was repeated unmistakably two days later. Sheryl and I were wandering in the 11th-century church in Saintes-Maries-de-la-Mer, the village by the sea where Mary Magdalene and her companions are said to have landed first in France. I was sitting praying in the lower half of the church. Sheryl had gone near the altar to look at the paintings on the side of the apse and was taking photographs of them with her phone. She came and sat down next to me, smiling broadly, and handed me her phone.

"Flick it on and tell me what you see."

The phone lit up with a painting I had not noticed, of Jesus sitting calmly in a boat. He was painted in profile—the same profile, the same face, as the painting she'd given me. The same face as the wonderful young man we had seen in the cave.

I said, "Who will ever believe this?"

She chuckled. "That's not the question. Do we believe it? Do you?"

"Yes," I said to her. "Finally, I do."

I went outside to leave Sheryl to pray on her own and to try to gather myself. I sat down on a slightly unsteady plastic chair in the small square outside and put my head in my hands. When I looked up, I saw a gypsy woman, in her 50s perhaps, dressed in a whirlwind of red and black and gold, gazing fiercely at me.

"I don't want your money," she said. "I just want to tell you two things which you must remember. Finish the work you have begun, however difficult it will sometimes seem, and whatever happens." She repeated, "*Whatever happens.*" Then she said, her face and eyes suddenly stony, her voice louder and rasping, "Never forget what you have been shown."

It is now clear, from the journey you and I have taken together in this book, who I and many others believe Mary Magdalene to be—Jesus's wife, his co-equal, his conscious partner in and pioneer of the sacred marriage, with the astonishing possibilities this book will continue to open up.

It is important, however, to acknowledge before we go further that short of the discovery of an actual document or an unambiguous archaeological relic, what I am proposing cannot be proved indisputably. Those who wish to cling to the safety of orthodoxy will have two millennia of authority behind them and will always be able to dismiss those of us who challenge it, either nuancedly or out of hand. I disagree with this response, but I respect it.

The vision of the Jesus of the Gospels, after all, and a large part of the mystical tradition inspired by it, have exalted countless lives and continue to do so. While I and many others believe that Jesus's relationship with Mary Magdalene is an indispensable and marvelously illuminating part of his story and journey, it is not his whole story, as is sometimes claimed by some of the Magdalene's most fantastical celebrators. To say, as I heard one famous Magdalene expert claim recently, that "Jesus is just Mary Magdalene's front man and mouthpiece" is absurd and dangerous.

An obvious counter-correction to established views, which substitutes a new biased orthodoxy for the old one, rubbles both the mystery and the potentially revolutionary implications of their sacred union. This mystery and these implications do not in any way limit, deflate, or circumscribe Jesus's teachings, example, or the mystical vastness of the journey he underwent on humanity's behalf. Those who revere the tradition as I do, but believe in its capacity to integrate new revelations and perspectives, can never be swerved from undertaking potentially controversial adventures. We are not deterred by rigid respect for the old or lacking in the kind of courage the great Christian mystics displayed, especially, I believe, the women mystics such as Mechthild of Magdeburg, Julian of Norwich, Hadewijch of Antwerp, and Elizabeth of the Trinity.

Cynthia Bourgeault, in her masterpiece, *The Meaning of Mary Magdalene*, stands firmly and exaltedly in this tradition. I shall never forget the cries of joy and recognition that broke from me when I first read these words in her book that continue to inspire me by both their balance and their wise daring:

> If Jesus shows us what the completed human being looks like in male form, she, Mary Magdalene, models it for us in its female version. Together they become the Christosophia, the androgynous archetype of human wholeness. And because her human heart and lover's passion are so central to this transformation, she teaches us not to be afraid of these things in our own spiritual striving. The path to the fullness of being lies through human intimacy, not away from it.

As we approach Mary Magdalene in her role as anointer, and the potential radical possibilities it can open to us, we cannot go forward without risking again and again the largest and most inspiring possible vision of Jesus's and Mary's love, even in the face of orthodox derision and the lack of indisputable evidence I have spoken of. In the decades I've been meditating on and researching the evidence of their love, one question has constantly haunted me. If the vision of the Christ's and Mary Magdalene's love is, as I and other Christian mystics believe, so transformatory, why has the Divine not made it more indubitably obvious, especially in a time like ours, when it's so needed?

I cannot possibly claim to know the definitive answer, but I am beginning to suspect from my own painful and miracle-filled writing of this book that part of the answer may lie in the nature of our contemporary agonizing and amazing evolutionary crisis. The way it is teaching many of us to go beyond all traditional formulations in all mystical traditions, and to dare to trust in our deepest soul intuitions, mystical experiences, and revelations of human intimacy and intimacy with the creation.

The evolutionary transformation or transfiguration that humanity will have to go through to survive cannot depend only on orthodoxy, dogma, or tradition, however profound, but will have to depend on the courage and visionary receptiveness of each individual's choice. The evolutionary path ahead is a new and unprecedentedly rich and complete vision both of God and ourselves. While our inherited traditions have essential truths we cannot afford to jettison or overlook, their subtle patriarchal and tribal dualisms and limitations block us now from precisely that discerning and radically humble and experimental courage we now need to go forward.

If we do, through grace, discover this courage or choice within us and dare to reaffirm it in the unassailable depth of our own soul and experience against all odds and opposition, externally and internally, we will be rewarded with new revelations both of divine and of human potential.

As Father Bede once said to me, echoing Shams of Tabriz's exhortation to Rumi that "the world of God is a world of endless expansion," "Never rest in even the highest and deepest realization you may have reached. If you do, you will be fixed in it and your evolution subtly congealed."

The nature of the Divine is, as Shams and Gregory of Nyssa said, *epektasis*, endless growth. Every step of that endless growth has to be consciously chosen by a soul to whom grace has revealed what was revealed to all the evolutionary mystics in all traditions: There is and will always be more.

The Context of the Anointing

TO UNDERSTAND AS FULLY as we are able the significance of Mary's role as anointer, we need to approach it, I believe, in two interrelated contexts: that of Jesus and Mary's sacred union and that of the extremely dangerous, tumultuous three years of Jesus's brief life and mission that Mary Magdalene shared with all her being.

Seen in this way, the Magdalene's anointing of her beloved acquires a far richer private and cosmic significance and forms an exalted and radical part, both of her and his continually unfolding legacy.

First, the sacred union.

The central insight of Cynthia Bourgeault's magnificent exploration of Jesus's and Mary's love, derived from Boris Mouravieff, the depths of the Christian esoteric tradition, and her own experience, is that Jesus and Mary in their love together birthed what Mouravieff calls "an abler soul that guided and informed their sacred evolution and shared mission and suffused them both progressively with its all-unifying wisdom."

I believe this vision, both from my own inmost experience and because it is confirmed in different and related language, in both Islamic and kabbalistic mysticism and also by the alchemical and Eastern tantric traditions, that when two highly evolved and sacredly dedicated beings come together in surrender, in adoration of their being to each other in the Divine, "a third" is created. This third being makes possible three interlinked and astonishing transformations.

First, the lived experience of complete holy passion guided by the third unifies the opposites in both—transcendence and immanence, light and shadow, body and soul, masculine and feminine. Second, this progressive unification engenders in both what the esoteric traditions call "the subtle body," and some tantric traditions call the radiant or golden body. Third, the more illumined and conscious this subtle body becomes, the more the actual physical body opens itself to the mysterious process of what Orthodox Christian mystics call *theosis*, which means transfiguration or divinization, and great Hindu and Buddhist tantric mystics and the great universal mystic Kabir call *engoldenment*.

Such a vision will inevitably meet three interlinked forms of resistance. All three may be arising in you as you read this. The first is the resistance we have identified in many ways in all the exoteric traditions to the radical and transformative equality of the sacred masculine and feminine in the one.

The second related resistance both in traditional exoteric Christianity and in all patriarchal exoteric traditions is to the inherent divinity of the creation, matter, and the body itself. The highest and most inclusive mystical wisdom of all the traditions proclaims the indivisibility of transcendence and immanence, the mysterious unity in difference of matter and spirit, creation and source, body and soul, the world of transient form and eternal presence. While this tremendous secret of what Caroline Myss memorably calls "organic divinity" is known in Buddhism, Taoism, and Hinduism, and has been experienced by the most awake mystics in all traditions, its revelation has not yet informed deeply and richly enough the exoteric traditions they belong to.

The third resistance intimately entangled with the other two is the most serious and difficult one both to acknowledge and discerningly transcend. We must be unshrinkingly aware of the first two resistances and the ways in which they have consciously and, more importantly, unconsciously contaminated and limited our vision both of the Divine and of human potential. Otherwise, any vision that claims a Divine at once utterly transcendent and utterly immanent infinitely beyond all story and history, and completely involved in an organic and evolutionary expansion of both, will seem absurd and even blasphemous and heretical.

What this view will reveal is what the Christian mystical tradition secretly knows, that the evolutionary progression of Jesus's own life and path from birth to baptism to Transfiguration to Crucifixion to Resurrection, Ascension, and Pentecost gives a complete, astounding, stringent, and exalted template for our own evolution from humanity to divine humanity.

Beginning to open to this truth opens to another challenge that again does not deny traditional Christian orthodoxy, but expands it in moving and glorious ways. This challenge springs from the deepest secret of the Christ path, one still largely unknown and unexplored by the Western churches and the majority of Christian mystics inspired by them. But it is known and celebrated at the heart of orthodoxy as *theosis*, or divinization, by which a human being becomes human and divine, just as Jesus was—not only in soul, heart, and mind, but also in body. All the Orthodox churches, especially the Russian, celebrate a feast of the Transfiguration when mystics like Gregory Palamas and Saint Symeon the New Theologian believe Jesus manifested his incarnate glory to the disciples, not only to reveal the majesty of his own truth, but also the goal of the new creation, his mission, and life inaugurated—that of the potential all-inclusive divinization of those who love and follow Christ.

As Gregory of Sinai puts it most comprehensively, "Every person who has been renewed in the Spirit and has preserved this gift will be transformed and embodied in Christ, experiencing ineffably the supernatural state of deification."

While the Western churches for the most part envisioned Christ consciousness as a purely mystical and spiritual process, the Eastern Orthodox mystics realized an even more astounding truth, that Jesus as incarnation offered those who loved him their own miraculous birth into the Transfiguration, their own birth as the complete transcendent and immanent divine human, what the Gnostic Gospels call the Anthropos, a being born of the marriage of all opposites, divine and human, male and female, heart and mind, body and soul, mystical and active.

While the Eastern Orthodox mystics celebrated this vision of theosis with unique precision and intensity, this vision of the divinization of the whole human is not unique to them, or even to the transfiguration lineage that stretches from the Desert Fathers to the 11th and 12th centuries, to Saint Seraphim of Sarov in the 19th century, and to Bede Griffiths in the 20th. What 30 years of intimate experience and dogged research into the depths of all the major mystical traditions has made clear to me is that this secret of transfiguring birth into the fully human and fully divine is the central and most important and galvanizing secret of all of the major traditions, awaiting rediscovery and radical unveiling and returning in its demand and splendor to us now, to guide us through the evolutionary challenge of our global dark night.

It is this secret that Shams transmitted to Rumi of a "new kind of love, neither above or below," a love both transcendent and immanent and beyond both. It is this secret, as Henry Corbin has shown, that illumined the 14th- and 15th-century Iranian mystic's vision of the "Man of Light." It is this secret that inflamed the Shaivite mystics of South India, such as Tirumular and Manikkavasagar, who worshipped the golden Shiva of their central shrine at Chidambaram as not only a supreme icon of the Divine, but as the sign of their own potential total divinization through adoration and the grace of the Golden Dancer. It is this secret that Moses de León and other kabbalists explored in dazzling imagery of the sacred marriage. It is this secret that esoteric Taoist alchemy proclaims as the ultimate gift and realization of the Tao. It is this secret that Jung celebrates in his masterpiece *Mysterium Coniunctionis*, as Jung reveals it at the heart of the alchemical process of birthing what alchemists called the philosopher's stone, which is not—or not only—a magical formula for turning lead into gold, but far more radically, the mysterious birth of a fully embodied, fully divinized being forged in the fires of inner alchemy and imbued with vast new holy powers. It is this secret, too, that the Dalai Lama unveiled in teachings he gave in Australia in 2016 that I had the honor to attend, when His Holiness made clear in intricate and precise ways that it lay at the golden heart of the Vajrayana path of Mahayana Buddhism and its cultivation in certain advanced adepts of "the rainbow body," a body capable through profound meditation and long irradiation by the clear light of emptiness, of dissolving into "rainbow lights" at the time of death. It is this secret also that has guided the pioneering and still too little known work of the modern evolutionary mystics, especially Sri Aurobindo, the Mother, and their brilliant successor, Satprem and also Teilhard de Chardin, whose vision of the progressive transfiguration in the "Christic" of the whole universe is rooted in and inflamed by it. I believe it is this secret too, as we shall see, that is transmitted to us from the true love of Jesus and Mary Magdalene in ways that do not contradict the ascetic transfiguration vision of the Desert Fathers and Orthodox mystics, but supplement it to make it potentially available to everyone, and at a time when its richest, deepest, most daring embodiment may hold one of the crucial keys not only to human survival, but to the potential birth in our dark night of a new human race.

The Alternative Transfiguration Process

WE ARE APPROACHING TOGETHER what I believe to be the crucial and amazing illumination that could guide us into the meaning of Mary Magdalene's anointing of Jesus and her hidden but essential role in his ministry, Crucifixion, and Resurrection—and, even more importantly, into the evolutionary power of the love they lived. The Divine creates by uniting; the third that Jesus and Mary Magdalene formed by and in their sacred union birthed a new force of full-bodied, full-souled evolutionary love that Mary Magdalene restores to us. The return of the unedited and empowered Divine Feminine she incarnated is now accessible to all of us who can find the courage through grace to acknowledge, celebrate, and embrace it.

What I have just shared with you, the witness of the Orthodox tradition of theosis (the divinization process), raises another extraordinary possibility—that the full-bodied, full-souled love Jesus and Mary Magdalene live birthed *an alternative transfiguration process*. This process does not in any way deny the splendor of the ascetic transfiguration path that has flowered secretly but splendidly from Saint Macarius in the 2nd century to Bede in the 20th, but complements it. It also opens the crucial mystery of the birth of the divine human to anyone who realizes the holiness of the body's and the heart's affections, and the potential divinization of sexuality through fearless and abandoned love dedicated to the Divine.

This is of course a momentous and radical claim within the inherited terms of the Christian mystical tradition. Yet we must keep remembering that the tradition, glorious though it is, was shaped by a writing out or ignorance of the truth of Mary

Magdalene, of Jesus's sexual nature, and of the full embodied Godhead, the sacred feminine.

A tradition, however hallowed, that cannot embrace fully and humbly the liberating vision of the Mother side of God and the divine sacred marriage cannot be completely empowering, and cannot activate the full evolutionary power of Christ consciousness. Christ consciousness is not only spiritual or transcendent, it also involves and makes possible the growing divinization or "oneing" of the whole human being with the Divine—the birth, in fact, of the divine human.

Understood and lived in this way, Christ consciousness reveals itself as the birthing power of a new human race, enabled through progressive transfiguration to collaborate with the Divine and birth in this world the all-embracing justice and passionate compassion of the kingdom-queendom. Such a birthing power cannot anymore be contained and interpreted within any patriarchal institutions or traditions. It will either reshape and reforge them drastically or they will die out for freer modalities of worship and practice to be born.

My beloved teacher, Father Bede Griffiths, understood this but believed, as I have come to do, that there are sources within the Christian tradition itself that could refashion it to make it open to this rebirthing force of Christ consciousness if reinterpreted expansively and in relation to other revelations with a mature and balanced realization of the sacred marriage.

Bede stressed two of these constantly throughout our conversations on Johannine mysticism (especially rooted in John, Chapter 17) and Trinitarian mysticism.

I shall never forget the morning when Bede, in one of the prophetic lucid hours his last ordeal graced him, recited to me from memory these verses from John 17, which he said many times was for him the cornerstone of true Christian mysticism:

"Jesus lifted up his eyes to heaven and said, Father, the hour is come, glorify thy Son, that thy Son also may glorify thee. . . . And now, O Father, glorify thou me with thine own self, with the glory which I had with thee before the world was. I have manifested thy name unto the men which thou gavest me out of the world. Thine they were, and thou gavest them me, and they have kept thy word.

Neither pray I for these alone, but for them also which shall believe on me through their word, that they all may be one as thou, Father, art in me and I in thee, that they also may be one in us, that the world may believe that thou hast sent me. And the glory which thou gavest me I have given them, that they may be one even as we are one. I in them and thou in me, that they may be made perfect in one, and that the world may know that thou hast sent me and hast loved them as thou hast loved me."

When Bede finished, tears of bliss were shining in his eyes, and he was so overcome with joy, he couldn't speak.

Then he collected himself and said, "What I have come to understand is that when Jesus asked to be glorified, it was not because glory was in any way lacking in him, but because—and this is crucial to understanding what Saint Paul calls the superabundant grace that flows from the Christ to the ones who love and adore him—Jesus longed to glorify with himself all those he would draw to him."

He paused and then said, "The greatest words that Jesus, as incarnate love, speaks in all the scriptures, the words that have expanded in their meaning as I myself have been expanded, are, I believe, these. Listen to them again."

Father, I will that they may be one in us as you, Father, are in me and me in you.

"The limitations in much of Christian mysticism so far come from interpreting these words purely spiritually. They are meant spiritually, of course, and speak of that identity of the human soul and the Godhead that Meister Eckhart and so many of the Christian mystics uncovered and celebrated.

"But they are not merely transcendent. The incarnation of the Divine that Jesus is, and is willing us to become in him and with him in the Divine, is also both radically embodied and radically active in works of healing and justice. This embodied and active dimension, which has deep roots as I have discovered in the sacred feminine, has been limited or neglected altogether with the disastrous consequences we see all around us.

"It is time to embrace the full evolutionary and revolutionary truth of incarnation that, as this passage from John shows us, belongs not to Jesus alone, but potentially to all those who take sincerely the Christ path. This embrace could usher in the real Second Coming, which, as you know, I do not in any way see as the return of the Christ, but as the birthing of incarnate and active Christ consciousness in millions of beings."

Bede paused, then continued, "One block to this birth I am seeing clearly now lies in the word *Father.* For most of my life, I found no problem at all in addressing God only as Father, but my own recent experience has confirmed for me that God is as much Mother as Father.

"Until God as Mother as well as Father is recognized and its implications accepted with the help of other great mystical traditions and explored and integrated within the tradition, the full birth that authentic Christ consciousness makes possible will be aborted. Jesus himself, the Gnostic Gospels make clear, worshipped the Divine as both father and mother. When you study the Gospels deeply, you discover Jesus identifying himself repeatedly with Hochmah or Sophia, divine wisdom, drawing on the practice of prophets like Isaiah and Jeremiah. Sophia is the breath of the power of God, the brightness of the everlasting light, the unspotted mirror of the power of God.

"Jesus's whole life and mission was, as his identification with Sophia shows, inspired by this vision of the feminine, especially perhaps by Sirach in [verse 2 of Chapter 8] the apocryphal books of the Old and New Testaments.

"'*I loved her, the spirit of wisdom, and sought her out from my youth. I desired to make her my spouse, and I was a lover of her beauty.*'

"What this verse suggests is what I believe to be the essence of the identification with wisdom Jesus stressed so often.

"He did not only seek her, he wanted to make her his *spouse*. He wanted to be *married* to her in all her transcendent and embodied dimensions, and so become in himself a full expression on earth of the marriage between Yahweh and Hochmah."

Later that afternoon, I found myself again alone with Bede in his hut. This time, he spoke to me thrillingly about his continuing exploration of the Trinity, and how this interpretation of what he called "the most inspiring of all mystical evocations of the nature of God" needed to be expanded and grounded to become at once more revelatory and more accessible.

Our conversation went on for two hours and remains one of the richest experiences of my life. For our purposes here, however, two of the many themes that he developed are important. Firstly, Bede emphasized the necessity of embracing the sacred feminine in all three persons in the one, so as to release our understanding of the Trinity from the subtle patriarchal constrictions of conceiving it as Father, Son, Holy Spirit, where all persons are considered masculine.

Secondly, he stressed how the central insight of Trinitarian mysticism—that God is interpersonal relationship—needed to be grounded in ordinary life, so that its fullest implications for us can become real.

Let me synthesize for you these two themes in his words.

"The Trinity is not a revealed dogma. It arises out of centuries of contemplation on what we talked about this morning, Jesus's relationship with the Divine and his mission to share its glory with us. The formulation of Father-Son-Holy Spirit that arose from this contemplation was a marvelous beginning, but inevitably limited by patriarchal emphasis. You may not know this, Andrew, but for the first two centuries after Jesus's death, the Holy Spirit was conceived as a feminine force, much like the Hindu vision of Shakti. Tragically, this got lost.

"What this initial understanding, when reclaimed, invites us now to imagine is integrating the Divine Feminine into all three persons. What has been called for two millennia the Father, the transcendent ground of all reality, needs to be reimagined as both Father and Mother, since transcendence is constantly birthing and living in all worlds. Similarly, the ancient knowledge of the Holy Spirit, the force of love transcendence emanates to create and evolve all worlds needs to be celebrated again as a fundamental mother force of cherishing, sustaining, evolving love. The Son, that is the creation grounded in and saturated and interpenetrated by transcendence and the force of love, needs to be formulated in such a way that enshrines the truth of the marriage of opposites in all processes, both of creation and divinization. And this can only be done by embracing the feminine on all levels of reality.

"This expansion of our current understanding of the Trinity to embrace the feminine dimension of all three persons could potentially, I believe, have two radical consequences. The most important is that it restores the Divine Feminine to equality with the Divine Masculine, and so reflects the ancient intuition of the sacred marriage as a rich and balanced vision of reality. The second is that it helps us experience the Trinity not only as a model of how the Divine works and creates and permeates every atom of its creation, but also as a way of understanding our ordinary life and our relationships as revealing and reflecting intimately the Trinitarian life of God and Jesus himself.

"The key to ground and realize the truth of the Trinity in ourselves and in our lives is to understand as deeply as grace makes us able that the diamond at the heart of the vision of the Trinity is that the being of the Divine is essentially interpersonal relationship. This insight resonates with what modern quantum physicists are discovering about how subatomic particles relate and react to each other in the field across vast distances.

"It also helps us ground the exalted vision of the Trinity in the core of our real lives. After all, for the great majority of us, personal interrelationships are the crucial experience in our lives. We experience ourselves in relation to our parents, to our wives or husbands or partners or lovers, to our children, to our pets, to our friends and associates.

"This is what makes up so much of human life for most people. And to say that the fullness of life, indeed the life of the Divine itself, is the fullness of interpersonal relationship is to describe what the Trinity is on all levels. It is, in other words, radical communion in knowledge and communion, personal communion. The revelation that the ultimate reality of God is intercommunion in love is, I believe, the diamond, the crown jewel of Christianity, and to me reveals the depth of the whole mystery."

As I transmit Bede's words on Johannine and Trinitarian mysticism to you now, 30 years later, in the context of exploring the transfiguring powers that the birthing field of Mary Magdalene and Jesus's love open up for all of us, two linked visions present themselves for our potential embrace.

The first vision dissolves millennia of demonization of the body and its desires by showing us that the embodied glory that Jesus of John 17 is praying to God to give to us, as it was given to him, potentially floods and divinizes all of our loves and desires, revealing them to be not blocks to our becoming our complete selves in God, but manifestations of the deepest desire the Divine has rooted in us—the desire for the beloved, the longing for the one who is love.

This vision invites us to experience all of our relations with friends, lovers, partners, animals, and all the manifestations of the creation as both gifts and revelations of the grace of divine love itself, to be lived in a sacred discernment and gratitude that will progressively unify our whole being with the one. The more we love all beings and things, the more love itself will possess, irradiate, and transfigure us.

The second vision illuminates directly the one I am exploring with you of the nature and power of Mary Magdalene and Jesus's love, and its implications for us now and for a future humanity that embraces its possibility.

What this vision shows us is that in Jesus and Mary Magdalene's love, what is revealed to us in all its beauty, passion, truth, and evolutionary power is a sacramental form of sexual relationship that mirrors the life of the Trinity itself, and recognizes, fosters, and celebrates noble human passion as a living expression and grace of the Holy Spirit, and so allows its mother force to circulate through and in us, and transform all of us, just as it did them.

Mary Magdalene and the Transfiguration

WE ARE ALMOST READY TO EXPLORE together Mary Magdalene's anointing of Jesus in a new and expansive way. Before we do, however, we have to face again that the Gospels give us no real clues as to the depth of Mary Magdalene and Jesus's love or Mary Magdalene's unique role among the disciples or of the second alternative stream of transfiguration I am suggesting was birthed by Jesus and Mary Magdalene's sacred marriage. None of this should surprise us. We have shown how Mary Magdalene is almost entirely written out of the canonical Gospels and the multiple and complex reasons behind this omission.

I want to turn now to the work and tradition outside the Gospels I have myself found most illuminating—the Sophian Gospel, as portrayed by Tau Malachi in his book *Living Gnosis*. I quoted earlier the Sophian Gnostic's account of Mary Magdalene's meeting with Jesus in Capernaum. Here I want to emphasize what the Sophian Gnostic tradition tells us about Mary's role in the Transfiguration.

The Sophian Gospel is said to be communicated in an unbroken tradition from Mary Magdalene herself, and focuses, as I have done, on her role as Jesus's wife, co-equal, and teacher of the Divine Feminine, as well as his most inspired and receptive disciple. It claims among other things that Jesus taught Mary Magdalene wisdom he shared with no other disciple, she accompanied him when he withdrew into contemplation, and she prayed and meditated and shared many "secret wonders" with him. The Sophian Gospel reveals that when Mary Magdalene and Jesus made love, these wonders would occur as though in them Yahweh and the Shekinah were crystallized into a physical union and "blessings and light poured into the world."

What could confirm the truth of what I am proposing is what the Sophian Gnostic tradition informs us about the Transfiguration, which opposes the canonical Gospels.

As Tau Malachi writes, "According to legend, when the male disciples fell unconscious, overwhelmed by the display of fluid reality and divine glory, Mary Magdalene remained fully lucid and conscious, and she received the light transmission the Lord intended, so she also shone with supernal light . . . as the story goes, the evening following the Transfiguration of the Lord on the holy mountain, Mary Magdalene took three of her inmost women disciples into a cave and was transfigured before them. . . . It is said that the women had to hide their faces for several days because they shone with visible light, for unlike the men, they remained completely conscious and were illuminated by the divine revelation of the Woman of Light."

Tau Malachi goes on to describe how the story of Jesus and Mary Magdalene's co-mission alternate Divine Masculine and Divine Feminine images to celebrate what he calls "the true and full equality and co-labor occurring between them." This is clearest and most provocative perhaps in the imagery of their two transfigurations: Jesus's Transfiguration takes place on the phallic holy mountain, while Mary's transfiguration takes place in the cave, a feminine image of the womb.

As Malachi writes, "It is as though Mary Magdalene is the earth womb into which the seed of light is cast, through which all receive the light transmission. It is as though Lord Yeshua is the light and Lady Mary is the prism of light through which the light passes, becoming rays of rainbow glory."

Please, dear friend, pause now for a long moment, and allow all that you have been reading to crystallize in the depths of your heart.

I invite you now, with all you are now experiencing, to refocus your attention on the scene of the Anointing, and begin to see it with vastly expanded vision.

Now at last, we are ready to contemplate Mary Magdalene's anointing of Jesus in the days leading up to the Crucifixion and begin to see it in its full significance, a significance that embraces traditional approaches but transcends them.

First, let us place Mary's glorious act in its context, the tumultuous and dangerous life she and Jesus and the other disciples lived together.

In AD 27, shortly after their meeting and marriage, Jesus fled Capernaum because of a death threat by Herod Antipas. Four years of wandering followed, first in Gentile territory east of Galilee and then to the west. Traditional scholars claim that Mary Magdalene did not always accompany him, given her vulnerability as a woman, and that he worked mostly with his male disciples. The Sophian Gospel and other Gnostic texts suggest strongly otherwise, making clear that from the beginning their relationship transcended all convention, emphasizing Mary's warrior-like courage as well as the depth of her passion for her beloved.

If this is accepted, Mary Magdalene's love for Jesus becomes even more moving. She shared unshrinkingly the difficult and harassed life he had to live to fulfill his mission that was now their mission, feeding and strengthening and instructing him with her love, courage, and wisdom; renewing him and herself in the sacramental fires of their mutual passion; and experiencing with him the revelations of progressive transfiguration that it birthed.

She intimately shared all the anxieties, even terrors, that swirled around Jesus from the first sermon he gave in Nazareth, announcing the liberty and equality of the kingdom-queendom that so angered his audience that he only narrowly escaped with his life. What he suffered, she suffered. What threatened and assailed him threatened and assailed her.

From the beginning of her love for him, she must have known from everything she heard and everything he told her about why he had come, that his life was always in danger, as was now potentially hers. Their love would have to traverse zone after zone of threat and betrayal and extreme difficulty. Mary's love of Jesus, and her total giving of herself to their love, could never be only a private affair. They were enacted to transfigure human life and the world.

The love of Mary Magdalene and Jesus was in fact part of this revolution, its secret personal fuel for both of them, the living water in which they both bathed again and again to renew their whole being for the ordeals ahead. It offered a model for all revolutionaries of love in action, of how intimate union between two sacred lovers can illumine, strengthen, and even continue to transfigure both, to be able to serve truth and justice unstintingly, whatever the sufferings that arise and whatever defeats have to be endured on the road to victory.

In AD 31, Jesus made a momentous decision. As Bruce Chilton writes, "The opposition of Herod Antipas had only strengthened Jesus's appeal to Galilee's disenfranchised Jews, some of whom wanted the charismatic rabbi to head a violent onslaught against Antipas and his Roman protectors."

Jesus and Mary Magdalene knew that the kingdom-queendom could never be established through violence; that would only engender more violence. He had rejected in the temptations in the desert all lures of merely worldly power. He and Mary both knew that what had to be birthed now, for the reality of the kingdom-queendom to become possible and real in all human relations and works and institutions, was not a physical but an all-transfiguring spiritual revolution. This revolution would need to dissolve all fears of death and all the demented fantasies of separation that enslaved humanity and kept the structures of tribalism and exclusiveness going, which aborted the force of Christ's consciousness in its fullest splendor and the radical regeneration that would follow its enactment.

Everything Jesus and Mary had lived and worked for had come to a head.

The momentous choice that Jesus made, some reputable scholars believe, was to concentrate not on rebellion against the Romans but on a drastic renovation of the life of the Temple, where, Bruce Chilton writes, "He believed he and his followers could change the world and welcome God's kingdom into the land of Israel by offering sacrifice on Mount Zion in the way that the God of Israel desired . . . Rabbi Jesus believed that true sacrifice would bring both the end of Israel's oppression and the opening of the Temple to all humanity, both Jews and non-Jews."

While this view might partially explain why Jesus acted the way he did, both in overturning the tables of the money changers and choosing to enter Jerusalem and the Temple during Passover, when both would be thronged by crowds from the countryside, it does not go far enough. For one thing, it demeans Jesus's spiritual intelligence. Could he really have believed, given all he knew both of Roman power and Jewish religious corruption, that such a radical transformation of Temple life could be possible?

The real danger of such a precise explanation of Jesus's actions that led to the Crucifixion and Resurrection is that it misses their cosmic and universal significance, which would have been clear, even foremost, in the heart minds of both Jesus and Mary Magdalene. What this cosmic universal dimension reveals to those who contemplate it is that the logic of Jesus—and Mary's mission with him to birth the full Christ consciousness—had reached a decisive moment. He and Mary would have to risk everything to birth on the earth and in the universe a new reality, a new creation.

Only such a birth could begin to reverse the destructiveness of the Roman-Jewish conflict, along with the dark loveless desires for power and domination of all kinds that afflict all human history. It would ensure that the birth of a new humanity, one fully alive with the "glorious liberty of the children of God," could take place. Much more, then, than a renovation of temple life was at stake.

Jesus and Mary Magdalene knew, from their own drastic experience, the limitations of what could be accomplished in a world mired in limiting religious beliefs and entrenched patriarchal structures. However glorious their love had been together, and however thrilling Jesus's teachings and healings and miracles had been in their manifestation of the powers that flow from Christ consciousness, the situation in Israel revealed to them that something utterly new and even more transformatory had to be attempted. It would at once crystallize everything that had come before and birth, both in earth life and the life of the universe, the all-transforming love force they both knew was the one force that could change everything.

They could not know definitively how this birth of a new evolutionary level of all redemptive love would take place. They could not know for certain that Jesus would be resurrected, whatever happened; if we believed they knew this, it would, I believe, dim the intensity of their vision, their courage and trust in the mystery and the courage and vision their example is challenging us to embrace.

What they must have known, however, given the ordeals and revelations they had already repeatedly lived through, were three things: that the new adventure they would have to risk now would unfold in sometimes brutal and always unforeseeable ways; that it would, given the spiritually revolutionary nature of full Christ consciousness, drag them both through new and extreme dangers, even the death of one or both of them; and finally, that divine life, and the love that they knew was divine in its source, power, and passion, would have the last word, whatever it turned out to be.

These three hard-won realizations form the unshakable foundation of their resolve to risk everything for the birth of a new creation, and their surrender to whatever love would demand.

The Anointing

WITH EVERYTHING WE HAVE EXPLORED so far vibrant within us, we can now turn and see the anointing of Jesus by Mary Magdalene in a revelatory new way. Yes, it is an act of sublime adoration that prepares Jesus's body for burial, but it is also an initiatory empowerment of him by an incarnation of the Divine Feminine, at the moment when he enters the ultimate mother mysteries of death and rebirth in his Passion and Resurrection.

As you will see, approaching the mystery of the Anointing in this way expands our understanding of who Mary is in the real, as yet untold, story, and what their relationship is dedicated to. And it expands our knowledge of Jesus's own accomplishment on behalf of the whole human race and the universe itself, an accomplishment in which Mary—as woman, wife, healer, Anointer, adept of the mysteries of embodiment of the mother—plays a secret and holy role as co-transfiguratrix, co-redemptrix, co-birther of a new humanity and a new creation.

From everything we have already explored together, we can now see that Mary Magdalene's act of anointing Jesus is a diamond of seven interrelated, interpenetrating facets that embrace all of the different aspects of their relationship, both in its intense and passionate humanity and in its ultimate divine meaning.

Exploring these seven aspects together will begin to open us up to what the example and fruition of Jesus's and Mary's story makes available to all of us now. These seven facets of the one radiant diamond of anointing are in interdependent ascending order.

When my condo burned down, killing my beloved cat, I found myself in a state I had never known before—both annihilated and ecstatic. As I walked to the house of a friend who had offered to take me in, I heard Father Bede's soft, penetrating voice in my heart say, "Now is the time for you to say Mary Magdalene's mantra: *om nama Maria Magdalenaya.*"

I started to say the mantra immediately, and my whole being filled with a dynamic, vibrant peace that continues to dance in me.

I recommend, dear friend, that at this moment of our journey together, you bow your head to your heart, imagine Mary Magdalene anointing Jesus in whatever way is most vivid for you, and start chanting the sublime love, power, and wisdom it releases for yourself. Now you are ready to receive the full richness of the Magdalene as Anointer.

As you read the following description of these facets, try as far as you can to bring to them everything we have explored of Jesus and Mary's love up to this point:

The seven facets, I believe, are:

- Mary as woman and wife, anointing her husband for the ordeal they knew inevitably lay ahead.
- Mary as the paradigmatic Anointer of the Christian tradition, crystallizing and expanding and renewing through her act the rich feminine Jewish tradition of healing and anointing she was adept in and represented.
- Mary as wife and partner in Christ consciousness, preparing Jesus not only for burial, as the Gospels proclaim, but also for the possible and as yet unimaginable birth through that death of a new creation.
- Mary as beloved of the beloved, inspired by the first temple and the Song of Songs mystical traditions, both celebrating and reaffirming through her sacred act the revelations their sacred union had flooded them both with. She symbolically and actually poured into Jesus's being all the ecstatic powers of her own realization of the force of true love for his journey and her journey with him into death and rebirth.
- Mary as conscious incarnation of the Divine Feminine of Sophia, blessing and infusing Jesus with the full mother wisdom he would now need at the moment

they both knew he was about to descend as part of his divine mission into the ultimate mother mystery of death and rebirth, dismemberment, and regeneration.

- Mary as incarnation of the mother-father, blessing Jesus as incarnation of the father-mother in their sacred marriage, affirming her divine human determination to live out their marriage through whatever the mystery of divine love would now demand of both of them and unfold in them in time and eternity.
- Mary as co-birther with Jesus of a new stream of transfiguration, as co-transfiguratrix, reaffirming through her act the power of what they had lived already. She sacramentally infused Jesus at a new level of urgent intensity with that power the moment he would need all its divinizing strength, to realize their shared mission of birthing a new humanity, empowered at last to co-create with and in the Divine a new world.

It is this last ultimate facet—in which all the significance and power of all the other facets are consecrated—that will give us revelatory clues. The clues are to Mary's secret part in Jesus's mission and Resurrection, as well as to the role she enacted after his Ascension, in a progressively more ecstatic and embodied union with him as cosmic Christ, simultaneously in space and time and beyond both.

We can never remember enough that the journey that Jesus and Mary's love compelled them to take and unfold was not only for them in their own unique and uniquely empowered grace roles. Rather, it was enacted on behalf of all of us, and in a mysterious sense *as* all of us, as we could and will be when we are ready to believe in, open to, and work toward our own birth through love into divine humanity.

Mary Magdalene and Jesus enacted all the transfiguring potential of the sacred marriage to infuse the whole human race and creation with its always-expanding power, and gave all of us a rigorous map of its possibilities. At the moment, we need this map as richly, precisely, and deeply as we can imagine it, to be able not only to survive the global dark night we are now enmeshed in, but also to collaborate with its intended goal—the conscious and consciously unfolding birth in us of what was seeded in us through them, and the multiple revelations that love reveals.

In order to honor what Jesus and the Magdalene birthed through their sacred marriage, we must claim—through recognizing, accepting, and evolving in and through grace—our own embodied divine consciousness, our own radical equality with Jesus and Mary. It is not sufficient to marvel at and celebrate them, however passionately, if we do not claim our own divinely given capacity to emulate them and become our own unique and transfigured versions of them, our own Anthropos.

Adoration of Jesus and Mary prepares us to receive the fullest possible transmission of the love force they birthed for us, but it must be taken into the mysterious depths of amazed unity with them. Otherwise, that adoration can become the subtlest but most powerful obstacle to us realizing the deepest truth of their message to us, separately and together—that they are us as we will be when we allow the evolutionary love force of the father-mother to heal, unify, and transfigure our whole being.

If we distance and exteriorize Jesus and Mary, even in subtle reverential ways, the astounding alchemical possibilities of nondual relationship with them in the core of our psyches, souls, lives, and beings will continue to be aborted, as it has largely been throughout Christian history. Jesus and Mary did not risk again and again, and in increasingly terrible circumstances, their whole realization and being, to birth a transfiguring love force for us and in us, merely to be adored and worshipped.

They wanted as many of us as possible, and urgently, to embrace their extraordinary story as our own; their divine human passion as our own; their hunger to see our beings and our world transformed utterly, and their seamless enactment of both inner divinization and outer sacred action, as our own.

If we are truly to learn from the Magdalene and the Christ's journey, we have to be brave enough to claim it now, as a rigorous map of both our own potential divinization and of the secret meaning and potential of the crucifying dark night on every level our species as a whole is now enduring. We are all both challenged and secretly empowered to birth together now, through faith and the richest mystical information and relentless practice, a new divine human race, liberated from the tribalism and dogmatism and suicidal self-separation of the past.

Mary and Jesus—who took this dangerous, humbling, and exalted journey with splendor of being and courage before us—are among a small handful of humanity's most reliable and empowering guides, whose transfiguring, liberating wisdom is now not a luxury for a select few, but a necessity for all of us who can begin to grasp it and begin to dare to live it.

Accepting our radical equality with Jesus and Mary—as beings gifted like them with inherent divinity, and so intimately connected to and self-revealed in every aspect, level, and unfolding power of their journey—may sound initially thrilling. In practice, however, realizing and living this acceptance requires repeated leaps into mystery; repeated commitment to sometimes bewildering and deranging inner experience; and relentless shadow work on freeing ourselves from all the inherited cultural, scientific, and narrow religious voices that continue to intertwine and reverberate in our being to convince us of our doomed and ordained limitations.

To claim perhaps the most comprehensive, rigorous, and exalted map of divinization we have ever been given as our own, and then to interiorize it systematically in the core of our lives and practice, asks of all of us to open repeatedly to an ever-renewed, ever-expanding courage. The path of transfiguration that Jesus and Mary Magdalene opened, lived out, and birthed in dazzling finality for us cannot be just intellectually or even spiritually acknowledged as possible. It has to be acknowledged not only in our hearts and minds and souls, but lived inwardly, step by integrated step; outwardly, step by integrated step; in increasingly potent sacred action, just as they did.

To dare to live Jesus and Mary's increasingly revealed truth—and to dare, whatever the obstacles, ordeals, bewilderments, or sabotaging or deriding inner and outer voices, to do the inner work to remain ever more naked and open to their grace—is a work we must attempt. This is not only for ourselves, but for the world and cosmos that both mystics and quantum physicists know we are inseparably and organically interconnected with. The potential birth of a new divine humanity out of our global dark night depends on it. This new divine humanity that Jesus and Mary birthed together could potentially be capable of creating a world that mirrors kingdom-queendom consciousness in its institutions, arts, sciences, politics, and economics. It can also consciously participate in the progressive divinization of all the matter and substance of all the universes, the ultimate growing Christ, as Bede said, and Teilhard de Chardin came to experience viscerally, in amazed awe.

Andrey Sinyavsky, the great Russian mystic, wrote, "It is not a question of overcoming nature, but of replacing nature with another nature unknown to us."

It is this "unknown nature," with its organically enfolded and evolutionary supernatural powers, that Jesus and Mary were united with in their sacred marriage and will progressively unite us with—if we dare to let them and claim them ourselves, and show ourselves worthy of their demand.

Realizing and committing ourselves to live this, as Jesus and Mary's beloved brothers and sisters—whatever our religion or spiritual persuasion, whatever our age or sexuality—is perhaps the greatest and most transformative task we can attempt in our circumstances. What we also need to do is believe this, and then live our belief, whatever the cost. The great birth Jesus and Mary pioneered is, I know now, real.

It is beginning in me, and I suspect in many of you. Its fiery green shoots are cracking open the black concrete of our desolation, and its outrageous sun is piercing through the storm clouds of our willed devastation. The success of this birth, however, is not certain. The birth is offered, but we have to pay its price to embody its glory, to enjoy, spread contagiously, and enact the glorious liberty of the children of God, the children of the sacred marriage, of Jesus, the divine human word, and Mary Magdalene, the divine human feminine, Sophia, and bride.

And with their love and example and challenge and grace, fully alive in us, we can.

Two Essential Words

THREE YEARS BACK, I was sitting with an old yogi with knotted hair by the Ganges in Varanasi. He had been a wealthy banker and given everything away to his family to wander the holy city.

We used to meet every evening after the rituals by the Ganges and shoot the breeze. That evening, he asked me, "What are the two words you would love everyone to know the depth of?"

No one had ever asked me such a question. There was a sudden seriousness in the way he asked it that I knew that for him, a great deal depended on what I would say.

We went into meditation, and then I found myself saying, "My two words are *noble* and *sublime*. For me, from what I have learned through the grace of the Divine, is that how we open to imagine and feel these two words and apply them to our own essential selves as richly as possible determines much of the state of our consciousness, our knowledge of the Divine, and the reach of our actions."

He smiled broadly and ruffled my head tenderly. Then he said, "To begin to know the sublimity and nobility of the soul and to begin to know, too, that our highest purpose is to incarnate that nobility and sublimity into every part of our being and all our thoughts and activities, is the beginning of divine life on earth."

A slim crescent moon was coming up over the Ganges, and we smiled together, savoring its shimmering on the river.

Then he said, "When did you last hear anyone say those two words?"

"I can't remember."

"That tells you everything about the world we live in." We both chuckled ruefully.

A wonderful way to start entering this stage of Mary and Jesus's journey together is to reflect as deeply and many-sidedly with your full being and full life experience, first on the word *sublime* and then on *noble*. Write each one in your own handwriting on separate pages, and as you do so, commit yourself to allowing yourself to be irradiated by ever deeper realizations of their meanings. Don't be put off by any resistances you may feel to either word, or to opening to claim them as descriptions of your own essential self: recognize them as they arise and work through them with confidence and with joy.

My friend Caroline Myss has spoken brilliantly about what she calls holy language and the need to savor its truth as far as we can, to enable us to live sacred lives, and to allow ourselves truly to experience the transforming graces that emanate from it.

What better words could we find for Jesus than noble and sublime? With what better words could we celebrate the Mary Magdalene we are discovering together: lover, prophet, warrior, co-transfiguratrix? What more accurate words could be used to describe Jesus and Mary's love for each other, lived out in terrible times and circumstances, with such fearlessness in the face of disbelief and opposition from many of the male disciples? What richer words could we possibly find for the revelation of the power of true and total love that their love is unfolding to us and in us?

What Jesus and Mary are showing us is that divine human passion between two awakened and acknowledged equals is sublime in its transcendent origin, inspiration, and rapture of adoration, and noble in its commitment and expression. It is sublime because it is suffused completely with the wild and exquisite tenderness of full-souled, full-bodied worship, and noble because it is lived not only for the lovers themselves and their own liberation, but also simultaneously for the transformation of all life in all realms.

What I have discovered is that opening as far as I can to Jesus and Mary's nobility and sublimity of love connects me to my own most sublime and noble intentions, to the hidden royalty of my and everyone else's soul. It helps me to believe that such a love as theirs is possible, and that it is possible to be irradiated by the grace of *their* passion—and to have my own powers of noble and sublime love awakened, healed, strengthened, and subtly but marvelously expanded. With this expansion, a mystery of intertwined, nondual relationship with Jesus and Mary Magdalene starts to unveil itself.

A Practice of Mental Prayer

WHEN YOU HAVE CONTEMPLATED these two words—noble and sublime—and begun to claim them as the powers and characteristics of both Mary Magdalene and Jesus and your own essential soul and capacity for love, let me suggest that you plunge now into what the Catholic Church calls mental prayer. When you practice mental prayer with faith and sincerity, it enables you to find yourself in direct intercommunion with both Jesus and Mary in their story and in the core of yourself.

This is what a great 17th-century Spanish mystic, Peter of Alcántara, writes of this potent practice:

"In mental prayer, the soul is nourished with charity, continued in faith, strengthened in hope. The mind expands, the affections dilate, the heart is purified, truth becomes real and obvious, the senses are made new. Out of mental prayer comes, like living sparks, those desires of heaven which the soul engenders when inflamed with the fire of divine love. The excellence of mental prayer is a sublime one, great are its privileges. To mental prayer heaven is opened, to mental prayer heavenly secrets are manifested and the ear of God is always attentive."

The sustained exaltation of such a passage may be unfamiliar, even a little off-putting at first, because our culture has made such idols of the down-home and ironic. But if you practice mental prayer with sincerity and simplicity of soul, you will find out for yourselves that what Peter Alcantara is describing is real and actual and, over time, accessible.

So what is this practice? Mental prayer is the use of inspiring and central scenes in Jesus's life story to connect us directly beyond words to both his humanity and divinity, and helps us focus our will to become like him in our whole being.

I invite you to enter, armed with this practice of mental prayer, all of the scenes and visions we will be experiencing together by including Mary Magdalene with Jesus.

Throughout my preparations for composing this journey, at each stage that I needed to connect with Jesus and Mary beyond words in any scene in which they are both present, I have practiced a short invocation of each in the fullness of what they are showing themselves to be. I always started by invoking the Magdalene, the Divine Feminine, for the simple reason that she has been so little invoked in this way. I believe now is the time of the full reception of the bride back to where she has always secretly been, by the side of and equal to the bridegroom.

Then with my being filled by grace, I have turned in my inmost being to Jesus, the bridegroom, and found that my heart is immeasurably expanded by Mary to begin to see Jesus as she saw him, filled with "fire and light and truth."

In my own exploration of this new formulation of the ancient practice, I have found the following two invocations particularly potent.

For Mary Magdalene, I use these words of Saint Anselm, who wrote them originally for Mother Mary. For me they apply also to Mary Magdalene and the great renewal her return to us prepares:

"OH WOMAN, FULL AND COMPLETE, POUR YOUR GRACES ON THIS WORLD AND MAKE ALL CREATURES GREEN AGAIN."

The force of Divine Feminine streaming to us now from the returning bride is a force that greens, refreshes, reconstructs, resurrects anew our entire being. In both Christian and Sufi mysticism, the color green represents the eternal, eternally fresh springtime, not only of the sacred heart and its intelligence, but of the whole increasingly transfigured being, greened by that beauty and revelation.

Hildegard of Bingen wrote often of what she calls *viriditas*, the greening power of the Holy Spirit. In one of her prayers to the Virgin, Hildegard refers to the Virgin in the following way:

"OH GREENING BRANCH, YOU STAND IN YOUR NOBILITY LIKE THE RISING DAWN."

The same words apply to the Magdalene in the rising dawn of her return.

The invocation I have found most powerful for the Jesus I am celebrating here is a phrase I found years ago in Paris from the greatest of all Marian mystics, Louis-Marie Grignion de Montfort, whose works you will find both prophetic and revolutionary. As with Saint Anselm, they were written for Mother Mary, but my belief is that they also apply, perhaps even more pungently, to the Magdalene we are uncovering together. Altered for Mary Magdalene, this phrase from de Montfort reads, "FOR YOUR KINGDOM TO COME, O LORD, MAY THE QUEENDOM OF THE MAGDALENE COME."

This moves me profoundly because it crystallizes in a few words the essence of the transmission of the sacred marriage I have dedicated our journey to. By invoking both Mary and Jesus in this way, before entering into the scene that I wish to practice mental prayer in, I have discovered something that it is hard to put into words. What I'm coming to know is that by invoking them first separately and then together, I connect with them in the scene I choose to meet them in. Yet I am also bringing them into my deepest self, as the two forces that need to unite in me for my full embodied divine self, my Jesus Magdalene, to be born in the bridal chamber of the sacred marriage.

Allow for such an extraordinary possibility to be open to you too. As you continue to practice mental prayer, to enter the map that Mary Magdalene and Jesus are offering us, be alert to sudden quantum shifts of understanding, unimagined quick new openings, electric dreams, rushes of an unfamiliar and wild joy, sudden glimpses of the beauty and sublimity inherent in all things. These are the signs of the marriage of Mary Magdalene and Jesus taking place within you, the music that you hear when you open the door to take your place at celebration of their sacred marriage, and your own.

Birthing the Sacred Marriage Now

THE RADICAL INTIMACY that the practice of mental prayer will give you will not only help you experience mystically and viscerally the truth of Jesus and Mary's sacred marriage, but it will also give you holy keys to the sacred marriage of your own inner Jesus and Mary that birth you into your own unique divine human.

And there is more. Mental prayer will reveal to you, as it has revealed to me, why the revolutionary return of the Magdalene to the heart of a new vision of Christ's consciousness is happening at this moment of our human evolution. You will discover why trying to understand and celebrate as richly as possible the Magdalene's obscured but crucial role is essential not only for human spiritual growth, but for the potential birth of a new divine humanity out of our global dark night.

Put simply, the whole of humanity, whether many of us know it or not, is standing as Jesus and Mary were in their terrible time, before an almost unimaginable ordeal, even crucifixion, of our being and our world. All the old structures of thought and practice are collapsing. Some of us now believe what humanity's greatest evolutionary mystics and pioneers have told us, that our dark night is potentially the birth canal for a new creation and a new humanity, but we also know, with ghastly clarity, that the road to such a birth passes through unprecedented suffering, death, and destruction. We know that it could be aborted in a number of ways—through climate collapse, nuclear war, a global rise of authoritarianism and fascism—that would make any real and radical solutions to our predicament impossible. All of us are where Mary Magdalene and Jesus were in that room, when his divine human consort anointed him for the unforeseeable, both terrifying and potentially glorious, journey ahead.

Mary and Jesus both knew that the transfiguring force of love their union had birthed was capable of miracle. They had experienced this in the secret depth of their relationship, which they knew mirrored in time the laws and powers of the sacred marriage and the one in eternity. What they did not know is what such a miracle might cost, or even whether their great divine dream of being co-parents of a new humanity would be realized.

Everything Mary and Jesus had lived separately and together taught them that it was possible, but it had never been "done" before, and all the obvious facts of a violent, corrupt, dark world stood against it. What they did know, as many of us are beginning to know, is that there was no time left to lose—they had to give and risk everything in an abandon of divine human love beyond reason and all limited hope.

Understanding this not only deepens our love and admiration for Jesus and Mary, it can show us what will be required of us to collaborate now with our whole increasingly unified being with the mysterious evolutionary force of love. If Mary and Jesus are *us* transfigured, every scene and detail and revelation of their mutual journey into Resurrection and beyond gives us priceless information for our own journey, separately and together, through crucifixion to a hardly imaginable, yet potential, birth.

It is at this moment when we are about to enter a detailed and close reading of the anointing scenes in the Gospels that the transformative practice Mary V, an adept of the Magdalene, gave me will be most useful to you in birthing yourself as the Anthropos, the sacred androgynous human divine child of the sacred marriage.

It has four stages.

First, breathe in the golden transfiguring light, and let it penetrate your whole being. Do this calmly nine times.

Second, imagine Jesus and Mary standing together facing each other in the core of your heart center as your own sacred masculine and sacred feminine.

Third, imagine your own sacred masculine as Jesus honoring your own sacred feminine as Mary Magdalene and placing a golden light crown on her head. Do this slowly, richly, in your own inspired words, bringing together all the themes of this book. Then with equal reverence, do the same with Mary Magdalene. Do not rush. The more slowly you do this stage, the more revelatory it will be.

Fourth, rest in what will by now be becoming clear in your whole being, beyond words. Say, "I am the Anthropos, human and divine, male and female in a mystery of embodied engoldened presence, beyond both."

The Alabaster Jar

NOW, WITH THIS EXTRAORDINARY PRACTICE uniting your whole being in the One, let us turn to and contemplate together what is for me the richest and most suggestive of the anointing scenes, that in Saint Mark's Gospel (Mark 14, verses 3 to 9), realizing it is happening in you and to you.

In none of the four Gospel accounts of the Anointing is Mary Magdalene mentioned by name, for reasons that should be clear by now. Since Pope Gregory I's homilies in the 6th century, however—the very same homilies that paradoxically characterized her as a prostitute—tradition has named the woman with the alabaster jar as the Magdalene, preserving for us a diminished and doctored version of her role that we can now begin to see for the first time in its full implications.

Mark's Gospel offers us the earliest, most complexly textured account of this ritual event, in an anointing set in Bethany, the base of the Jesus movement and the last months of Jesus's life and mission. Here is Bruce Chilton's translation:

> He was in Bethany in the home of Simon the Scabby (not really a leper, as in the traditional translation), recumbent, and there came a woman who had an alabaster of genuine expensive nard ointment. Smashing the alabaster, she poured it over his head, but there were some angry among themselves. "Why has this waste of the ointment happened, because this ointment could have been sold for more than 300 denarii and given to the poor," and they were upbraiding her. But Jesus said, "Leave her. Why are you making problems for her? She has done a fine deed with me. Because you always have the poor with yourselves, and whenever you want, you can do them good, but me you do not always have. She acted with what she had. She undertook to oil my

> body for burial. Amen, I say to you, wherever the message is proclaimed in the whole world, what she did will also be spoken of in memory of her."

In his commentary on this passage, Bruce Chilton makes clear that Mark's withholding of Mary Magdalene's name, in seeming contradiction of Jesus's statement, "What she did will also be spoken in memory of her," may have been part of what Chilton calls Mark's "rhetoric of the unspoken." As Chilton writes, "The woman's identity evidently did not remain a secret to those who first heard Mark's Gospel. Her name and personality were hidden only temporarily, until Mark's hearers could become acquainted not only with the gospel as recited to them, but also with the now-lost oral gospel that enriched their instruction . . . Primitive Christianity was an oral movement, not a book club, and therefore some of its deepest truths were not committed to writing. The identity of the nameless anointer is a case of Mark intimating more than is literally said."

As Chilton later makes even more clear, "The contradiction to her identity appears later in Mark's text. What's important to understand at this point is that Mark identifies Mary Magdalene as the principal figure among the women at the mouth of Jesus's tomb after his Crucifixion, and that she undertakes a key ritual action associated with interment, anointing, Mark 16 and 1.

> *And when Sabbath elapsed, Mary Magdalene and Mary of James and Salome purchased spices so they could go anoint him.*

"Among these three women, Mary Magdalene foremost had observed where Jesus had been interred by Joseph of Arimathea. She is the indispensable character in Mark's account of the Resurrection, the pivot of the action around whom the final events turn.

"She, by name and by action, embodies the connection between Jesus's internment and the angelic announcement to the same Mary Magdalene that Jesus has been raised from the dead. She connects his death and Resurrection not only by who she is but also by what she does. Mary Magdalene established the place of anointing as a central ritual in Christianity, recollecting Jesus's death and pointing forward to his Resurrection."

This is as far as the most astute scholarship can take us. Yet, as I have made clear already, we must risk going far further, if the full richness of Mary Magdalene's act is to be revealed to us and in us.

Let us look again together at Mark's text and note three essential clues which will help us on our journey into Revelation.

The first clue is that in Mark's version, Mary Magdalene pours the expensive perfume over Jesus's head. He is shown as recumbent, and when she anoints him, she is implied to be standing above and over him. This is profoundly revealing. In the account in Matthew, Jesus is not recumbent but sitting at table. In the account in John, Jesus is at table and Mary Magdalene anoints his feet and wipes them with her hair. In the account in Luke, Jesus is reclining on the sofa to eat and Mary Magdalene stands initially behind him weeping and then wets his feet with tears, dries them with her hair and kisses his feet and pours the perfume on them. Such variations in detail are not incidental. They are clearly attempts to diminish Mary's stature, her equality with Jesus, and the authority the earliest version in Mark preserves—in which she stands above the recumbent Jesus and pours perfume over his head. Kings and high priests in Israel were ritually anointed on their head. Prophets also sometimes anointed their chosen successors in this way.

What Mark's account reveals to those with eyes to see is that Mary in this sublime act is showing us who we are discovering her to be—imbued with divine authority as Jesus is, queen to his king, high priest to his high priest, prophet in her own right, through the depth and reach of her own charism and transfiguration. In the first public act the Gospels depict her as performing, one the male disciples clearly regard as outrageous, Mary Magdalene is revealed as what Chilton calls the paradigmatic Anointer of the Jesus movement. She is certainly what the mystical tradition of both Western and Eastern Christianity has celebrated her as, a supreme guide to adore the Christ with abandoned, lavish love. But she is also a divine human woman to Jesus's divine human man, imbued like him with royal, priestly, prophetic authority in her own person.

The second clue to the deep meaning of the Anointing lies in the mean-spirited reaction of some of the disciples. The reason Mark gives for their reaction—that the perfume Mary poured on Jesus's head could have been sold and the money given to the poor—might not have been the only reason. Everything we have learned from our study together of the Gospels and the mention of her in them suggests that behind the apostles' narrow-minded fury at the Magdalene's extravagance lurks a darker and colder envy of her unique relationship with Jesus. It is revealed to them scandalously, as one in which she was free to anoint him as queen, high priestess, and prophet in her own truth—that was, as Mark's account shows, not only welcomed, but uniquely celebrated by him.

The third clue can be found in Jesus's celebration of her. It cannot be emphasized enough that there is no comparable example anywhere in the Gospels of Jesus celebrating anyone or any act of any disciple with such lavish praise. He alludes to Mary's prophetic clairvoyance, which she undertook "to oil my body for burial," and in a way he implies none of his male disciples understood. Jesus then adds in words that will always humble and thrill all lovers of the Magdalene: "Amen, I say to you, wherever the message is proclaimed in the whole world, what she did will also be spoken in memory of her."

It was this unique celebration by Jesus of Mary's action that made it impossible—even for those who might have been tempted to do so out of spite or misogyny or incomprehension—not to include her act of adoration and empowerment in all the accounts of his ministry and journey.

This should lead us to ask a key question. Why would Jesus have been so extravagant in his singling out of Mary's action? For me, the answer is both astounding and clear.

Jesus knew the hostility to and incomprehension of the disciples to his relationship with Mary. He also knew that the accounts of his mission would be recorded by men who might share that hostility or incomprehension. And he knew the full significance of the Anointing to what lay ahead for him—a knowledge he had shared and would share only with her for all the reasons our journey together has uncovered. He wanted to make certain by his insistence that Mary Magdalene's anointing would never be either completely diminished or written out altogether.

Jesus would also have known that even though his glorious words in praise of Mary would ensure that her act of adoration would endure in memory, the most revelatory meaning of that act would have to wait a long time to be fully unveiled. Just as the fullest implications of her place in his mission and Passion, Crucifixion, and Resurrection also would have to wait until the world would be ready to receive them.

It is these implications we must now turn to and explore as courageously as we can.

The Only Revolution

AS WE BEGIN OUR EXPLORATION of these implications and make ourselves ready to receive them in all their radical nobility and sublimity, imagining them with the fullest powers of our sacred imagination and attempting to integrate them with intimate mystical and prayer practice, let us pause again for a long moment. Let us crystallize in our being everything we have discovered together of who Mary Magdalene is revealed to be to us and in us—and what the evolutionary divine human love between her and Jesus in their sacred marriage reveals to us of the power of love to birth us into our own dynamic and ecstatic divine humanity.

It is only through such a crystallization, repeated again and again, as more and more of the mystery of their union is unveiled to us and progressively in us, that we will be able to see them as who they were and are. This also allows them, in a rapture of ever-widening recognition, to have their marriage within us, to birth within us the divine human, the one who fuses all opposites within the One.

This birth of the divine human within us is not only a private liberation. It is a revolution in our knowledge and experience of our own powers, inner and outer, to collaborate and co-create in and with the Divine a new creation and a new world, to put the wisdom and passion of love into transformative action both inwardly and outwardly. It is to birth the real world, the world revealed by divine law and divine love, the world of the kingdom-queendom, of radical equality, reverence for all life, active compassion for all sentient beings, justice not only for human beings but for all created creatures, and for the rights of nature herself, the body of God.

This is the only revolution that will not birth its potentially monstrous opposite, as all the secular revolutions, however noble their aspirations, have done. And this is not only the revolution that Jesus and Mary Magdalene dedicated themselves to, but also the revolution that the evolutionary threshold we have reached in humanity as a whole demands of us now. It offers us as our last but most transformative hope.

The hope and empowerment this revolution brings to those who dare to believe, experience, and increasingly enact it is not accessible to even the most illumined reason, which will always be subtly inhibited by its inherent need for coherent order. Jesus's life and teachings and the Magdalene's example show us that such a hope can only be won and integrated by those who dare to *unknow*, as Mary Magdalene and Jesus did, even their highest realizations in total surrender to the terrible and redemptive powers of divine love—a love that will take us, as it took them, through Crucifixion and death to Resurrection, to the lived experience of what Gregory of Nyssa called *epektasis*, endless expansion.

When Saint Paul speaks of the sublime madness of Christ Consciousness, inaccessible to all forms however honorable and convincing of worldly wisdom, he is not, of course, speaking about emotional excess or mental aberration. He is celebrating the true sanity of what Jesus and Mary Magdalene's life and example unveiled to us of God's excessive, redemptive, evolutionary love.

It is this sane madness that possessed and guided Jesus and Mary. It is this sane madness that has both grounded and expanded all the greatest Christian mystics and sacred activists. It is this sane madness and the experience of it that births the glorious liberty of the children of God and erupts in the scandalous extravagance of Mary's anointing of Jesus in all its multiple significances.

Those aware of the offered birth of a new humanity and nature from the unraveling and destruction of the old now need to allow themselves this *sane* madness, to experience and enact it beyond dogma or convention, beyond any patriarchal formulations of salvation or enlightenment. They must know its price, of derision and incomprehension and sometimes extreme suffering, and be more than willing to pay it, as Jesus and Mary Magdalene were, in order to experience and progressively incarnate the gifts only such a sane madness can give—gifts of vision, peace, sacred passion in all its uncurbed glory, hope, and fiery and tender and divinely excessive charity.

As Hadewijch of Antwerp writes, "God commands us never to forget love. Isn't it shameful robbery when we deprive love of anything or keep anything back? Think deeply on this word, neglecting nothing, to promote love above all things."

Hadewijch adds, speaking directly to all of us throughout history, but with a special intensity to us in our predicament now, "Be leaders and protectors for others who have not attained this state . . . With the vast fierceness of your unified burning life, they will be enkindled. With the flames of your blazing charity, they will be irradiated."

These are the words we will hear if we listen from the eternal Jesus and the eternal Magdalene in their union that is authentic Christ consciousness. These are the words that if we respond to them, believe them, give all of ourselves to enact them in the depth of our consciousness, in our sacredly inspired creativity, and in our own actions, will birth us into our own divine humanity.

Two Essential Mysteries and the Seven Marriages of Jesus and Mary Magdalene

I WANT TO CONCENTRATE NOW ON TWO of the seven mysteries that I have detailed about Mary Magdalene's anointing of Jesus.

It is these two mysteries that for me offer further essential clues to the work of transfiguration of ourselves and our world that Jesus and Mary are calling us to. First is the mystery of the mysticism of the Song of Songs that the Magdalene is invoking and enacting when she breaks the alabaster jar over Jesus's head. Then there is the even more important revelatory mystery that she is the living incarnation, the full and fully empowered divine mother feminine in all its paradoxical evolutionary magnificence, which she activates, implants in, and radically initiates Jesus into through her anointing of him. She prepares him for the ultimate mother mystery he is about to enter as the consummation of both their sacred marriage and their shared heroic mission, the mother mystery of death and rebirth, Crucifixion and Resurrection.

Before we begin our exploration of these central two mysteries, I want to share with you an unforgettable conversation with Mary V, who gave me the inner sacred marriage practice I have shared with you. Please bring to my distillation of our conversation all that mental prayer and this practice of inner union has given you.

I lived in Paris throughout my 30s when I went through my first bewildering and ecstatic mystical awakening. One of the greatest gifts I was given in that period was a friendship with Mary V, a woman in her 70s, who at the time I met her was starting serenely and stoically to go blind. She lived in a calm, white flat in Saint-Sulpice. Just before she died, she sent me a letter describing her lifelong passion for Mary Magdalene and a vision she had of her in which Mary Magdalene herself told her the following:

"Everything I'm about to say to you has always been seeded in you. Because everything I am and Jesus is, and we are together, is already in you, waiting in you to help you in your own unique evolution and incarnation of the Fire of Love.

"Jesus and I have had seven ascending marriages in our marriage in the One. Six can be spoken of, for the seventh there are no words, but silence will teach you its mysteries directly when you are ready.

"The seven marriages unfolded in the following way. I am going to say them briefly and invite you to meditate on each stage as long as you are alive.

"Our first marriage took place when Jesus and I first gazed at each other and our souls, hearts, and bodies merged as One.

"Our second marriage, that was the marriage at Cana, was dedicated to the Sacred Marriage of the Father and the Mother and married us in the One to It so the One could work in us separately and together.

"Our third marriage, the total abandoned love we lived in private, married progressively our souls and hearts in the love fire of the One to every cell and muscle and bone in our bodies, unifying both of our beings separately and together, birthing Jesus deeper into his human divinity in me and me deeper into my human divinity in him.

"Our fourth marriage occurred at the Anointing. At the Anointing, I blessed him as his human wife, his Divine Feminine other self, and as the Mother blessing the Father. In the Anointing I symbolically married him again as he and I together prepared to face the price of birthing the powers we now knew and embodied, as he and I together prepared to face the price of birthing the powers we had experienced of love for everyone and for the universe.

"The fifth marriage that married our whole human and transcendent being to each other in a love both ultimately painful and ultimately joyful unfolded as he and I lived together his Passion and

Crucifixion. The male disciples, apart from John, abandoned him. I remained. I suffered his betrayal and torture, the horror that was inflicted on him, the agony of the universe itself, both with him and in him and in the depths of myself. There was no separation at any moment. I accompanied him as he descended into hell and liberated its prisoners. This was the most terrible part of our journey, and after the liberation from hell I knew or could know nothing of what would unfold next. We had known that love could do anything from what it had done in us. Because I was still embodied and subtly limited by my embodiment, I could not follow him any further. That is why I came into the Resurrection Garden weeping.

"The sixth wedding was in the Resurrection Garden. I was irradiated with the new light of the new creation to begin my own Resurrection in him, in me. After he left in the Ascension, the sixth marriage unfolded both in time and beyond it in light after light, revelation after revelation, glory after glory in the last decades of my life in the cave in France. That cave was the womb of the birth of our true child, the child of our true and total love, the child of the endless transfiguration process for all beings and all the matter of all the universes. I had to stay on the earth to ground this work in this world, in this reality, while Jesus from within me, both in this reality and one with the One, guided me and helped me guide myself.

"The seventh marriage began when I left the body and united with Jesus in all dimensions forever in the One.

"Once again, I say to you, my daughter, everything I am saying that was revealed to me can be revealed to you. We have never been separate, and you've come to the time in your evolution when you are ready to claim your inseparability from me, in me, in you. Whatever you do not understand or cannot understand now, love will teach you directly and make plain to you."

Before we go forward, I invite you to read the Magdalene's words describing her seven interlinked marriages with Jesus twice again.

The first time, read them as a step-by-step revelation of what a beloved–beloved relationship can accomplish and unfold both in time and history, and beyond them. Allow waves of astonishment, gratitude, and calm empowering ecstasy to sweep over you.

The second time, interiorize the seven marriages slowly within yourself as a revelation of what the progressive union of the sacred masculine and feminine within yourself will initiate you into—an endlessly unfolding transfiguration, first in time and history, then in eternity.

I have done this practice countless times and each time more and more of the truth that enflames all evolutionary mystics with deathless joy has become more amazingly alive in me: The transformations in divine love can never end, because love is infinite.

Now we are ready with vastly open hearts and minds to plunge into the Anointing and all the sacred marriages between Jesus and Mary Magdalene that followed.

As a woman who loves her man, as a wife who is absolutely committed to her husband, as the living incarnation of Shulamith in the Song of Songs, and of all the forms of mystical knowledge and rapture that total love reveals, Mary Magdalene anoints Jesus, her beloved, her bridegroom, her divine human, noble, and sublime co-equal.

Mary Magdalene anoints Jesus with the precious perfume of adoration and royal respect with which the lovers in the Song of Songs anoint each other, and she does so scandalously in public—outraging the disciples as we have shown, unveiling for the first and only time in the Gospels her primacy in Jesus's life—at the moment when he is to go into the mystery of extreme ordeal they both knew would come.

Mary Magdalene's anointing is at once a healing, a coronation, and a transmission from her to Jesus at the moment he would need it most of all, of her love and their love, to irrigate his whole being at a new level of power and strength. As Jesus says, it prepares him for burial—who but a wife and beloved could prepare him in this way—and prepares him for the potential unknowable birth his dying could engender. It manifests the truth for all who have eyes to see of what Matthew Fox writes in his masterpiece, *The Cosmic Christ*.

"The Cosmic Christ might speak thus on the topic of sexuality: 'Let religion and the churches abandon their efforts to be "houses of sublimation." Instead, reenter the cosmic mystery that sexuality is and teach your people, young and old, to do the same, remembering justice, remembering responsibility as intrinsic to the mystical experience. All lovemaking (as distinct from "having sex") is Christ meeting Christ. Love beds are altars. People are temples encountering temples, the holy of holies receiving the holy of holies. Wings of cherubim and seraphim beat to the groans and passions of human lovers, for the cosmic powers are there eager to enhance the celebration.'"

In order to realize the reach of the revelation of sublime sexuality through Jesus and Mary Magdalene, it is essential to emphasize, as Fox does, that those who enter the cosmic mystery of sexuality must also remember, as Jesus and Mary Magdalene never forgot, justice and responsibility. Justice and responsibility are rays of the sun of kingdom-queendom consciousness, and when lived, fueled by the transfiguring power of love, help birth the kingdom-queendom in time.

Mary Magdalene is not anointing Jesus only as her beloved and co-equal. She is anointing him for the ordeal ahead and the realization of what their total love was for, and all sublime sexuality lived in their name is for, to empower him and her with him to realize the deepest purpose for which they had met and loved, the birth of that new creation that their love was birthing in them.

The Anointing, then, not only crystallizes and focuses everything they had learned and known of love, it crystallizes and focuses those revelations at the moment when they would both need them most. Jesus would go forward into the potential birth that could flame from what would be a terrible death, and Mary Magdalene would accompany him, literally and mystically, through everything, united with him on every level.

Mary V's vision of the Magdalene reveals to us that her anointing of him was a remarrying of him at the moment when the golden fruit of their love would either be annihilated or brought to cosmic fruition. Imagine Mary's and Jesus's hearts saying wordlessly to each other these sublime and noble words from The Song of Songs:

Set me as a seal upon thine heart
As a seal upon thine arm
For love is as strong as death.
Jealousy is cruel as the grave.
Its flashes are flashes of fire
A most vehement flame.
Many waters cannot quench love.
Neither can floods drown it.
If a man would give all the wealth of his house for love
It would be utterly scorned.

Mary Magdalene knew, as Jesus knew, that without their union being renewed at yet another level of depth and intensity, all would be lost for both of them. With that renewal installed, the truth of love being stronger than death and undrownable by the floods of the worst torture and evil—the heart of the revelation of the Song of Songs—would be realized in them and as them.

But there is more. In the Song of Songs, Shulamith says of her beloved:

When I found him whom my soul loveth
I held him and I would not let him go,
until I had brought him into my mother's house,
and into the chamber of her that conceived me.

Mary Magdalene was anointing Jesus not only as Shulamith, but as Asherah-Shekinah-Sophia, and as a full Divine Feminine incarnation of the Christ, anointing the full Divine Masculine incarnation of the Christ.

As we have seen, Mary had already brought Jesus into her "mother's house," fulfilled and completed his embodiment by initiating him into the mother mysteries of free and total love. Now, at this stage of their love, at the moment when he was about to enter the ultimate all-fertile darkness of the mother mystery of annihilation and re-creation, death and rebirth, Mary Magdalene, the female

Christ, anointed the male Christ, pouring into him both symbolically and actually all her own lived knowledge of that mystery.

Mary had already been crucified and resurrected in her own life, resurrected by him and the light splendor of their divine human passion. Her own humanity had been tortured beyond endurance and then miraculously renovated through what had transpired between them. She knew, as he could not yet completely know—because of the elevation and installation of divine consciousness in him from birth—just how drastic and unspeakable the agony he would experience would be as he descended into the final depths of human vulnerability to evil.

She knew, too, that he would now need, as a man, everything that she knew as an awake divine human woman. In her anointing him, she filled him with all her powers, powers she had been given by the motherhood of God, powers he would now need to be irradiated by and guided by to become in the final ordeal, both of his humanity and divinity, the mother of a new creation.

If my celebration of Jesus as Mother of the new creation seems extravagant, listen to what a 12th-century prioress, Marguerite of Oingt—one of a group of women mystics who celebrated Jesus the Mother that include the sublime Julian of Norwich—wrote with searing intensity.

"Are you not my mother and more than my mother? The mother who bore me labored in delivering me for one day or one night, but you, my sweet and lovely Lord, labored for me for more than 30 years. Ah, with what love you labored for me. . . . But when the time came for you to be delivered, your labor pains were so great that your holy sweat was like great drops of blood that came out of your body and fell on the earth. . . . Ah, whoever saw a mother suffer such a birth, for when the hour of your delivery came, you were placed on the hard bed of the cross and your nerves and all your veins were broken and truly it is no surprise that your veins burst when in one day, you gave birth to the whole world."

What Marguerite of Oingt could not say, although she may well have suspected it or secretly believed it, was that Mary Magdalene helped prepare Jesus for this cosmic motherhood.

As we as a human race enter the last stages of our own evolutionary journey that will either end in death or the birth of a new humanity, we are entering, each in our own way, our own Passion, Crucifixion, and Resurrection through and in the motherhood of God. If we do not integrate the full powers of the Divine Feminine with the full powers of the Divine Masculine within us—our inner Mary Magdalene with our inner Jesus—the birth offered us cannot take place. The mother anointing of Jesus by Mary Magdalene to unify, strengthen, and embolden him with the sacred powers of the motherhood of God, to be able to bear the mother's annihilating, re-creating energies, has to take place within us at ever greater depths of faith and abandon if we are going to be reborn.

A New Vision of the Eucharist

As we explore further the unfolding of Jesus's cosmic motherhood, blessed, initiated, and empowered by the Magdalene as the embodied Divine Feminine, let us look with new vision at the Last Supper now and Jesus's transmission at its end of the Eucharist. Unless it is realized that the Eucharist is above all feminine mystery, much of its matchless mystical power is lost. In David James Duncan's commentary on Judith Ernst's translation of the Song of Songs, Duncan speaks of what he calls "the eroticism of loving sacrifice" revealed between the bride and bridegroom. Duncan adds, "In taking the beloved in love, one consumes her. In offering oneself to the beloved, one is consumed." Duncan tells us, invoking the richest depths of Jewish and kabbalistic mysticism in the Song of Songs, "What one is offering and receiving and celebrating here is not just one person in the sexual act—the herds of the holy hills, the figs, fruits and spices, the orchards, honeycomb, milk, secret gardens, so emphatically seen as components of the body. The beloved's body is not just like these divine gifts. The gifts can be literally touched, felt, and tasted in her body. Through each other, lovers literally drink, eat, and know the holy gift that is the land."

In the Eucharist, Jesus both crystallizes and expands cosmically and universally what he had lived with Mary Magdalene—to invite all who love him with their whole being to be flooded with divine light power. We do this by taking him into every part of ourselves, heart, mind, soul, and body, as Mary had done, and so unifying ourselves with the cosmic Christ and the new creation.

In the years I have been writing this book, I have gone to a local Catholic church to receive Mass every Sunday. Every time I receive the body of Christ in the bread and his blood in the wine, I pray to

Mary Magdalene to be able to receive him as she did, both in his glory and all his humanity, in every corner of my soul, in every cell and bone and muscle of my body. I have always loved and believed in the divine power of the Eucharist. For me, transubstantiation, the belief that Christ is truly present in the bread and the wine is not a dogma, but an ecstatic reality, one that millions of human beings have experienced throughout the last 2,000 years.

Yet now, through what I have lived and experienced of Mary and of the liberating power of her and Jesus's love, I have found that invoking her passion and wisdom to bless me as I participate in the Mass lifts my experience of it into another dimension of intensity, both more glorious and more visceral.

As I have tried to show, Mary blesses Jesus in her anointing of him with all her unique knowledge and experience of the mother mysteries. In the transmission of the Mass, as the great women mystics of Christianity knew most richly, Jesus is not only elevating the mystical truth of the eroticism of loving sacrifice that the Song of Songs celebrated, he is showing to all those who can see that he is as much, perhaps even more, mother as father. Nothing could be more explicitly maternal than Christ's words over the bread and wine: "This is my body and this is my blood."

Some male mystics understood this mystery also. Saint John Chrysostom writes in his Catechesis, "As a woman nourishes her child with her own blood and milk, so does Christ increasingly nourish with his blood those to whom he has given life."

A mother feeds the embryo within her by the forces and powers of her body and through her blood. Jesus, through the intense earthiness of the symbols he uses for the highest mysteries of transmission, makes clear that for him his sacrifice, like a mother's for her child and a lover's for his or her lover, is an absolute one involving the entire being, and so demanding the involvement of the body and blood of the one who receives the mystery.

Jesus is setting up the bread of his flesh and the blood of his extreme love for us to eat and drink, to take into the body and blood of our own deepest earthly being, so as to birth us into being sacred mothers of the new creation. In this way, we become beings who have learned how to give extreme love like a mother, and to live in a love that wants at all moments to give away everything, so that the whole of life can become pregnant with divine creativity and power. The Eucharist is in its depths a feminine mystery. Not to see this—or how, therefore, the transmission it involves and makes possible is fundamentally connected to the motherhood of God—is to miss its true nature, divert its authentic power, and so cripple the most powerful mystical transmission ever given humankind.

For the Eucharist to be revealed in its full power, I believe, we need to restore the tradition that existed in the first two centuries of Christendom until it was banned by Origen as part of the Church's growing etherealization of Jesus and its enshrining of body and sex hatred as revealed truth.

Far too few Christians know that for the first two centuries, to receive the Eucharist, the priest and the whole congregation danced together. They did not do this only for the sheer joy of celebrating the miracle that is the mass; they did it because Jesus had himself danced after transmitting the Eucharist at the Last Supper, a revelation that was written out of the canonical Gospels but preserved for us in the Gnostic Acts of John.

Before you read and interiorize for yourself the passage from the Acts of John I am going to offer you, realize where you and I find ourselves now in world history, increasingly clear-eyed before the prospect of multiple disasters unfolding both in America and in the world. What more powerful and empowering teaching could the Christ give us all, out of the heart of the sacred marriage he lived with Mary Magdalene, and his own divine genius? The greatest of all evolutionary pioneers, conscious of the agony and horror that lay before him, did not despair or grow numb. He danced and celebrated his deepest truth, the truth of the universe and God, showing us all the way to meet our own painful and potentially amazing destiny:

> Before he was arrested, Jesus assembled us all and said, "Before I am delivered to them, let us sing a hymn to the Father and so go to meet what lies before us." So he told us to form a circle, holding one another's hands. Jesus stood in the middle and said, "Answer Amen to me."

"So he began to sing the hymn.
Glory to You, Father, Amen.
Glory to You, Mother, Amen.
I will be saved, and I will save, Amen.
I will be loosed, and I will loose, Amen.
I will be wounded, and I will wound, Amen.
I will be born, and I will bear, Amen.
I will eat, and I will be eaten, Amen.
I will mourn, beat all your breasts, Amen.
The Holy Eight sing in choir with us, Amen.
The twelfth Number dances on high, Amen.
The entire universe belongs to the Dancer, Amen.
If you do not dance, you don't know what is happening, Amen."

The way to transfiguration is a way of dancing. The transfigured one, the Anthropos, as the Acts of John reveals, is a dancer of paradoxes and marriages of opposites on every level. The dancing that was celebrated after the Mass for two centuries kept alive alchemical and visceral knowledge, as well as making it electric in every cell of the body. The true goal of the Eucharist is to make increasingly transfigured divine and embodied dancers of us all, one with the great dance of the father-mother's evolutionary love. As Jesus says, "If you do not dance, you do not know what is happening."

The Fifth Marriage, Passion, and Crucifixion

WE BEGIN TO ENTER THE MYSTERY of the fifth marriage that the Magdalene revealed to Mary V—the marriage through the passion of hers and Jesus's whole human and transcendent being to each other in a love both ultimately painful and ultimately joyful in the passion and crucifixion. We need to plunge into mental prayer as deeply and richly as we are able. This is hard, because if you truly expose yourself to this mystery, you will discover yourself trembling before what it exposes of the truth of the evolutionary love Jesus and Mary are birthing. The truth is that total love involves an acceptance of sometimes unimaginable suffering and eventually the crucifixion of all separation on every level, and that the vast and all-redeeming love for such surrender engenders explodes all those who encounter even a small part of it, as it did Jesus and Mary Magdalene into its realm of fiery and majestic limitlessness.

What I have found most revelatory in my own journey into the mystery of the fifth marriage as it took place in Mary Magdalene is yet again the writings of one of Christianity's great women mystics, Elizabeth of the Trinity and Mechthild of Magdeburg, for both of whom Mary Magdalene was a crucial inner and outer inspiration.

Elizabeth of the Trinity died at 26 in 1906 after suffering both her own crucifixion through the horror of a yearlong agony of Addison's disease, and her own transfiguration and Resurrection in and through that agony, which sanctified her and many of those who witnessed the manifestation in her of the power of divine love. In 1978, folded and slipped into one of the leaves of her personal diary, compilers of Elizabeth's collected work found her most personal and most revolutionary account of what it meant for her to be as she became on entering the Carmelite Convent at 21, a bride of Christ, as Mary Magdalene had been.

Do not read Elizabeth's words too fast. Each sentence is a potently radiant revelation of what awaits you, as your inner marriage of her-and-him continues to unfold.

"To be a bride of Christ, this is not only the expression of the tenderest of dreams, it is a divine reality, the expression of one entire mystery of similitude and union. . . . Bride signifies everything that this name presents to her of love given and received, of intimacy, fidelity, and absolute devotion. . . . To be bride is to be handed over as he is handed over. It is to be immolated as him, by him, for him . . . it is the Christ making himself ours entirely and us becoming entirely the Christ's. It is to know nothing else but loving, loving in adoration, loving in repairing, in praying, in asking, in forgetting yourself. Loving always in all love's forms.

"To be 'wife' is to keep your eyes in his, to keep your mind haunted by him, your heart seized and invaded entirely by him, as if out of itself and passed into him, your soul full of his soul, full of his prayer, to keep your whole being active and surrendered. . . . It is to enter into all his joys, share all his griefs."

Then, astonishingly, Elizabeth writes these words, which take us into the heart of the mystery of the fifth marriage in the Passion and Crucifixion that Mary Magdalene lived in and with her beloved. Again, read them slowly, integrating in yourself their outrageous promise Elizabeth herself realized in her own dying, and as many of us as possible need to realize for our own dying into love in the middle of, and on behalf of, a dying and resurrecting world.

"To be bride is to be fecund, co-redemptrix, to birth souls in grace, multiply those adopted of the father and redeemed by Christ, the co-heirs of his glory."

In that last sentence, Elizabeth of the Trinity takes us into the heart of Mary Magdalene as she lived with Jesus, their passion and crucifixion. Mary Magdalene is, as Elizabeth of the Trinity discovered herself to be, also "fecund, co-redemptrix, birthing souls in grace, multiplying those adopted of the Father and redeemed by Christ, the co-heirs of his glory." Elizabeth of the Trinity is writing unforgettably from the revelation of the bride of her own (and our own) inner Magdalene. To be able to enter the mystery of the fifth marriage and be instructed beyond words by its overwhelming beauty, agony, and power, we will need to enter, communing simultaneously with both our inner Magdalene and our inner Jesus separately and together in the full Christ they are both one with.

This is hard, and anyone who attempts it will find themselves reeling both from what they uncover of the heroic nature of true love and from what they uncover of their own innate nobility and sublimity and its final demands.

Who you thought you were before you began to allow this mystery to expand in you will not be who you are when you arise from its initiation. If, whatever your resistance is, you persist, you will discover three things.

The first is the revelation of Mary Magdalene and your inner sacred feminine in union with your sacred masculine as bride, co-redemptrix, and co-birther of souls into grace and co-heir of the full Christ's glory.

Whatever sex or sexuality you identify with, this will revolutionize your understanding of yourself and initiate you by degrees into an identity beyond any self-identification and both alert you to and prepare you for your own inner marriage in this fifth mystery to be able to become in Jesus and Mary Magdalene, with them and for them, co-redemptrix birther of the new fire of love they progressively birthed.

The second revelation is of the nature of truth of evolutionary love—the love Mary Magdalene and Jesus lived out in all its realms of unfolding to birth in us and for us, and that is arriving in the revolutionary return of the sacred feminine in Mary Magdalene to the heart of Christ consciousness. What this will reveal to you and in you is both the heroism that true love requires, if we are going to birth it in our finally devastating time, and the joy that such a willingness to be annihilated in love as love for love prepares.

Third, if, fortified by faith, you persist in allowing yourself to be invaded and possessed by what invaded and possessed Mary Magdalene and Jesus in this fifth marriage mystery, an all-new transforming and empowering new vision of the Resurrection it prepared will arise in you.

What this third revelation will make as clear as fire to you is that Jesus's Passion and Crucifixion, and Mary's in him and with him, are not as they have been described in Orthodox Christianity, centered on the atonement of human sinfulness, depravity, and evil. This is far too limited and constrained to describe the love you will discover through uncovering it in them, in yourself. As you in mental prayer accompany Mary and Jesus together throughout the terrible ordeal of the passion and their crucifixion, love herself will reveal to you the secret of their marriage journey at this stage. This passion and crucifixion are lived by both of them in an abyss of both ultimately peaceful and ultimately agonized surrender and unconditional forgiveness—not to atone for human sin and evil, but to transfigure them through suffering. They transfigure human nature itself, with its propensity for darkness and self-destruction, by divinizing it.

It is this greatest of alchemical miracles that the love of Jesus and Mary Magdalene is dedicated to birthing in those who guide their journey by this sun. Coming to see this sun shining in the night sky of the evolution of our world, as it faces its all-defining crises, changes everything if we let it. Over time, it builds in us the divine human strength to love as they did, embracing as they did, the suffering of extreme transformation in surrender and forgiveness with our whole being fixed as theirs was on its final ecstatic goal. Nothing less is asked of us. We aspire to be in and for them, ourselves co-redemptrix and co-birthers of a new creation and a new humanity.

Our most noble and sublime guide into what Mary Magdalene lived, witnessed, and suffered during the crucifixion of her beloved, is again one of Christianity's greatest woman mystics, Mechthild of Magdeburg. Allow this amazing description of the Magdalene's passion by one of her most inspired mystical daughters guide you through her inspired words beyond all words. Please read slowly, with awed attention:

She bears her cross along a sweet path
Because in all her suffering
She gives herself totally to God . . .
She is nailed so firmly to the cross
By the hammer of omnipotent love
All the creatures cannot release her . . .
Her body is killed in living love
And her spirit raised up
Above all human senses . . .
After this, she descends into hell
And consoles despairing souls
With her prayers of God's goodness
Though her body knows nothing of it.
She is pierced in her side
By a blind man
With a tender spear of innocent love
And from her heart
Pours a flood of holy teachings.
She hangs on the cross of love
In the pure air of the Holy Spirit
Facing the eternal sun
Of the living Godhead
And parched bare of all earthly things.
Then in a holy ending
She is talked down from the Cross and says
'Father, receive my spirit. It is perfect.'
She is buried in a sealed grave of final humility . . .
She also rises joyfully on Easter day
After grieving ecstatically in the night
With her lover on their marriage bed.

The Sixth Marriage in the Resurrection Garden

NOW WE ARE BACK WHERE WE BEGAN our vast journey into the Magdalene and the Gospels, with Mary Magdalene in the Garden with the resurrected Christ. And we will see with all our journey and now integrated within us, its revolutionary magnificence and promise.

Perhaps the greatest blessing of my relationship with Bede has been the vision of the Resurrection it gave me. We had many conversations about it, both when we were filming the documentary on his life and later when he was dying. Here is the essence of what he shared with me out of his own growing experience of being transfigured.

"The traditional Christian vision of the Resurrection as the key event, not only of Christ's ministry but of human history, has great and timeless strengths. It celebrates in the Resurrection the triumph of divine love over sin, over evil in all its most ferocious forms, and most importantly, over death itself. It celebrates, too, the victory of the transcendent in the immanent, the perpetual primacy of the transcendent in and over the immanent, and reveals to all those who recognize its truth and turn to it in gratitude and awe that we, too, through superabundant divine grace, have the force of divine love and wisdom within us, a force that promises us, too, a Resurrection of our whole being like the Christ and in the Christ. This promise has inflamed with its reality countless believers and the entire Christian tradition.

"But there is, I am discovering and you will discover, far more. When the transfiguration process began in me, I started to realize the truth of what the Orthodox mystics like Saint Symeon described as *theosis* and realized, too, beyond words, that it is this process of divinization and its potential activation in all of us, not only Christians, that the Resurrection makes possible. Jesus's Resurrection did not only birth Jesus into the new being of the new creation, it birthed potentially all of us.

"What I am seeing and knowing now is that the Resurrection not only birthed the Christ into light matter, into a body that could appear and disappear as was needed, passing through walls and suddenly walking with the disciples on the road to Emmaus, it seeded that birth potentially in the depths of the cellular structure of the human being and in every atom of the matter of the entire universe.

"When understood like this, Christ's Resurrection is revealed as the evolutionary destiny of the whole of humanity, and as Teilhard de Chardin has explored with such fearless brilliance, the destiny of the created universe itself, that will become, as Saint Augustine said, of the mystical body of Christ in its ultimate state, *unus Christus amans seipsum*, one Christ, loving Christ. What the unimaginable miracle of the Resurrection makes possible, then, is a double Resurrection—of the human race and of the universe itself.

"What is truly astounding, I am discovering, is that these two Resurrections are *interlinked*. Every time a person enters the transfiguration process, through his or her own profound inner work and divine grace, that person participates directly and consciously, not only in his or her own divinization, but also—and this is what is awe-inspiring—in the divinization both of humanity and the universe itself. A Resurrection first births us into the new creation and, as we grow, makes us ourselves co-birthers in the growing Christ of a new humanity and a Christed universe. We become, in Christ, with Christ, for Christ, through the grace of Christ, a co-redemptor or co-redemptrix."

To many Christians, this may seem blasphemous, but to me it is the secret of secrets and the ultimate revelation of Jesus's boundless and endlessly transforming love.

What this secret shows is the Resurrection seeds possibility of a quantum leap in human evolution and the evolution of the universe into union on every level with its dynamic light source.

Bede continued: "The possibility of this quantum leap is known in different ways in each of the great mystical traditions. If you look deeply enough, you will discover this knowledge as the secret of secrets at the heart of all the revelations and in the work of the mystic scientists of evolutionary mysticism, like Ibn Arabi, and Aurobindo. No other mystical system that I know of, however, has at its heart waiting to be discovered such a precise template of endless evolution as the one the Christ lived out and lives.

"Because it is so precise, I believe, it is also both grounded and ecstatically joyful. If people on all paths or their own direct path can meditate on it and integrate it into their own inner reality, miracles will be possible, fulfilling the promise in Revelations of 'a new heaven and a new earth.'

"The Bible begins with the creation of heaven and earth and is brought to its climax with the Second Coming, the coming of a 'new heaven and a new earth.' In Revelations, it is said, 'I saw the holy city, the new Jerusalem, coming down out of heaven from God, prepared as a bride adorned for her husband.'

"This new Jerusalem is not the universal theocratic state that many blinded Christians believe in and would be a demonic nightmare. The new Jerusalem is a symbol of redeemed, unified, increasingly transfigured and divinized humanity and the new world it will co-create in and with God."

This transmission from the Christ through Bede to me has been my secret bread and wine for 30 years and suffused everything I have tried to be and write and do.

What writing this book has revealed, however, is that there is one crucial piece missing from Bede's vision, the one our journey together is dedicated to adding—the role of Mary Magdalene as herself in her own Divine Feminine right and in her intimate sacred collaboration with Jesus for the Resurrection birth to be possible. When Revelations describes the new Jerusalem as coming down from heaven as "a bride adorned for her husband," that cosmic-embodied bride to the cosmic-transcendent husband is prefigured in Mary and her role in Jesus's life. There can be no Second Coming, no redeemed, unified, increasingly transfigured, and divinized humanity, no new Jerusalem, without the full return and inmost reception of the Bride, of Mary in all her splendor.

Mary Magdalene is the one the Song of Songs is celebrating: "Who is she that looks forth like the dawn, fair as the moon, clear as the sun, and terrible as an army with banners?"

Mary is the incarnation of the full sacred feminine, sensual and transcendent, humble and majestic, beautiful and terrible as an army with banners, who in union with Jesus, births the love force that changes everything, forever.

The most powerful and illuminating way of entering the mystery of the sixth and sacred marriage in the Resurrection Garden, I have found, is to ask and explore together slowly, as deeply as we can, five questions in ascending order.

These five questions are:

Why is Mary Magdalene weeping when she enters the garden?

Why does Jesus say to her initially, *who* are you looking for?

Why does Jesus call her by her name?

Why does Mary Magdalene, when she stunnedly recognizes Jesus, call him *Rabboni,* little master?

Why does Jesus say to Mary Magdalene, *do not touch me*?

These are not academic questions. Each of the possible answers radiate, as we will discover together, subtle revelations that, integrated together, unveil final and liberating truth.

Over two decades I have read hundreds of commentaries from some of the finest male mystics of the Catholic and Orthodox traditions. While they contained holy truths, they were all contaminated by patriarchal bias. In the great majority of them, Mary Magdalene was portrayed as weeping because she was a woman, and all women are, of course, hysterical and overemotional.

Even when these commentaries acknowledged her sublime courage as being the one who remained throughout the horror and abomination of the crucifixion while the male disciples scattered like terrified mice, and Peter, supposedly Jesus's unique successor, betrayed him three times, the depth of their unconscious, tragic misogyny blinded them to the truth of her tears. One of the great blessings of the time of Mary Magdalene's return is that now we can see the answer to the first question—why was she weeping?—more clearly.

The glorious poem of Mechthild of Magdeburg that I have already shared with you reveals that the already divinized visionary heart of the Magdalene was accompanying Jesus on the cross in surrendered union with him, consciously birthing in and with him the miracle of what they both knew from their inmost experience was possible, the Resurrection in the new creation. The human woman wife-lover in her, however, was burnt to the bone by having to witness the abomination of her divine beloved's body being tortured systematically, and with all the lethal precision of patriarchal Roman cruelty, while being mocked and spat at and humiliated by the human instruments of demonic forces determined to abort a possible great birth. A multidimensional horror then, greater by far than the one that had led her to meet him in the first place as we have seen, now again shook and shadowed both her sanity and the certainty of her divine prophetic consciousness.

When my condo burned down and the beloved of my life died, my divine intelligence knew immediately that the crucifixion of such naked atrocity could only be a necessary blowing open of the door to a new being and a new reality. The human part of me, however, was ablaze with the heartbreak of an intensity I had never experienced before.

And when at last I was alone, I sobbed for two days in a state that fused together two extreme opposites—a bliss of gratitude for all the perfect love my beloved and I had lived together, and that had transformed us both, and an agony of grief of my whole being for the loss of the one I had loved with all of myself, and who had loved me with all of herself, in a way I knew was incomparable and unique, and in a way I knew I would and could never experience again.

It wasn't only my mind and heart that were weeping. My body, every muscle, every bone, every cell was sobbing too. Parents who hold a dying child in their arms, grandmothers who hunt for the scattered limbs of their grandchildren after a bomb explosion know this state, and in my experience of it, I joined and join them now, forever.

A month later, I am beginning to understand and live a second reason for why Mary Magdalene had to endure this fusion of extreme opposites to participate fully in the miracle of the Resurrection, a miracle that is now living in me. The amazing clue both to the new life I'm beginning to live, and I know now through her grace, is revealed in the vision of Mary V, which I have shared with you. In this vision, the Magdalene revealed that she was weeping as she entered the garden, because she did not yet know if the divine dream of her and Jesus's love to birth a universal, all-transforming, all-transfiguring love force had been completely realized.

She had been able to accompany Jesus through the agony of his crucifixion and into his descent into hell to liberate its prisoners, but even her powers, Mechthild tells us, had not enabled her to go further.

There is a reason, I believe, for this. Extreme grief and uncertainty had to empty her ruthlessly and completely for her to be able to receive the fullest possible empowerment from the birth she had helped to make possible. Just as in the Song of Songs, the ecstasy of the union of the lovers is made even more glorious and revelatory through the shocks and sudden baffling separations it had to confront and endure, so Mary Magdalene had to be brought to the emptiness of near-total despair for the Resurrection light of the bridegroom to flood her and transfigure her in its fullest possible intensity of joy and amazement.

Now, let us turn to the second question. Why does Jesus say to her, *who* are you looking for?

The answer is revelatory.

When Jesus initially meets the disciples who are going to be his beloved and sometimes faithful companions in John 1, he asks them, importantly, not *who* they are looking for, but *what* they are looking for (*tize teite* in Greek).

This "what" clearly refers not to a guide or master, but to a principle, a vision, a mission they could ground their whole being in to satisfy and fulfill the hunger of their soul and their passion to employ their sacred masculine energy in serving the world.

When Jesus, as yet unrecognized by her, says to Mary Magdalene as the now resurrected Christ, *who* are you looking for (*tina zeteis* in Greek), he is responding to the truth of their divine human marriage. Mary Magdalene, from her first astounding meeting with him, had not only been looking for a new life, vision, and mission, her soul had been famished to meet as well the way, the truth, and the life in a person divinely ordained for her, for her healing and transfiguration.

At the amazing moment Jesus asks her this question, he knows even more completely than he knew before that Mary Magdalene is the one destined to transmit, radiate, and ground the Resurrection light in humanity and birth its evolutionary truth in the cells of every human being. Mary the mother, when she first held her divine child in her arms, was the first to contemplate Jesus in the splendor of his divinity.

Mary Magdalene would be the second. She had seen it in their first meeting, in a way none of his beloved brothers had, his divine essence. As his wife and divine human beloved, she had initiated and been initiated into the great alchemical mystery of their marriage and the sacred marriage.

And in a way now that she couldn't yet know, the intense intimacy of their shared sublime passion would make her, and not the male disciples who had only partially understood his being and message, who had slept in the garden of Gethsemane when he had begged them to stay awake and accompany him in his agony before his destiny, and had either deserted or betrayed him at his crucifixion, the destined witness, transmitter, and birther of the mystery of the Resurrection. His mother was the one who witnessed his glory at his birth. His wife was the one who witnessed, as she had in all the ways we have already described, prepared and midwifed it, his second birth, and would with unique authority not only be reborn in it herself, but, as we shall see, birth and ground it in humanity, its evolutionary journey, and the evolutionary unfolding of the universe.

Dare, my friend, to imagine now the bliss and honor and unspeakable gratitude with which the resurrected Christ must have looked at the majestic, indomitable woman who had loved him as Jesus, as he had loved her as Mary, a Mary destined soon to be transfigured and resurrected as the female Christ.

If you do as I have suggested, you will discover another holy and amazing answer to the question, who are you looking for? With a sublime divine wit, the resurrected Christ is preparing Mary for the revelations to come in the Resurrection Garden.

How could even Mary Magdalene, with all her intimate and mystical knowledge of her husband and all her experience of the great alchemical work their love had been dedicated to, even begin to imagine the unimaginable that would soon be revealed to her, that the Jesus she had known was utterly changed now into the resurrected Christ? She might well have imagined Jesus resurrected, but even the highest and most loving mystical imagination, which she certainly was possessed by, could not possibly imagine realistically the Resurrection miracle he had now become. In the state which she was in, still aghast at the loss of her human divine beloved, she could not yet begin to imagine, as no one before her in history could have begun to imagine, the "who" she was destined soon to meet, when, at the ordained time, her eyes were opened by revelation.

Understood in this way, Jesus's question becomes at once a celebration of Mary Magdalene's unique relationship with her, and his unique knowledge of her, and a tender indication of what would be required of her as co-birther of the birthing force of the Resurrection. The "who" Mary Magdalene would discover Jesus to be would be a revelation too of the "who" she would become in yet another miraculous unfolding of their union.

Now let us turn to the third question: Why did Jesus the Christ call his beloved by her *name*? Our greatest illumination comes, paradoxically, from Pope Gregory, who grounded in the patriarchal Christian tradition the myth of Mary Magdalene as "the repentant prostitute." In Pope Gregory's Homily 25, he writes, "Jesus said to her, Mary, before he had called her woman, a name common to all her sex, and she did not recognize him, and now he calls her by her name." Gregory goes further and compares this specific naming of Mary by the resurrected Christ to Exodus 33, verse 12, "And Moses said unto the Lord, 'See thou sayest unto me, "Bring up thy people,"' and thou hast not let me know whom thou wilt send with me.

Yet thou hast said I know thee by name, and thou hast also found grace in my sight."

Gregory comments, "Man is a common name for us all. Moses is a proper name. And the Lord affirms that, yes, he knows Moses by his name, as if to say to him clearly, I know you, not in the global way I know all the others, but in a very specific way."

In this extraordinary reflection, Gregory the Great links Mary Magdalene's being called in a very specific way to Moses's prophetic intimacy with God, and therefore implicitly celebrates her as the Moses of the new creation.

And now we are ready to enter the sanctum of the mystery of the answer to the fourth question. Why did Mary call the resurrected Christ *Rabboni*, my beloved master?

In Exodus, Moses does not talk back to the God who has called him intimately by name, because he is overwhelmed by Yahweh's glory. In Mary Magdalene's case, however, she does.

She calls the resurrected Christ, whose self-revelation both astounds her and confirms the radical truth of everything they had lived, *Rabboni*, my beloved master, affirming as she does so the direct link between the human divine being she had adored as her beloved husband and teacher and the glorious resurrected Christ she was now being irradiated by.

The great majority of the patriarchal commentaries on this scene use Mary's calling of Jesus Rabboni as evidence of her feminine sentimentality. It is supposed to show her inability to see his full divinity and glory, unlike even doubting Thomas, who calls Jesus after his encounter with him, *my Lord, my God*.

Something far deeper, however, than the ancient patriarchal commentaries could grasp is implied by Mary's tender use of the diminutive after being prophetically called by name. Moses's prophetic relationship to the divine is a relationship to transcendent glory, and the law he was destined to transmit streams from this relationship in all its majesty and precision. Mary's prophetic calling is inextricably interwoven with her sacred marriage to her Rabboni, the Jesus she had loved with all her being in both his humanity and divinity, and who now stood before her, resurrected, yes, but still just recognizable as her beloved, her husband.

The law that streams from this sacred marriage relationship cannot be formulated precisely, because it is sourced from ever-deepening and ever-expanding states of radical intimacy and union, each one of which conjures its own set of inspired and appropriate behaviors. The Magdalene is the Moses not of a set of commandments but of a progression of states of unity with divine love that lead from transfiguration to Resurrection and beyond, states she herself incarnated and embodied for us in union with Jesus in her sacred marriage with him.

Mary does not call Jesus even at this astonishing moment my Lord and my God, as doubting Thomas did, because her relationship with him is not hierarchical. Her awe and amazement at his fulfillment in resurrection of the dream of their love does not drown the long and radiant intimacy of their union. Calling her beloved Rabboni, my beloved master, links both the glorious resurrected one to the one she loves and has loved definitively and radically. No wonder the patriarchal commentaries I have mentioned try to humiliate Mary. Had their authors dared to explore the real meaning of her calling Jesus Rabboni, they would have had to abandon everything they championed to reimagine not only the story of Jesus but the nature of Christ consciousness.

What if the true law of Christ consciousness is not another slew of dogmas and prohibitions but an ever-expanding unfolding of states of union as exemplified and embodied by both Jesus and Mary Magdalene in their sacred marriage? Then all patriarchal emphasis on human sinfulness and the need for obedience and adherence in faith to accepted dogma would be unveiled as sterile and bankrupt evasions of the real challenge Jesus and Mary and the Christ consciousness they birthed together poses us to marry in ourselves our sacred masculine and feminine and so be born into our full transfigured and resurrected divinity.

Now we are ready to begin to answer the fifth question. Why did Jesus say to Mary after calling her by name, *do not touch me*? Patriarchal commentaries on this have universally proclaimed that this is the resurrected Christ separating himself from all contamination by Mary's sensuality or her claim on his person. This is absurd, as everything in this book claims.

The real reason for Jesus saying *do not touch me* is that in his newly resurrected form of light matter, he would be dangerous to her. Jesus was not rejecting Mary Magdalene. He was warning her with the utmost and most beautiful tenderness and protectiveness.

His Resurrection body was fresh-minted and, as he says, about to ascend to the Father. His entire being was filled with and radiating the glory of the light that had resurrected him. If Mary Magdalene touched him at this moment, she would be annihilated. Later, Jesus in his resurrection body could be touched by Doubting Thomas, but at that moment his beloved was ordained to meet him, the glory alive in him would have destroyed her.

There is, I believe, another linked reason he warned her tenderly not to touch him. He knew that the resurrection glory would flood her and begin to resurrect her and reveal to her what was revealed to him, and that then she would no longer need to touch him because soon, very soon, she would know he was alive in every cell of her being, and that every cell of her being was alive in him. Just as she in him had helped Jesus birth himself as the resurrected Christ, the resurrected Christ in her would, as we will see, birth her into full female Christhood and resurrect her.

Nothing about so momentous an event as the meeting of Jesus and Mary Magdalene in the Resurrection Garden can be incidental. We have explored together the First Temple and Song of Songs mystical traditions, informing and infusing Mary Magdalene and Jesus's love from its ecstatic first meeting and through all its unfoldings.

In the First Temple tradition, Asherah, as divine mother consort to Yahweh's father, was worshipped as the embodied godhead in fields and groves and gardens and ecstatic festivals that were celebrated in wild nature. In the Song of Songs, the lovers, as you know, adore and worship each other in multiple images drawn from the creative world, mirroring the interpenetrating worship of the father-mother in the First Temple tradition.

With that revelation intact in us, we can now enter Chapter 2 of the Song of Songs, and hear how the ecstatic summons of the bridegroom to the bride infuses the full cosmic significance of the Resurrection Garden and the birth of a new creation it makes possible. Here is the quotation from the Song of Songs:

Rise up, my love, my fair one, and come away.

For lo, the winter is past.

The rain is over and gone.

The flowers appear on the earth.

The time of the singing of birds has come.

Now, dear friend, with the whole of the journey alive in you up to this moment, let us dive into the first line: *Rise up, my love, my fair one, and come away.* Jesus rises up, and so through her love for him and her meeting of him in the garden, does Mary Magdalene. The love of the lovers of the Song of Songs has engendered a new creation that both reveals the evolutionary power of that love in the matter of the universe and in the lovers themselves who rise up together.

And now let us dive together into the second and third lines, which proclaim *the winter is past* and *The rain is over and gone.* What this reveals to us is the truth of what you could call the eternal springtime that the sacred marriage of Mary Magdalene and Jesus engenders in the Resurrection, the springtime that dissolves both the winter of humanity's subjection to evil and death, and with them, the winter of all patriarchal religious systems that deny the power of divinized human love and the inherent sacredness of the body and the essential ever-fertile goodness of the creation.

With these realizations vibrant within us, let us contemplate the fourth line, *The flowers appear on the earth.* The transcendent and immanent love of the lovers of the Song of Songs and of Jesus and Mary Magdalene births a new world in which flowers appear, flowers of a new divine humanity, of whom Mary Magdalene is the first, and of new revelations born from the father-mother, sourced in and drenched by the tender, triumphant, ecstatic joy of their union and the ever-unfolding birth that gushes from it.

Now look at the last line, *The time of the singing of birds has come.* The eternal springtime the Resurrection in the garden births in tender, triumphant, ecstatic joy is not for the lovers who have midwifed and incarnated it alone. It is for the whole of humanity, disempowered by the brutal visions and systems of the winter and rains of the past, and now inconceivably empowered and singing for joy of divine life, lived in a unity of body and soul, human and divine. The Resurrection is both a personal and communal and universal evolutionary event. It empowers the scorned and marginalized and those fighting for justice and compassion in the cruel world, and it floods them with a new energy of love.

Those who awaken sing not only for themselves, but for all the universes of matter now flooded by the new light of the new creation. Both a new humanity and a new creation are singing what Revelations called the new song, the *canticum novum* of the golden world, the sacred marriage, the new Jerusalem.

Now we all can see why the Magdalene supposes Jesus at first to be the gardener. Commentators who claim this proves her limitations as a woman have entirely missed the mystery. Her first perception of Jesus as the gardener may be partial but is not wrong. It is an initial but revelatory glimpse of the comprehensive springtime glory of the Resurrection event, and of the essential truth of the Resurrection consciousness that it engenders.

The resurrected Christ, in other words, is *a Gardener,* creating a new order to reveal a new wonder and power in the garden of human consciousness and in the depths of the universal garden of matter.

In the Talmud, there is a story of four men—Ben Azzai, Ben Zoma, Elisha Ben Abuyah, and Rabbi Akiva—who enter a garden (*pardes*) and are dazzled there by states of wonder and revelation. In some kabbalistic traditions, these texts are read in terms of a visionary ascent to consciousness that leads to a revelation of all worlds being God's always evolving, always regenerating garden. *Pardes* is interpreted in various ways—as the garden of Eden, or the heavenly and earthly temple, or even heaven itself, the heaven that the first chapter of Enoch reveals as a dwelling the elect and righteous live in.

The Resurrection reveals the aboriginal truth of reality as God's good and glorious garden, the ever-blossoming manifestation of Yahweh and Asherah's holy marriage.

The winter of patriarchal traditions that split transcendence from immanence, masculine from feminine, the body from the soul, matter from the light consciousness that creates it, is over, and the springtime of the Resurrection Garden reveals the original garden truth and garden face of reality.

If reality is the garden and Christ Consciousness is the gardener, then the intention, skills, and inspired powers of divine creativity constantly evolve that garden into both ever more complex and ever more unified revelations of divine beauty, magnificence, justice, and majesty.

The aboriginal nature of the creation as garden, then, reveals itself in and through the Resurrection, and reveals what follows it as open to endless evolutionary transfiguration by the gardener, endless epektasis.

Now, let us turn to the last line, *The time of the singing of birds has come*. When the first truth I've shared begins to be absorbed, it awakens in all those flooded by its splendor both an indescribable joy and an ecstatic new level of creativity, grounded in the softly volcanic birthing energy of the new creation. This creativity has through its source a divine comprehensiveness.

If it is experienced, integrated, and unleashed, it can transfigure the whole of earth life, from the arts and sciences and religions to, and critically, political and economic philosophies and institutions. The divine creativity grounded in and sourced by the gardener's Resurrection light can regenerate everything, and through both its inner and outer expressions, birth what Jesus called the kingdom and what I call the garden on earth. To connect as deeply as we can with this eternal springtime garden energy is essential now, not only for the survival of humanity in our terrible time, but for the realization of the Divine's dream of humanity's resurrection through its current and necessary and inevitable crucifixion.

The job of the true lovers of God now, I believe, is to be singing birds, visionary activists like Jesus and Mary Magdalene, singing the song of their lives to the music of the *canticum novum*, the new song, singing out fearlessly the song of the Resurrection Garden in the middle of the darkening winter of our global dark night, not only to inspire others but to intoxicate them with the glorious liberty of the children of God and so draw them willingly into a total commitment to transform all of reality into its essential glorious truth.

The Resurrection Garden is at once Origin Restored, Origin Reinvigorated, and the new Eden of the new divinization process of the new creation of both humanity and the universe. Jesus is the new Adam and Mary Magdalene the new Eve, not passively obedient as in the old Eden, but both consciously fully alive, human and divine, both irradiated by the new light that new union has birthed.

In the year since I realized these truths, I dived back into the tradition to find out if any of the great Christian mystics had had a similar intuition. I knew the vision of Jesus as the new Adam was familiar to Christian mystical theology, but where in all the hundreds of commentaries I devoured was the new Eve, the bride to Adam's bridegroom, the mother to his father?

Once again, as at the beginning of this book, the visionary genius of Romanos Melodus comes to our illumination. In the fourth hymn of the Resurrection, Romanos Melodus has Mary Magdalene say to the disciples who are bewildered by Jesus appearing to her first and not to them, "You who love him with a truly fervent love, do not think like that. Be patient. Do not lose courage. *What has happened is a divine grace for women. The first in the fall is the first to see him resurrected.*"

Romanos Melodus's Mary Magdalene does not claim to be the Eve of the new creation explicitly. She knows the apostles would have reacted to such a claim with outraged derisiveness. Instead, with both awed humility and a hard-won canny and strategic compassion, Mary Magdalene goes as far as she can to open to them the mystery of the Resurrection Garden by describing a revolutionary role as messenger, as a divine grace for and blessing on women in general, and implicitly the Divine Feminine in general, and the redemption of the fall and of human history in particular. The disciples could not hear what she was saying to them, but now after all we have experienced together, we can, and with astounding joy, free from the wintry slaveries of the patriarchal past.

In order to help you become drunk with the joy of Jesus and Mary as the new Adam and the new Eve meeting in the Resurrection Garden, allow me to share with you a practice of mental prayer that I have evolved.

The moment in their meeting that I have chosen to contemplate is the moment after Jesus calls the Magdalene by name and she says, "Rabboni," and before Jesus announces her mission as messenger. In this timeless moment, I see Mary and Jesus, the new Eve and the new Adam, standing and gazing at each other in a mutual ecstasy of recognition and gratitude in the middle of the Resurrection Garden. For me, this gaze echoes and immeasurably expands that first electric gaze that united them in Capernaum.

Just as that first gaze married their souls forever, so this gaze begins what Mary Magdalene described to Mary V, her and Jesus's sixth marriage, the marriage with the universal cosmic Jesus beyond space and time that Mary Magdalene would live out for the rest of her increasingly transcendent and embodied life, as Eve to his Adam, Asherah to his Yahweh, Shulamith to his bridegroom, Sophia to his Divine Masculine, female Shakti to his transcendent Shiva, as the living grail, radiant with Christ's resurrected and resurrecting light blood.

Every time I practice this contemplation, I see Jesus and Mary at once more precisely human and expansively divine, and realize my own being more clearly as the Resurrection Garden in which my own inner Jesus and Mary Magdalene stand facing each other in rapture, in gratitude, united now forever in the all-transfiguring golden lights that emanate from the new Eve and the new Adam, and now is beginning to live in me as it is in you.

After the Resurrection, Mary Magdalene, Mary the Tower, became the spiritual leader of the esoteric church that was forming in centers all over the Middle East, Europe, and in Egypt.

Jesus's original plan was for the Magdalene to guide the inner mysteries, which would be protected by the esoteric church. As we have seen, this did not happen, with the disastrous consequences we have explored. Throughout the Gnostic Gospels, rediscovered in Nag Hammadi in 1945, we find exalted descriptions of her real status after crucifixion as "The woman who understands the All."

Mary Magdalene traveled widely, teaching the secrets of the sacred marriage she had lived and increasingly embodied in what many scholars believe to have been a sacred marriage mystery school that instructed adepts in the stages of a way that leads to oneness with the one through the union of opposites in what the Gnostic Gospels call the "bridal chamber." The aim of her teachings was not to exalt herself or even Jesus, but to present them both as Way-showers, who lived a path available to anyone who undertook it with passion, devotion, and progressively expanding inner revelation.

This is the path she has guided me to invite you to embrace in *The Magdalene Revolution*.

After Mary Magdalene's irradiation by the Resurrection Light, her already majestic realization continued to expand in embodied radiance and sacred power, as ours will also if we enter fearlessly the way of the sacred marriage she and Jesus show us.

Two sublime and interconnected mysteries need to be explored to complete our vision of her work and its eternal legacy, so her Pentecost can be as initiatory and all-inclusive as possible. The first is the mystery of the Magdalene's ascension.

The second is the mystery of the birthing cave, that cave in Saint-Baume in the South of France, where I had the vision of her in her golden, transcendent, and immanent splendor that began our journey, where she lived the last years of her life.

The Revelation of the Magdalene's Ascension

IN 2010, A DEFINITIVE BREAKTHROUGH in our knowledge of "the woman who understands the All" occurred. Mary Magdalene's own gospel, written by her in Alexandria in the Greek of the 1st century after the Resurrection, and subsequently taken by her when she went to France, where it was guarded in secret by the Cathars, was finally translated, published, and brilliantly and movingly annotated by Jehanne de Quillan.

The revelations of *The Gospel of the Beloved Companion: The Complete Gospel of Mary Magdalene* confirm everything we have integrated so far on our journey. There are six of them that irradiate the vision of *The Magdalene Revolution*.

First and astoundingly: The marriage at Cana was Jesus and Mary's marriage.

Second, Jesus did not, in Mary's gospel, call himself the son of God. He called himself and was called by her "the son of humanity."

Third, the Jesus of Mary Magdalene constantly stressed his union with the motherhood of God ("my true mother gave me life").

Fourth, "the single one" Jesus was and Mary became, the Anthropos that his and her teachings were directed to helping birth, is, as we have proclaimed on our journey in this book, the child of an inner marriage of opposites that births "the male and female into a single one so that the male shall not be male, nor the female, female."

Fifth, *The Gospel of the Beloved Companion* confirms, as do some rediscovered early Gnostic Gospels, modern writings on the Magdalene, and the message of authentic channelers and visionaries, that it is Mary Magdalene, not John, who leans tenderly against Jesus's breast at the Last Supper. And it is, *The Gospel of the Beloved*

Companion proclaims, Mary Magdalene, not John, to whom Jesus from the cross confers the care of his mother, symbolically making Mary Magdalene his "sister," and mystically revealing her as the daughter of the divine human embodied mother, his mother Mary.

These six revelations would be revolutionary enough, but there is a seventh and culminating revelation that lifts our understanding of who and what the Magdalene became, and was and is: the revelation of the Ascension process that Jesus out of his love opened to her in her, in yet another unfolding of their sacred marriage, to birth her forever into female Christhood.

It is to this, to a precise, reverent, and profound exploration of this ascension process, that we must now turn. In the text of *The Gospel of the Beloved Companion*, Mary Magdalene gives us no precise indication as to when Yeshua revealed to her and in her the Ascension process she describes, whether before the Resurrection when still in a body, or after it in a divine vision.

My belief is that Yeshua revealed the process in the last weeks of his earthly life, leading up to the Passion, Crucifixion, and Resurrection, to prepare his beloved as completely as possible for the horrors and ordeals that would be necessary to endure and transmute for the birth in the Resurrection Garden. Remember what we have already read in Mechthild of Magdeburg's glorious description of Mary Magdalene's inner state during Jesus's Passion. Only a Mary Magdalene initiated already into her full divine humanity, I believe, could have embodied such steady radiance while witnessing and participating in Jesus's agony.

The Gospel of the Beloved Companion tells us that at the end of the first week after the Resurrection, "when all the disciples had gathered in (her) house in Bethany," the Migdalah (Mary refers to herself now as the Tower after what she had just lived and experienced with the Christ) came to them and told them what she had seen and what Yeshua had said to her privately.

The disciples were desolate, grieving, and afraid. "How shall we go out and preach the gospel of the kingdom of the Son of humanity? If they did not spare him, how will they spare us?"

The Tower stood up, saluted them, and raising her right hand, proclaimed from the depths of her innate nobility and fearless truth, now irradiated by the Resurrection-birthing Light of the New Creation, what she, in and through her Pentecost is also saying to all of us in our dark night:

"Only from the truth I tell you, do not weep, and do not grieve or be irresolute, for his grace and the grace of the one who sent him will be entirely with you and will protect you, but rather let us praise his greatness, for he has prepared us and made us truly human."

Then Peter, acknowledging at last the Migdalah's unique mystical authority, if only briefly, says:

"Sister, we know that he loved you more than any other among women. Tell us the words of the rabbi which you remember, which you know and understand, but we do not, nor have we heard them."

Encouraged at last by Peter, whom many Gnostic Gospels portray as jealous of her and antagonistic to her witness, Mary Magdalene progressively begins to unveil not only her real nature and status after the Resurrection, but also what she had been recognized as by Yeshua himself.

"My master thus spoke to me, 'Miryam, blessed are those who came into being before being came into being, and whose eyes are set upon the kingdom, who *from the beginning* has understood and followed my teachings.'"

Clearly the divine human woman, who had seen the resurrected Christ in the garden and been given by him specifically the task of spreading the glorious "good news," is here implying, with both divine pride and divine humility, that announcing her own reality as the one who both understood and lived and continues to live his teachings was part of the message of the Resurrection Garden, inseparable from the full power and truth of its revolution. This, of course, changes everything.

What is also to me profoundly moving is the subtlety and tact with which Mary Magdalene refrains in front of the male disciples, and especially Peter, from proclaiming her full inner splendor.

Mary Magdalene always knew, with her exquisite and tender Divine Feminine intelligence, how far she could go without exciting the latent misogyny of most of Jesus's male disciples. She does, however, hint at her secret, authentic co-equality with Jesus when she reports Jesus saying to her that she "came into being before coming into being." She hints that she too, like Jesus, was and is an ordained divine incarnation, one from birth with the One. This hint may well have slipped past the male disciple's understanding. Mary Magdalene suggests exquisitely without claiming emphatically what she knew was her essential role and mystery.

With the male disciples now firmly but gently prepared, she then unveils the unfolding of the Ascension process that Jesus, her equal and beloved, revealed to her in her.

After praising and recognizing her, Yeshua says, "Only from the truth I tell you, there is a great tree within you that does not change, summer or winter, and its leaves do not fall. Whosoever listens to my words and ascends to its crown will not taste death."

Jesus then shows her a vision in which Mary Magdalene sees "a great tree that seemed to reach unto the heavens." As she sees this astonishing vision, Jesus tells her that this great tree is rooted in the earth, which is *her body*. He reveals to her then that its trunk ascends from shadowed beginnings upward through the "five regions" of humanity to its crown, which is the kingdom of the Spirit, the formless, all-creating, all-infusing, divine light-force of the One.

As Annine Van Der Meer, in her brilliant commentary in *Magdalene's Ascension*, writes, explaining the sacred significance of this vision not only to Mary Magdalene but also to all of us: "The inner tree inside *every human being* shows itself in a much larger scale in a great tree outside of every human being. This great tree reaches from the earth to the kingdom of Spirit in heaven, *so the microcosmic tree is at the same time revealed as a macrocosmic tree*." (The italics are mine.)

In other words, Jesus and Mary are both implying that all of us are this "microcosmic, macrocosmic" great tree, with its roots in the muscles, bones, and cells of our body, with our spine, its trunk. Van Der Meer writes, "In ancient Egypt, the spine is erected from the reclining or sleeping position into the standing posture of the resurrected or awakened one."

The trunk also represents what could be called the middle region of the soul, that vaster reality we are all one with, whether we are conscious of it or not, which initiates us stage by stage, as you will see, to the realm where all duality dies into oneness. The crown of our tree extends even this dazzling realization to melt all we are, or imagined we could be, into living, ever-transforming, direct, ordinary, extraordinary union with the Birthing Formless.

The vision that Jesus gives Mary, then, sums up all the visions of identity with the Divine of the first axial age: in Buddhism, Taoism, Hinduism, early Kabbalah, as well as Shamanism, while transcending them all beyond any religion or dogma or system, and proclaiming all of our potential, endless, both transcendent and immanent expansion, in and through our original divine nature.

If Christianity and Christian mysticism had evolved from this all-comprehensive vision, this great, natural, original Yes, the horror of our global dark night, with its flames of hubris and demented dissociation closing around us and threatening to burn down our human and environmental house, would not be as terrifying as it is. Yet because this vision is eternal and original, its restoration in its fullest power and glory through the Pentecost of Mary Magdalene and the knowledge, love-energy, and resolution it restores to us can, if we embrace it, still renovate and regenerate everything.

Jesus, after describing the great tree, now tells his beloved who will be revealed as Eve to his Adam in the Resurrection Garden, the Migdalah-Eve, who is revealing it to the disciples in her house in Bethany, and through the rediscovered and now available-to-all text of *The Gospel of the Beloved Companion*:

"There are eight great boughs upon this tree, and each bough bears its own fruit, which you must eat in all its fullness. As the fruit of the tree in the garden caused Adam and Chav'vah (Eve) to fall into darkness, so this fruit will grant to you the light of the spirit that is eternal life."

In other words, the apple that caused the downfall of Adam and Eve in the old creation, in the new creation that began with his and her ordained incarnation together and erupts in its full, all-changing power in the Resurrection Garden, will grant not only to Mary Magdalene, who eats it first for herself but also for all of us who recognize the timeless truth of what the male incarnate Christ is saying, "the light of the spirit that is eternal life."

It is crucial at this moment to remember that this "eternal life" Jesus is speaking of does not begin, as traditional Christians would have it, only after death. It is always available to us now, on the earth, in a body, in history, in time. The true and revolutionary meaning of the phrase that echoes through the Bible of "God made the human in God's image," known and lived by Mary and Jesus themselves, by some of the Gnostics, and a handful of Christian mystics, is that life in the body is through its light source already eternal, already wholly good, and blessed, and entirely, in all its particulars, sacred, waiting to be recognized as such and rejoiced in with humble amazement by all those willing to do the work necessary to enter authentic "kingdom consciousness," oneness at all levels and in all levels, simultaneously and normally in the One.

Jesus then tells the Migdalah, "Between each (of the eight boughs) is a gate and a guardian who challenges the unworthy who try to pass."

He then tells her that the leaves at the bottom of the tree are thick and plentiful so no light penetrates. He adds, "If you do not free yourself from the world, you will die in the darkness that is the root of the tree, but if you free yourself you will rise and reach the light that is the eternal life of the spirit." As Mary Magdalene absorbs the majesty of what Jesus is unveiling to her and in her, she writes, "I felt my soul ascend." She then ascends the great tree, bough by bough, fruit by fruit.

It would be glorious to explore in detail each stage of her ascent, but for our purposes, a simple description of each stage until the final astounding revelation on the final bough will be, by now, with all we have already integrated and been illuminated by, enough.

I will describe the first five stages that lead to the growing ecstatic freedom of the last three precisely. If you want to relate what I describe to what you have been through already in your life and quest, treat each simple description as a kind of Zen koan. Take it in spiritually, intellectually, emotionally, and let it reveal to you secret diagrams of your own evolution so far.

Imagine yourselves now in that room in Mary Magdalene's house, sitting with the disciples, listening with their mouths open, their hearts racing, their minds swirling, as the woman Jesus loved, the first direct witness of their beloved's Resurrection, unfurled the humble splendor of her soul before them. Imagine the sacred intensity of the atmosphere in the room, the stillness of the embodied silence in her radiating from her, the golden Jerusalem light pouring in, birds singing in the beginning of spring. Now enter calmly the Magdalene's account of the "ascension journey" yourself.

The First Great Bough: This great bough bears the fruit of love and compassion, which, as Mary claims, is the foundation of everything. The guardians of the fruit are judgment and wrath: "And I heard the voice of the Lord of wrath calling to me, but I denied him, and he had no part in me."

As you read those words, look at the anger and judgment that still boil in you. With your head bowed, say the mantra, "Om Nama Maria Magdalenaya," and offer them up to the Divine to be transmuted into fierce compassion and loving discernment.

Imagine now a golden light apple appears before you, the light apple of the new creation, like a tiny sun. Take it into your heart and feel how it irradiates and expands your heart. Bless your enemies and abusers. Release those you continue to judge out of pain or fear. Feel the strength and tender fearlessness, the love and unconditional compassion you are now beginning to radiate.

Please use this simple practice with all of the first four boughs, until we arrive together at the fifth bough with Mary Magdalene, when we will no longer need it.

The Second Great Bough: This bough is weighed down with the fruit of wisdom and understanding and guarded by ignorance and intolerance: "And I heard the voice of ignorance call to me, but I knew him not and my soul did go thus unchallenged."

The most powerful and challenging way of passing the guardians of ignorance and intolerance is to choose to contemplate a group of people you find horrifying or extremely dangerous.

Our world, as you know, has a plethora of such groups, wreaking havoc everywhere. Do not give up your discernment or the fierce clarity of conscience such a group provokes in you, but meditate deeply on three things: that the group of people that agonizes or outrages you is made of your own brothers and sisters; that they also are children of the Living One, however dark their works; that they, in the oneness field of the sacred marriage, *are* aspects of your own self-identity. Now, fearlessly offer these aspects you fear in them that you discover in yourself to divine grace for transformation, and see those who you have found terrifying with the eyes now of wisdom and understanding, and imagine them as they could be if they were drenched by the grace now drenching you. Continue to oppose what they do, but peacefully, with no hatred, and you too will eat the golden light apple of wisdom and understanding.

The Third Great Bough: This third great bough bears the fruit of honor and humility. Its guardians are duplicity and arrogance. "Arrogance called to me saying, 'You are not worthy, go back,' but my soul was deaf to him, and so moved onward and upward into increasing light."

In a world like ours dominated by liars and lies, it is shaming and humbling to face in ourselves the way we often lie to protect ourselves, fit in, or get what we want.

Remember three recent lies you have told, however small or large, and open up to divine grace whatever you discover in yourself that made you first tell them, and then excuse them, or even justify them.

Now do the same with your arrogance. Anyone still in their ego, however subtle, is arrogant. The very nature of the separate ego is arrogance. If you are foolish enough to believe you are not arrogant, try to realize with dry amusement that that is itself a dangerous form of arrogance. Just look now without flinching or self-laceration at your mind for one morning, and you will be humbled by how many unconscious entitlements and fantastical superiorities tango through it.

Choose three examples of your arrogance and entitlement again with no judgment but with naked honesty, and offer them up to divine grace to be transmuted into honor—of God, of others, of your own potentially royal and humble self. Dare to ask the light to continue to expose in you your own lies, your own vanity and arrogance at ever deeper levels, not from a morbid desire to expose your original sin or unworthiness, but from a longing to embrace original blessing and the essential radiant goodness of your own God-nature, and the honor and humility you will embrace in your own true self when you incarnate, embody, and start enacting it.

The Fourth Great Bough: This fourth bough blossoms with the strength and courage that come to you when the foundation of your life is love and compassion, when your heart-sun has expanded with the golden light apples the first and second boughs offer you and the third anchors in you. As you ascend to this fourth bough, you find yourself, often to your own surprise, strong, clear without being brutal, focused without being fanatical, and brave without the need to wound or humiliate or flaunt your "heroism" in many of the situations and responsibilities you once flinched from. Your true self at this stage is beginning to emerge, and you feel full of gratitude and wonder that you have it within you to face life's ferocious betrayals and ordeals without running into the false satisfactions of the false self.

The guardians of this bough, however, the weakness of the flesh and the illusion of your fears, will still continue to confront you in ever subtler but still dangerous ways. A strong and brave person can still be hobbled by the fragility of being human and the fear of abandonment, derision, or failure that can arise from it. At this stage we need, above all, relentless sacred practice and shadow work that makes ice-clear the limitations in us, the imbalances we have not yet healed, the ways in which trauma may still keep us locked fearfully in the prison of our private story, to keep purifying our strength from any desire for power over others and our courage from any secret disdain for or shaming of others for not yet acquiring or enacting their courage in the ways we believe they should.

This practice and shadow work is critical for sacred activists to help them avoid unconsciously perpetuating the very inner and outer power structures and dynamics they are trying to transform, and to protect them from shaming others into resistance through flaunting self-righteously their own truth and heroism. As Thich Nhat Hanh says, "If you want to heal the environment, heal the environmentalist."

The practice I suggest for our purposes now is to ask yourself, "How terrified am I of losing whatever inner and outer security, big or little, I may imagine I have?" When you awaken, you realize there is no security in being governed largely by corrupt, wealthy madmen, religions that denounce others, an economic system that is a glorified Las Vegas casino where even the canniest and most corrupt can lose everything, where there is no safety at all, except in your own consciously realized and embodied divine consciousness. Until that embodied enlightenment and the strength and courage only it can give is truly enshrined in us, we are all vulnerable and know it, and our potential magnificence is imprisoned by fears we need to make conscious now if we are to become, as Jesus and Mary did, Way-showers and Towers in a global dark night.

As you explore what I have said, offer up the insecurities you uncover to divine grace without self-condemnation, but lucidly, and fortify yourselves as ceaselessly as you can by prayer, meditation, and above all by the saying of the name of God, and when and if catastrophe strikes you, you will find yourself far braver and stronger than you ever imagined you could be or ever wanted to be.

As you do so, let the golden light apple of strength and courage melt into your expanding heart-sun and see its radiance expand from your body now to embrace in protective tenderness all sentient beings, the creation, and the universe.

Rejoice that you are now a midwife-warrior of Love-in-Action.

The Fifth Great Bough: This bough bears the fruit of clarity and truth. This bough's test, Jesus tells us, as all the greatest teachers have told us from their own grueling experience, is "the hardest gate of all." You will meet at this stage "the Master of the World," the Dark One unmasked. Only the strength and courage you have acquired by the journey to "oneing" with your innate midwife-warrior can ever give you the power to, as Jesus says, reject the "Deceiver," the "Master of the World." This Deceiver and Master of the World has two aspects. In the first aspect, the Master and Deceiver is the demonic intelligence behind what Saint Paul calls "the principalities and powers," impersonal forces of darkness within the One that enter into us through our own dark thoughts and addictions.

The second aspect is a more esoteric one. In this aspect, in its deepest sense, Deceiver and Master of the World means the part of us that still deceives us that we are separate from oneness. This subtle deception is very difficult to overcome, but it is lethal if we stay in it, because it aborts us from the full birth of our splendor and power in the field of oneness of the sacred marriage.

The journey up to this "hardest gate" has prepared you for what you need, but divine grace alone, as all mystics of all traditions know, can guide you through this gate. This "hardest gate" is the gate you can only pass through if you definitively die into life, truth, and unconditional service to all beings. This death can be tender and wonderful, but that is extremely rare. Most often—as in the Magdalene's own case, when she was dragged until in her early 30s through inner rooms of broken glass, until she was flayed and open enough to see and recognize the living one in front of her—dying into life is preceded by sometimes extreme suffering, the suffering of a relentless and authentic dark night.

If and when such divine violence is aimed directly at you for your crucifixion and resurrection, if you continue to practice what I am suggesting, you will find that your love of God and the grace of your practice will give, even in complete disaster, the strength and courage to know that disaster as divine mercy. Your last clinging to a separate identity will be burned down, and you will enter a new self, world, creation, the new creation of the Resurrection Garden with its "glorious liberty of the children of God." You will be crucified and resurrected, and then dead and for the first time fully alive and present simultaneously, normally, in total reality, transcendent and immanent.

This state is described in different but related ways in all the mystical traditions. Mary Magdalene, who was speaking in that upper room to the disciples, and who had gone even beyond this radiance of being, as we shall see, knew that all those listening to her and all those now reading this were and are as capable as she was of attaining her own exalted state. When you know as she did, when she came to gather the fruit of the fifth bough, that you are "a child of the Living Spirit," and that you can no longer "hear the voice of the world" and so become as silence, you see with both sober and ecstatic clarity that all other human beings, whatever their current distressing or even partially demonic disguise may be, are inherently divine, fearless, lovable, and worthy of compassion, whatever they do or have done.

The practice for this bough is to understand without shame how terrified you are of dying into life and how you will do and believe anything to avoid its necessity. Do not be ashamed of discovering this.

Even Jesus, after all, reeled in the Garden of Gethsemane before what he knew was inevitable. And even Mary Magdalene, with all that her great love had taught her and revealed to her, must have reeled inwardly when she anointed her beloved for the awful and glorious road ahead.

The mantra for this stage of dissolving the inner Deceiver and countering the Master of the World is always the equivalent of "more and more love, more and more surrender . . . not my will, but your will." Say this mantra, my friend. Offer up your terror of dying into life as you do so, and so prepare yourself for when your time to die into life comes. Prepare in this way, and you will get through "the hardest gate" by grace, and your heart-sun will fill with the now blazing golden light apple of clarity and truth and open fully forever.

The Sixth Great Bough: Many maps of enlightenment end in the bliss and freedom of what is unfolded through passing through "the hardest gate." For authentic evolutionary love consciousness, however, the love consciousness Mary and Jesus embodied to birth it in us, to be enlightened is the amazing beginning of another journey that never ends—the journey of infinite expansion in God.

The fruits of the sixth bough, healing and power, have no guardians to prevent you from eating them. The enlightened birth into your real, strong, and brave, dead, alive, true self means you no longer need them.

Even at this level, Mary tells us, the one who is graced to ascend here has one essential task before them—to use the force of healing and miraculous sacred power that flows naturally to them first on themselves, before they can most fully emanate them to others.

One of the most moving and reassuring aspects of the teachings of Mary and Jesus is their holy practical realism. Evolutionary revolutionaries cannot afford to float off into the unreal light of fantasy, however exalted, for their goal is the transfiguration of humanity, the world, and the universe itself, and the costs to body, heart, mind, and soul of pursuing such an exalted but gritty goal are immense.

This is why Jesus tells Mary at this level that she and all who follow her and the way to engoldenment must direct the force of power and healing they are now graced with to the healing of their own souls and hearts and bodies. This healing of the whole self is what, in the esoteric schools Mary founded, the tradition of anointing was devoted to.

The traditions of anointing of the mystery schools of Egypt and the secret Jewish traditions of First Temple and Song of Songs mysticism they infused, instructed, and inspired evolved rituals of chanting, sacred dance, and anointing with sacredly inspired mixed perfumes and unguents that together could fortify and regenerate initiates on all levels, but especially and crucially on the level of the sixth bough.

This is because, as Mary herself, standing in that room in Jerusalem, knew definitively after the Passion and Resurrection, and after everything she had endured as the beloved of the beloved, the wounds of the soul are the hardest and last to heal. Even after enlightenment, the soul is still scarred by everything it has had to suffer in an often horrifying world of lies and cruelty and conscienceless power, and from the ego that encased and shrouded it and dragged it through furnaces of suffering.

One of the things I am certain of is that one of Mary's supreme gifts to Jesus throughout their love was her sacred guardianship as one who knew the mystery of the anointing of his incarnate human divine body and soul. Jesus, a Son of Man and Son of God, knew exhaustion and despair and a heartbreak at human evil that only one who saw with no filter its horror and danger could experience. Jesus faced demonic malice, ignorance, and cruelty in all its human forms without the defenses of apathy, denial, or answering futile brutality we might erect. His incarnation, as hers, was finally vulnerable and exposed in its humanity. Through her anointing rituals, Mary Magdalene did not only guide him into the heights and depths of the sublime sexual bliss that unified them both. She also protected, adored, healed, and empowered him through her sacred anointing wisdom, constantly cleansing his body, constantly healing the inner scars that human depravity and betrayal and rejection carved on his soul.

Imagine a world in which devoted lovers of all possible kinds are instructed in anointing rituals that keep each other, whatever they go through, adored, healed, and divinely empowered in heart, mind, body, and soul. One of the greatest miracles of the Magdalene Pentecost is that that world is already here, in the authentic priestess schools of anointing that have emerged in the last 40 years, beginning to open their wisdom to women and men and all sexual and human varieties at the very moment when they will be most needed.

In Chapter 42, verse 11, of *The Gospel of the Beloved Companion*, Jesus, after speaking of the necessary healing of the soul at the stage of the sixth bough, then says, "This healing of your own soul . . . makes it ready to be filled with the fruits of light and goodness"—of the *seventh* bough. As Mary Magdalene writes, "And I saw my soul ascend again to be filled with the light and goodness that is the spirit."

Study both the Gospels and many of the Gnostic Gospels, especially that of Mary Magdalene, and you will discover, with both astonishment and grief, that Jesus's original and most transformative teaching, and the teaching of the Magdalene she evolved on her own and then married to his, contains no mention or suggestion at all of "original sin." How could original human nature and the nature of the created universe, birthed from the light-flesh of the birthing One, be anything but glorious and good and compassionate and imbued potentially with miraculous creative power and an infinite capacity for infinite expansion?

To be able to go forward through the hurricane flames of the next stage of the global dark night, flames that are perfectly designed to burn down the house the human false self erected in its misery, self-loathing, and consequent narcissistic addiction to fantasies of unlimited power, all of us are going to need what the seventh bough of the great tree will give us, if we follow the sublime marriage map the Magdalene's ascension process revealed to her.

The Seventh Great Bough: What are the fruits of light and goodness of the seventh bough? The most astounding fruit that radiates its all-healing golden light throughout the teachings and heroic example of Jesus and Mary themselves is that at this stage, evil is at once revealed as extremely powerful, but also as in its secret heart sad, helpless, self-ignorant, self-destructive, and also as—and this is the source of the smile on the face of the embodied and awake—ludicrous, idiotic, and unconsciously hilarious in its hubris and in the seriousness in how it takes itself. Remember the conversation I had earlier in the book with the chubby, tender exorcist on the train and how he told me that there are only two things the dark one cannot stand: a crucifix and being laughed at.

The divine hilarity that Aquinas and many others of all traditions characterize as the gift of true freedom is not in any way a form of exalted idiocy, divorced or ignorant of the agony of the world and the devastation evil always inflicts. It is final knowledge through grace of the way the divine goodness uses evil for its own sublime, fierce alchemy of evolution and resurrection in ways that can stun dumb even the most awake, but will, if they are patient, reveal to them its fabulous wonders. Every authentic mystical tradition guards this most empowering of secrets; the lives of Jesus and Mary Magdalene separately and together that took them through every imaginable kind of ordeal into and through the atrocity of the Crucifixion, into the redemptive glory of the Resurrection Garden and beyond—proclaims this secret with matchless and triumphant power and eloquence.

There is a second gift the fruits of light and goodness give us that I believe we all, wherever we are on the journey, need to align with as far as possible now, facing what we face ahead together. The teachings that Mary Magdalene gave in the esoteric schools she started and fostered all stressed calmly but emphatically that the only truly effective way of countering evil, while seeing clearly and with no illusion its power of annihilation, was through the process she and Jesus discovered, lived, and pioneered together—the process that makes you a Living Flame of Yes, the Yes of the Resurrection Birthing Light, the Yes that is born in you as your new you when you accept and surrender to anything, anything at all that is needed to birth you into it. This Yes has been known and lived by the greatest and humblest and most loving in all traditions: Jesus and Mary lived it in its utmost intensity and experienced through it a progressive stream of unimaginable miracles.

Their teaching of the fruits of light and goodness on the seventh bough and the teaching of "the Magdalene Revolution" can be stated simply, although, even for them as the Gospels show, living it will be grueling, exhausting, bewildering, even seemingly insane at times.

Please read the following slowly, integrating each linked message and aligning your deepest soul intention with what is revealed.

Take a long, deep breath. Breathe in the golden light of the divine enlightened wisdom of the fruits of the seventh bough, and breathe out anything in you that still does not believe yourself capable of incarnating what is yours through "original blessing" or anything in your subtle ego that wishes to cling to separation.

Now, listen with your whole being, radiant with golden light, to what the enlightened wisdom of "light and goodness" will reveal to us all when we arrive at this stage.

Always keep remembering the Divine is a fountain of miracles. Always believe, even when everything seems and is horrific, that Yes will have the last word as it had the first. Always have faith in the unfathomable grace and mercy of the one who created you in its own unified image.

Always remember, however shattered, humiliated, and oppressed you might find yourself now, the ingenuity of your father-mother to protect, heal, release, and liberate you is endlessly inventive. Always remember, too, your essential nature and the original nature of all the big and small Hitlers and Neros prancing now on the world's burning stage is originally blessed, holy, sacred, fearless, noble, sublime. Jesus and Mary's Christ-nature is my and your Christ-nature.

The miracles that unfolded from their embrace of peaceful and dynamic Yes-in-action on every level will unfold from you as naturally as it unfolded from them, if you follow the path they pioneered and keep asking them for the courage and adamantine resolution they obeyed, the Yes in every cell of their united being they never forgot to honor or follow through all the atrocious ordeals flung at them.

Resist evil firmly, but not violently; otherwise, you will become evil. Do not waste your God-given energies in hating evil in those who, in rabid and ultimately self- and soul-ignorance, destroy themselves by embracing it, but make ecstatic, grateful, energetic, constant progress in the good. Forgive your enemies unconditionally if you can, and if you can't yet, never cease to pray for that grace, the grace of unconditional love of the Divine to illumine you, to help you do so. Remember that unconditional love and the unconditional forgiveness that flows from it open the final gates to your liberation and ultimate self-recognition.

Understand that your worst enemies are in some ways your best teachers of patience, of the unconscious aspects of evil in yourself, of the heroic virtues of courage, strength, equanimity, and liberating forgiveness you could never have discovered in yourself without their malice, brutality, and sometimes life-threatening, soul-wounding, heart-savaging cruelty. When your enemies wound you most, ask Jesus and Mary to give you the divine madness to pray most passionately for their healing and ultimate liberation.

You'll be a living flame of Yes then, as Jesus and Mary were and are, birthing through your incandescent, playful, heroic, tender presence already the birth that is coming.

And now, dear friend, we are ready in the upper room in the New Jerusalem where Mary Magdalene is appearing in her tender golden splendor to tell us next what happened to her and what will happen to us after "we are filled with light and goodness" that is the Spirit.

Listen carefully. She is speaking to you and me now, facing an exploding triple dark night together—the dark night of the human soul, the dark night of the environment, the dark night of democracy. If you and I listen carefully, trusting the woman who, as the Gnostic Gospels tells us, understands it all, something even more wonderful is open now to all of us.

The darkness around us is growing stronger, but the miracle at the secret core of our time is that in getting even more shameful, famously vehement, and depraved, the darkness is birthing a great light in those who dare to open to it more that is more invincible in its truth and power than any that has come before. A light that, if many of us grasp this and do everything to incarnate in inner realization, guiding urgent, structured, strategic, sacred action, will birth a new divine humanity and a new world.

Mary Magdalene now speaks to us out of the transfiguring Pentecostal fire of that light to share the secret of secrets she knows cannot be hers alone, but is ours also to rejoice in and try to understand as far as we can now, while continuing to travel toward its full, astounding realization, when our own ascension rises to its completion of completions in us.

Mary Magdalene is filled with the light and goodness of the seventh bough and then tells us about the eighth:

"And I saw my soul now free of all darkness ascend again to be filled with the light and goodness that is the Spirit, and I was filled with a fierce joy as my soul turned to fire and flew upwards in the flames, from whence my Master showed me the eighth and final bough, upon which burned the fruit of the grace and beauty of the Spirit.

"And I felt my soul and all that I could see dissolve and vanish in a brilliant light, in a likeness unto the sun, and in the light I beheld a woman of extraordinary beauty clothed in garments of brilliant white.

"The figure extended its arms, and I felt my soul drawn into its embrace, and in that moment, I was freed from the world, and I realized that the fetter of forgetfulness was temporary from now on, and that I shall rest through the course of the time of the age in silence. And then, as if from a great distance, I heard the voice of my Master tell me, 'Miriam, whom I have called the Migdalah, now you have seen the All, and have known the truth of yourself, the truth that is I Am. Now you have become the completion of completions, and thus the vision ended. And open another.' This is what my Master has told me, and shown me, and only from the truth I tell you, that all that I have revealed to you is true."

When the Migdalah had told of all that Yeshua had said and done, she fell silent, since it was in that silence that Yeshua had spoken with her and revealed these truths.

Irradiated as we now are not only by Mary Magdalene's words, but by the silence of the woman who was and is the completion of completions, let us also here remember two truths recent scholarship has revealed to us.

The first truth is that no other ascension journey in classical world mysticism that has come down to us ends with an adept being blissfully embraced by a woman. Until Mary Magdalene wrote her account, the only other records of ascension were written by men. The woman, as several modern Magdalene mystics have pointed out, is Hochmah, wisdom, the eternal light in its feminine form, "father" transcendence showing his "mother" face.

Mary Magdalene reached in her ascension what in the Gnostic Gospel of Philip is described as the bridal chamber, the nuptial bed of transcendent and immanent love consciousness in whose clear unified ecstasy all opposites of heart and mind, soul and body, masculine and feminine, light and matter, dark and light, fuse and make love to each other and birth her as both a female Christ and as *The Gospel of the Beloved Companion* implies but never explicitly states, the mother with Jesus as the father of a new embodied divine humanity and a new creation.

Only when the full majesty, passion, life wisdom, and complete embrace of all stages and forms of life of the Divine Feminine are integrated with the authentic sacred masculine can the full force of Christ consciousness be revealed and the original intention of both Jesus and Mary's mission to birth a new human race, a new world, a new creation be realized.

The second truth is that not only is Mary Magdalene the only woman from classical antiquity to leave us this description of a sacred marriage ascension process with a revolutionary emphasis on the feminine, she is the only one who marries the ascension process with the tree of life.

The tree of life in all the many mystical systems it appears—from the Mayan to the kabbalist and certain secret forms of tantric Buddhism and Hinduism—is always a Divine Feminine symbol, a symbol of the feminine embodied life's consciousness that embraces and interlinks all realms of reality from the densest to the vast expanses of the formless.

This is especially true of the tradition of First Temple Judaism that survived secretly until Jesus and Mary's time, and as we have shown, inspired their sacred marriage.

As Annine Van Der Meer has pointed out, in the First Temple the Holy of Holies was in a tower, and *tower* in Hebrew is *debir*, which is derived from the word "to speak" or "to oracle." A tower, or *migdalah*, that is the site of ultimate revelation then, is also the site of the oracle and vision that Mary Magdalene, in her gospel, is representing and giving.

Van Der Meer also writes, taking us further into the mystery, "In the tower (of the First Temple), it is dark until the lights of the tree are lit." The tree gives light, and that light is reflected a thousandfold from the golden walls with which the Holy of Holies is lined. The return of the vision of Mary Magdalene and her experience of the ascension process has lit again the lights of the tree. Imagine yourself now in the debir, in the tower, the site both of revelation and oracle, in that upper room in Jerusalem, in the silence of the Migdalah as she finishes her great unfolding of the stages of ascension.

Imagine that the lights of the tree are now fully lit by our unfolding exploration of her precise and glorious descriptions of each stage. Imagine now that you are one of the myriad reflections of these holy lights, glittering and commingling and dancing off each other from the walls. Imagine now that in whatever way is most natural and alive in you, you start to rejoice that you know now who you essentially are and what you can now endlessly expand into becoming.

The Mystery of the Birthing Cave

THE MAGDALENE REVOLUTION begins and ends and begins again to go on unfolding now in us in the cave of Sainte-Baume, the birthing cave of a new universal evolutionary, revolutionary path that fuses together a path of divinization and divine love in action, as Jesus and Mary did in all the rich and passionate ways I have offered to you. When this path is understood and, even more importantly, lived with the same absolute commitment, fearlessness, and joy as Mary and Jesus did, it will birth a new humanity, a new world, and a new creation.

Bach's supreme masterpiece, *The Art of Fugue,* on which the structure of *The Magdalene Revolution* has been modeled, ends unfinished, not because, as some musicologists claim, Bach died before he could complete it, but because he knew he had gone as far as music and his own genius could go. The music would have to go on in those who really understood its unfolding forever in them, in their own unique instrument. *The Magdalene Revolution* ends and begins again, never to end, in the birthing-cave, that cave-womb that began it, the cave of Sainte-Baume, that translates as "Holy Balm."

Mary Magdalene's birth into female Christhood in the ascension experience she describes in her work, *The Gospel of the Beloved Companion,* did not end her journey. Just as the Christ's incarnation as Jesus in Bethlehem began the endless journey that we have described from different manifestations of divinity into cosmic Christhood and beyond, so Mary Magdalene's birth as the female Christ in the ascension experience began her endless journey.

Now a world teacher and Way-shower and Way-sharer in her own right, her journeys in France and elsewhere after Jesus's resurrection reveal her to us as a fully embodied female Christ, fountain of authoritative teaching and a worker of miracles, inner and outer, just as Jesus, the male Christ, had been.

In her last years, to complete and fulfill her particular Divine Feminine mission as "mother of a new humanity," she withdrew, first for periods of retreat and then finally into the cave of Saint-Baume. The revolutionary gift of the silent work she accomplished there, as we shall see, is arriving now in her Pentecost, in transfiguring tender fire.

Let us now unpack as far as words can this endless journey of Mary Magdalene after Jesus's Resurrection.

After her Ascension experience, Mary Magdalene, the Migdalah, the Tower, the female Christ, the woman Way-shower and Way-sharer, lived the human divine life now offered to all of us through her and him, demonstrating through her witness as Jesus does in his, the sublime powers we will embody ourselves in wonder and gratitude, when we know ourselves, whatever our religion or nationality or sexual orientation, as the brothers and sisters of Jesus and Mary in the sacred marriage. What they lived and knew, we will live and know: The path they unfolded will unfold in us, in all its rigor and demand and responsibility and miraculous amazement and joy.

I know the living truth of this now, in dazzled and awestruck bliss. The crucifixion I went through when my home and life burned down, and I lost the love of my soul and my life, my cat, as the Magdalene lost hers in the Passion, only to find both alive in her in a new and vaster way, has become a new life, the life of the Resurrection Garden. Everything has been quietly, normally, but utterly transfigured: the way I walk and know my body, the way I speak and teach, the way I eat and dream. I know, beyond reason or words or any need to justify or explain, the birth of a new humanity through love in action on all levels is not a fantasy. It is here.

This birth is happening now in the middle of our triple global dark night. I know that what I have been given will be given to anyone, anywhere, who risks the adventure. I know that the way Jesus and Mary birthed, that fuses commitment to engoldenment and to inspired sacred action simultaneously, is the one way that offers all of humanity the strength, force, power, love, and wisdom that it will now have to embody, not only to survive the hurricanes of destruction that are now inevitable, but to keep birthing in and through them the new world that is coming and that is already beginning.

With what I have just written aflame in your heart, dear friend, let us return now to Mary Magdalene, as she returned after her work of teaching and miracle working was completed, to the cave of Sainte-Baume to do, as the "completion of completion," one last great work for us all. Gather everything you have heard in the fugal music of this book, and in the inner graded revelations you have integrated in and for yourself through the practices that punctuate it, and realize as far as you can that every word that follows now is not only a description of what Mary Magdalene and her ascended and embodied Christhood did, but what you also can do through her and Jesus's grace in the ever-expanding birthing of the sacred marriage in the One.

In the womb of the cave of Sainte-Baume, Mary Magdalene at the end of her life incubated, grounded, and integrated the eternal light of the One, the eternal light released by the Resurrection, the seed the resurrected Christ had seeded in her and potentially in all of us and all the evolving creation and universe. She did not do this for herself.

Nothing our sublime brother and sister did was done for themselves. There was no "individual," either separate or separated self, left in her. In the womb cave of the Holy Balm, Mary Magdalene worked in ecstatic silence to marry the Resurrection light in a more and more grounded, practical, and indissoluble way into every thought of her illumined mind, every emotion of her shattered open and transformed heart, and most crucially and finally for us, into every cell of her now increasingly divinized body. She did this patiently, silently, with Divine Feminine realism, guided both by her transcendent mother self and by the male Christ, her human and now divine beloved, vibrantly, precisely, and expansively alive in all of her.

Mary Magdalene did this sublime and noble and sometimes grueling birthing work for all of us as the mother of a new divine humanity and a new world. Jesus, as the sacred masculine in its most complete and splendid and both human and divine incarnation, fulfilled his mission to birth—helped, inspired, nourished, and empowered by Magdalene—the Resurrection light and seed through it a wholly new evolutionary possibility for all of humanity, nature, and the evolution of the whole universe into ever-expanding oneness with its light source. Mary Magdalene, as the sacred feminine in its most complete and magnificent and both human and divine incarnation, fulfilled her divinely ordained mission in the cave of the Holy Balm—helped, inspired, nourished, guided by her divine and human husband, now the cosmic Christ, alive now in all of her—to birth and ground the fire seed of the Resurrection light in all of her and simultaneously and potentially in the hearts, minds, souls, and increasingly transfigured bodies of all of us.

Together in their unfolding sacred marriage, our brother-father and sister-mother birthed for us and potentially now through the second Pentecost of Mary Magdalene, whose initiatory power unites with and completes the first of what we now need most in our unprecedented triple dark night, a way forward that will help us fuse together for the first time in history both the ascetic and tantric streams of transfiguration and divinization we have explored and celebrated together and inspired and sacredly guided, calmly urgent activism, just as Mary and Jesus did in their marriage in time and continued to do in their marriage in eternity.

Words, like even Bach's music, end in full and astounded amazement before the mystery they help to clarify and install but can never either completely incarnate or even completely describe. You can read all the greatest mystical works of humanity: In the end you will have to burn them and stand in the acrid ashes of your burnt-away inner library as I did on May 2, 2025, and accept the challenge I am beginning to, of becoming yourself a living book, a living quintessence of what they all pointed to, as Mary and Jesus and all the great shamans and prophets and mystic tender incendiaries have done in the past and now you and I must do to be useful midwives and fearless warrior lovers of the great birth offered us.

Take your unique place now bravely, dear friend, as a growing and increasingly joy-filled "completion of completions" with all other human beings, conscious or not, who are also potentially "completion of completions."

Calmly step now in your heart-mind beyond all the religions and mystical systems of the past who, for all their glorious and heroic work of preserving essential holy truths, have inevitably been limited and partly corrupted by the patriarchal world they were born in. Revere their essential transmissions, integrate them with humility and gratitude, recognize without needing to condemn or hate their inevitable constrictions and the harm they have unconsciously done and the misery and agony they have unconsciously perpetuated in their need for control. Claim yourself now in the name of Jesus and Mary as fully human, fully divine while humbly committing yourself rigorously to the way Jesus and Mary birthed for you, which will progressively reveal to you what that claim means for you and in you as you yourself become "golden towers," "flame children" of the new humanity, of the birth that is already here and will expand now whatever the cost of the flame initiations ahead.

The "best wine" of the marriage of Cana, of the original and eternal sacred marriage of all opposites in the one, and of the marriage of Jesus and Mary now tenderly aflame in all dimensions and realms, is now being poured out for all of us in the marriage feast that all humanity is now invited to. Whatever and whoever you now imagine yourself to be, whatever religion you belong to, or path or no path you are on, whatever sexuality you now identify with, whatever mistakes or crimes or even abominations you may have committed, the "best wine" of Cana is poured out for you and will now through the return of the bride in full radiant equality with the bridegroom be poured out to you forever, if you truly desire it with your whole being and accept whatever unfolds and has to unfold to realize in your whole being what its blessing fire reveals. Do the practices I have been inspired to offer you by the

Golden Tower I saw 20 years ago before the Cave of the Holy Balm and the others her "singing flames" of her Pentecost have already prepared for you, and the greatest miracles will start to dance in you and around you, as they danced in and around Jesus and Mary who pioneered the way to help you live what they did and with them birth a new reality.

Here is one last sublime and noble practice the Magdalene has inspired me to offer you so you too can ground, incubate, and birth the resurrection seed light in your heart and mind and body temple cave.

Imagine now, dear friend, that you too are seeing as I was graced to see the Magdalene, the Golden Tower, at the beginning of our journey, softly ablaze with soft gold fire outside the cave.

With all the revelations of the Magdalene revolution alive in you, smilingly offer this book to her golden fire so all its words and pages burn away. Watch this book burning away and its ashes vanishing in a fragrant wind, the wind of the Magdalene's unknowable but present mystery.

Imagine that you are now your own living book, your own unique tender revolutionary of love in action. In whatever way that is spontaneously arising in you now, bless yourself in divine pride and humility for discovering yourself through grace as you truly are. Bless the Magdalene for showing you as she showed me who she truly and now always is for you in you.

Now imagine Jesus, the resurrected and cosmic Christ, coming out of the cave and joining his eternal co-equal, bride beloved, his cosmic woman who understood and understands and lives the All. Jesus too is a golden tower in a blaze of golden light. The blazes of golden light that surround Jesus and Mary separately now, in front of your astonished inner eyes, first touch, then expand, in a circle around both of them, which then explodes softly in a big bang of golden light that irradiates suddenly and finally everything—the cave and mountain behind them, the lush landscape of the creation beyond, and then the whole universe, and you too, drunk now on the golden light wine of their marriage—alive now in all of you, mind, heart, guts, muscles, bones, cells.

If you want, chant *Om Nama Cana*, meaning, "I celebrate my inner marriage with yours, eternal ones," with your hands on your ecstatic heart, expanding now to embrace all beings in the whole ever-birthing universe with the vast and unconditional Yes, beyond reason or words.

Rest in the glorious, grounded, ecstatic hope in the divine superabundant grace that this wordless, final Yes will fill you with.

Now in the final stage of our journey together, concentrate the steady embodied bliss, hope, and Yes you are now in the living core of your own sacred heart center, imagined now as a dancing golden sun spreading its birthing light upward to your crown center, beyond it to the unknowable, and down to the bottom of your feet, to the fire core of our earth.

Now start saying tenderly but firmly the mantra of the female Christ I have been given to offer humbly in her name to anyone who wants it to experience its miraculous power, as I have begun to: *Om Nama Maria Magdalenaya*. Start directing its power inwardly to all the trillions of cells in your entire body that have been wait ing for billions of years throughout your incarnations to receive the direct golden kiss that your saying of the mantra of the Magdalene will give them.

Imagine now with great joy as you continue saying the mantra in ever-growing amazement, your trillions of cells start to awaken as brilliant golden light diamonds dancing with and swirling around in ever more amazingly beautiful geometric forms that appear and disappear in ever more lucid and ravishing alignments and configurations. Imagine, too, that all your golden light diamond cells now join you and your awakened golden heart-sun in saying, *Om Nama Maria Magdalenaya* in ecstatic tiny voices, singing flames now in the Magdalene's Pentecostal birthing flame of love.

Dedicate all that you find you already are and all you will now go on becoming forever—both in time and history and beyond them in realms no one can yet imagine but will recognize and enter with rapture and wonder and adoration when they are revealed—to being a birther, a Way-shower, and a Way-sharer in this world and all others.

I wrote this chapter, "The Mystery of the Birthing Cave," on June 8, the day before my 73rd birthday. I wrote it in a nondescript bare hotel room in Oak Park, where I've been living since the fire on May 2 that ended one life and began another. On the afternoon of the 9th, my great friend Theresa Joseph, the most pure and authentic receiver of visions and messages from the Divine I know, who has guided me weekly in the last months of the crystallizing of this book, offered me a session as a birthday present on Zoom.

The session began as Theresa's sessions always begin with silence and quiet, focused breathing. Usually, Theresa stands behind her desk in her house in Connecticut, stretching out her hands in prayer. This day, however, she was seated with her fluffy white dog Gaia on her lap.

In all our many other sessions, Theresa would speak and tell me in her clear and naked way what she was seeing and hearing. This time, miraculously, I found myself in her vision with her, seeing and hearing as if through her eyes and ears.

I was seated on an old simple chair outside the entrance of Mary Magdalene's cave in spring sunlight. Mary Magdalene came out of the cave and stood behind me and touched my right shoulder gently with her right hand. Then she came and stood in front of me and showed me a beautiful, two-dimensional, meticulously rendered painting of her in Renaissance style.

The woman standing showing it to me was not the woman I saw in the vision that begins this book, not the Tower ablaze with Pentecostal golden light. She was a strong, broad-shouldered, older woman, hooded, her hair matted, dressed in a threadbare dark brown loose tunic, her weatherbeaten face staring at me with tender but piercing dark brown eyes. I remember thinking, *I have seen women with the same ordinary majesty in the streets of the Bronx, in villages in France or Turkey, in the mountains in Kashmir.*

She pointed to the Renaissance painting and said with an ironic smile, "This is how I have been depicted by both men and women. I am not this. I am a woman like other women: brave, passionate, sculpted by the joys and ordeals of life."

Then she said, "In these days people are terrified of aging. They do everything to avoid showing its ravages. They embalm themselves with creams and plastic surgery. Why embalm yourselves when you are alive? Wait until you're dead. How can you or anyone stop the art of completion? Every stage of life has its sacred beauty. What you wrote about me in the cave is true. Remember always, however, that I did what I did as the woman you see before you, and not only for myself, but as and for all women and men. I am all women and the woman in each man. The glory you have celebrated in me is waiting to be discovered in everyone. You know this."

Then Jesus came out of the cave and stood beside her.

Now I found myself walking with him down a narrow dark street in Jerusalem. We came to a simple door in a house indistinguishable from the others crowding it. He pushed the door open and I saw him seated at the Last Supper, surrounded by the disciples, with the Magdalene on his right, smiling calmly.

Jesus pointed to a little boy in rags, squatting in a corner, staring at him with lovestruck, shining eyes. "This was you," he said.

The joy of the little boy I was filled my old body. Then he lifted the cup in front of him. Now there was only him in the room, him and me.

Jesus said, and I quote, "Humanity is too immature still to find the chalice. If it did, it would idolize and idealize it, and continue to bury and ignore my true message."

Then, he said, "Mary Magdalene was the only one who did not need to drink my wine, my blood, my light essence from the chalice at the Last Supper. She had already drunk my essence, and she was already the chalice. Mary Magdalene is the true grail, not the object, the cup I drank from. Mary Magdalene became the grail first to reveal to every human being that they too can be living grails.

"To reveal this and the path for everyone to realize this for themselves is why we came. The time has come for this to be known and lived everywhere."

In Memoriam

My cat Jade.

BORN FROM A MOTHER rescued from a house burned down by Special Forces Marines in Tikrit, Iraq, in late 2007, who died in another burning house in Oak Park, Illinois, between 11:15 and 11:30 A.M. on May 2, 2025.

My baby, my playmate, my sweetheart, my best friend, my muse, my sacred healer, my teacher of peace, my guide into embodied tender, blissful, unconditional love, my serene initiatrix into the mystery of mutual adoration beyond all categories or words, my philosopher's stone with fur, my private paradise garden, my goddess with 108 secret names, my cat-Magdalene throughout her long life, my cat-Christ who surrendered her life mysteriously so her beloved could live on and who lives in me now as the best and sweetest part of me to steady, ripen, lighten, and ennoble me as she always did and, now, always will.

It is finished. It is begun again.

Mysterium tremendum.

Sanctus, sanctus, sanctus.

Acknowledgments

FOR JILL ANGELO, MY PILLAR, MY LIONESS. For Leena El-Ali, for all her holy precise wisdom. For Anne Baring, beloved revealer. For Anne Barthel, marvelous tuner of the music. For Cynthia Bourgeault, for her pioneering, heroic courage. For Roland Comtois, how could I ever thank you enough? For Stephen Dinan, for championing my work and his sacred brotherhood. For Elayne Doughty, anointed co-conspirator for her *sprezzatura*. For Matthew Fox, for his constantly amazing example. For Laurence Freeman, beloved friend in Christ. For Patty Gift, for her faith and sublime clarity. For Beth Grossman, publicist extraordinaire and heart friend. For Ellen Gunter, for all she gave and gives. For Miles Gunter, for his lucid friendship. For Robyn and Mike Fitzgerald, incomparable companions. For Theresa Joseph* for her amazing gifts of love and guidance. For Sheryl Leach, for everything always. For Annie Wilson, sister of my heart.

Special gratitude to Jehanne de Quillan** for the brilliance and fearlessness of her translation of and commentary on The Gospel of Mary Magdalene and the clear depth of her indispensable teachings.

Hosannas to all at Hay House who contributed to the layout, beauty, and dissemination of the message of *The Magdalene Revolution*. May she bless you all for your selflessness and expertise.

*Theresa is a gifted mystic, spiritual director, and healer. Query her at theresajoseph.com.

** If you are interested in attending a seminar or workshop presented by Jehanne de Quillan on *The Gospel of the Beloved Companion: The Complete Gospel of Mary Magdalene*, please refer to www.editionsathara.fr for a schedule of upcoming events.

Seven Essential Books

These are seven books that are essential to deepening our understanding of Mary Magdalene and the Divine Feminine.

Love Is Everything, by Hadewijch of Antwerp.

The Myth of the Goddess: Evolution of an Image, by Anne Baring and Jules Cashford.

The Meaning of Mary Magdalene: Discovering the Woman at the Heart of Christianity, by Cynthia Bourgeault.

The Gospel of the Beloved Companion: The Complete Gospel of Mary Magdalene, translated and annotated by Jehanne De Quillan.

The Resurrection of Mary Magdalene: Legends, Apocrypha, and the Christian Testament, by Jane Schaberg.

Ordinary Mysticism: Your Life as Sacred Ground, by Mirabai Starr.

Magdalene's Ascension: Mary's Journey to Becoming Light, by Annine Van Der Meer.

Sources and Resources

Sri Aurobindo, *The Life Divine*, Lotus Press, 2011.

Anne Baring, *The Dream of the Cosmos: A Quest for the Soul*, Archive Publishing, 2019.

Bruce Chilton, *Mary Magdalene: A Biography*, Image, 2006.

Henry Corbin, *The Man of Light in Iranian Sufism*, Omega Publications, 1971.

Matthew Fox, *The Coming of the Cosmic Christ*, HarperCollins, 1998.

Matthew Fox, *Sins of the Spirit, Blessings of the Flesh: Lessons for Transforming Evil in Soul and Society*, Harmony, 2000.

Bede Griffiths, *A New Vision of Reality: Western Science, Eastern Mysticism and Christian Faith*, Templegate, 1990.

Andrew Harvey, *Becoming God: 108 Epigrams from the Cherubinic Pilgrim by Angelus Silesius*, iUniverse, 2019.

Andrew Harvey, *Engoldenment: A Year with Kabir: 366 Timeless Poems*, iUniverse, 2021.

Andrew Harvey, *Son of Man: The Mystical Path to Christ*, Tarcher, 1999.

Andrew Harvey, *Teachings of the Christian Mystics*, Shambala, 1998.

Kerrie Hide, *Love's Oneing: A Book About Contemplation*, Austin Macauley, 2022.

Jean Yves Leloup, *The Gospel of Philip: Jesus, Mary Magdalene, and the Gnosis of Sacred Union*, Inner Traditions, 2004.

Jean-Yves Leloup, *The Sacred Embrace of Jesus and Mary*, Inner Traditions, 2006.

The Mother, *Mother's Agenda, 13 Volumes*, Institut de Recherches Evolutives, 1978.

Elaine Pagels, *The Knostic Gospels*, Vintage Books, 1979.

Satprem, *Evolution II: After Man, Who?*, Mira Aditi Centre, 1998.

Satprem, *The Mind of the Cells*, Mira Aditi, 2010.

Satprem, *Mother or the Divine Materialism: 1*, Inst. for Evolutionary Research, 1976.

Satprem, *Sri Aurobindo or the Adventure of Consciousness*, Lotus Brands, 2018.

Index

C

D

E

F

G

H

I

J

N

O

P

Q

R

S

T

About the Author

Andrew Harvey is a world-renowned spiritual teacher, evolutionary mystic, and sacred activist. His work is sourced from all the major mystical systems and is celebrated for its marriage of scholarly and personal fearless visionary witness. He has written 40 books, the most important of which include *The Way of Passion, The Return of the Mother, The Direct Path, Sun at Midnight: A Memoir of the Dark Night,* and *The Hope: A Guide to Sacred Activism,* which ignited and continues to guide a global sacred activist movement through his Institute for Sacred Activism. He has devoted a considerable part of his work to a radical reenvisioning of Christ consciousness for our time: *The Son of Man: The Mystical Path to Christ,* his groundbreaking translations of Hadewijch of Antwerp and Angelus Silesius, and now *The Magdalene Revolution.* All his work is dedicated to helping humanity, through a fusion of inner mystical passion and wisdom and urgent sacred guided action, birth a new divine humanity and a new world.

www.andrewharvey.net

Hay House Titles of Related Interest

YOU CAN HEAL YOUR LIFE, the movie,
starring Louise Hay & Friends
(available as an online streaming video)
www.hayhouse.com/louise-movie

THE SHIFT, the movie,
starring Dr. Wayne W. Dyer
(available as an online streaming video)
www.hayhouse.com/the-shift-movie

MARY MAGDALENE REVEALED: The First Disciple, Her Feminist Gospel & the Christianity We Haven't Tried Yet, by Meggan Watterson

A TIME FOR GRACE: Sacred Guidance for Everyday Life, by Caroline Myss

WISDOM IS BLISS: Four Friendly Fun Facts That Can Change Your Life, by Robert Thurman

All of the above are available at your local bookstore,
or may be ordered by contacting Hay House (see next page).

We hope you enjoyed this Hay House book. If you'd like to receive our online catalog featuring additional information on Hay House books and products, or if you'd like to find out more about the Hay Foundation, please contact:

Hay House LLC, P.O. Box 5100, Carlsbad, CA 92018-5100
(760) 431-7695 or (800) 654-5126
www.hayhouse.com® • www.hayfoundation.org

Published in Australia by:
Hay House Australia Publishing Pty Ltd
18/36 Ralph St., Alexandria NSW 2015
Phone: +61 (02) 9669 4299
www.hayhouse.com.au

Published in the United Kingdom by:
Hay House UK Ltd
The Sixth Floor, Watson House,
54 Baker Street, London W1U 7BU
Phone: +44 (0) 203 927 7290
www.hayhouse.co.uk

Published in India by:
Hay House Publishers (India) Pvt Ltd
Muskaan Complex, Plot No. 3,
B-2, Vasant Kunj, New Delhi 110 070
Phone: +91 11 41761620
www.hayhouse.co.in
